D0310247

50 Reasons to
HATE
The French

50 Reasons to Hate The French

or

Vive la Difference

Jules Eden

Alex Clarke

Copyright © Jules Eden and Alex Clarke

The moral right of the authors have been asserted.

Apart from any fair dealing for the purposes of research or private study,
or criticism or review, as permitted under the Copyright, Designs and Patents
Act 1988, this publication may only be reproduced, stored or transmitted, in
any form or by any means, with the prior permission in writing of the
publishers, or in the case of reprographic reproduction in accordance with
the terms of licences issued by the Copyright Licensing Agency. Enquiries concerning
reproduction outside those terms should be sent to the publishers.

Quetzal Publishing

60 Grove End Road
St Johns Wood
London NW8 9NH
Web: www.quetzalpublishing.co.uk

ISBN 10: 0-955346-70-3
ISBN 13: 978-0-955346-70-5

Print production management by Troubador Publishing Ltd, Leicester, UK
www.troubador.co.uk
Printed in the UK by The Cromwell Press Ltd, Trowbridge, Wilts, UK

> *"I have tried to pull France out of the mud. But she will return to her errors and vomitings. Even I cannot prevent the French from being French."*

CHARLES DE GAULLE, FRENCH GENERAL, WRITER AND STATESMAN (1890-1970)

EDINBURGH LIBRARIES	
C0044298838	
Bertrams	09/05/2011
	£12.95
CH	DC34

Contents

For Thomas,

JE

For Sir Percy Blakeney,

AC

50 Reasons to HATE The French

or, Vive la Difference

"De Saint-Malo j'avons parti
Sur une frégate bien jolie
Pour s'en aller dedan la Manche
Dedan la Manche vers Bristol
Pour aller attaquer les Anglais"

"From Saint-Malo I had gone
On a right pretty frigate
To sail away down the Channel
Down the Channel for Bristol
To go and attack the English"

FRENCH SEA SHANTY (EIGHTEENTH CENTURY)

In 1989, Salman Rushdie wrote a book called *The Satanic Verses*. Ayatollah Khomeini believed it to cast aspersions on Islam and called upon any one of the world's 1.4 billion Muslims to kill him. Rushdie sat out the '90s in a shack on the moors of Scotland, so jumpy he tested the postman with bacon sandwiches before opening the front door. He learned his lesson, legend has it, because a proposed sequel was never published, *Buddha: What A Bastard*.

The point is that these days it's just not in anyone's interest to flip off any social, political, racial or religious group with access to an AK-47, which is pretty much all of them (not including the Amish but they're more lawyered-up than the N.R.A.). All in all, we live in a world of different cultures, different peoples and different opinions where hate of almost anything, thank God, is taboo.

Except, of course, France and the French.

For all the magnificence of the Louvre and the Arc de Triomphe, for all the cultural joys of Debussy and Cézanne, for all the achievements of Joan of Arc and Napoleon, there just *is* something fishy about the French.

The desire to think better of the world only conceals reality, it doesn't change it. The reality of it, my reality as an Englishman in the twenty-first century, is that France and the French *are* different, and many of those differences are less than likeable. Around the world, animosity towards the French is still the dislike that dares to speak its name.

This is not just *un anglo* revulsion that you might find in Americans outraged that while Jacques Chirac was touring the United Nations to whip up opposition to intervention in Iraq, Jean-Bernard Mérimée, France's former U.N. ambassador and a special advisor to Kofi Annan, was receiving €133,970 ($165,725) in payments from Tariq Aziz, the Iraqi Foreign Minister. It's not even the perennial dislike you find in a Briton from "*la perfide Albion*" angered that 40% of the taxes paid into the agriculture budget of the 25-country European Union goes straight to French farmers. It's not even the delayed reaction of former French colonies like Algeria which has no income tax except for French residents. It's everywhere. As a young student, I once visited a ruined fort in Penang, Malaysia. A rusty old cannon still stood on the collapsed battlement. After wiping off the dust and weeds, I read the words engraved upon it: "This gun was positioned here to fight the French".

I have family in France and a home there. Where other writers, glad to have left the city life behind them for the slow Gallic lifestyle, relish the experiences of pleasant peasant neighbours, my reality left me wanting. In St. Marin de Lerm le Bourg, in the Dordogne, one dinner with French locals in this small village soon descended into a drunken row. Iraq. Algeria. The headscarf ban. Anti-Semitism. Collaboration. Corruption. Camembert. Personal hygiene. Gérard Depardieu. Rudeness. Little yapping dogs. Le *rock and roll*. Le *Roi Soleil*. Napoleon. The U.N. The E.U. Stuffed geese. Suppositories. Strikes. Speedos

My boozy French "friends" drank all my wine and left. With the exception of the local mayor, who collapsed in the garden. We left him under a blanket next to his dog. It all got me thinking about France's place in the world, past and present.

Why do the French condemn Coalition actions in Iraq while their own army rampages through the Ivory Coast?

How do they reconcile being such animal-lovers that Michelin-starred restaurants let dogs eat at table yet, every summer, they go hunting for songbirds to crush with large stones?

What exactly do they mean by "Liberté, Egalité et Fraternité" and how did these principles lead to the world's first guillotine-powered, slave-owning, totalitarian dictatorship?

When did the French, the most unhygienic nation in Europe according to their own newspapers, become home to some of the world's most fabulous scents?

The French are different, believe it. And no amount of wishful thinking or relativism makes all those differences congenial. That truth struck me the next day. Work needed to be done on the house, and it became apparent that I needed a wheelbarrow.

"No problem" I thought, I can borrow one off the farmer next door who was at the party. I knew he had three. He had spent half an hour the previous evening describing every last detail of his machinery to me.

"Puis-je emprunter votre brouette," I asked politely as he stood by them. "I need it for "juste une demi-heure?"."

"Non" came the shortest of replies and off he went to fill in his forms to claim more European Union subsidies. That's the reality of living in France and dealing with the French on a daily basis.

This book explores fifty such realities across French history, politics, culture, sport, show business, food, geography and cuisine. They don't make up a complete picture of the French but, who knows?, next time you meet a French person and walk away from the experience thinking "Was that guy for real?", you'll find the answer in here.

JE, DORDOGNE 2006

WELL, YES, IT'S WRONG. *The premise is wrong, the method is wrong, the conclusion is wrong. A book about hating any country, even France, is morally and maybe even legally wrong. In fact, the only thing right about this book is the facts.*

Though France may be a western democracy, a consumer society and a liberal economy, it is somehow distinct from other countries of the type. The French themselves take this difference as a given. They call it the "exception française", that special something that separates them from the rest of the world.

The facts we lay out in this book highlight that difference. True, they're selective and slanted. I'm sure any French reader with all the humour, modesty and generosity of their nation will see that this book is intended as a gentle joke. And, yes, we could have looked at these differences and interpreted them in a different way to produce a book called 50 (or 500 or 5000) Reasons to Love the French. Then again, we wanted to produce something that would sell.

AC, LONDON 2006

France
at a Glance

Where Did It
All Go Wrong?

Your step-by-step guide to the history, heroes and legends
of France from 25,000 B.C. to 2000 A.D. that made the
country what it is today.

28,000 B.C.: Cro-Magnon notation, possibly of phases of the moon, carved onto
bone, discovered at Blanchard, France.

2,500-50 B.C.: Celtic Bronze Age. France is populated by tribes of brutish, finger-
sniffing Celts. Life is so miserable the only fun is invading the neighbours. In 390
B.C. one tribe under Brennus pops over the Alps and sacks Rome.

BRENNUS: *The Sore Winner*
*"Quintus Sulpicius conferred with the Gallic chieftain Brennus and together they
agreed upon the price, one thousand pounds' weight of gold – the price of a nation
soon to rule the world. Insult was added to what was already sufficiently
disgraceful, for the weights which the Gauls brought for weighing the metal were
heavier than standard, and when the Roman commander objected, the insolent
barbarian flung his sword into the scale, saying 'Vae victis' – 'Woe to the
vanquished!'".* Livy, Ab Urbe Condita

52 B.C.: Lutetia is built, the future Paris.

58-51 B.C.: The Gallic Wars With 43,000 men, Julius Caesar over-runs the place, conquering 800 towns, subduing 300 tribes and selling one million people into slavery. Finally, he defeats a union of Gauls, under Vercingetorix at Alesia. Gaul is absorbed into the Roman Empire.

VERCINGETORIX: *The Main Feature*
Chieftain of the Arverni Gauls, led the great Gallic revolt against the Romans in 53-52 B.C. Breaking a previously given allegiance to Rome, he unified the tribes with a dramatic new strategy – systematic retreat from fortification to fortification after burning towns and crops before the Romans' advance. Caesar eventually caught up with him at Alesia. Vercingetorix surrendered and was imprisoned in Rome for five years, before being publicly displayed at Caesar's triumph in 46 B.C. As a show-stopping climax to the celebrations, Caesar had him strangled.

400 A.D.: With the Roman Empire in decline, Gaul suffers raids from tribes over the Rhine. One set of tribes, the Franks, beats off competition from Vandals, Visigoths and Huns to claim the place. Merovingian King Clovis weans the inhabitants from worshipping rivers and sacred pigs to Christianity.

CLOVIS: *The Headbanger*
"The soldiers had borne away from a church, with all the other ornaments of the holy ministry, a vase of marvellous size and beauty The king pointed to this vase, and said: 'I ask you, O most valiant warriors, not to refuse to me the vase in addition to my rightful part,' One of the soldiers raised his battle-axe aloft and crushed the vase with it, crying, 'Thou shalt receive nothing of this unless a just lot give it to thee' When a year had passed he ordered the whole army to come fully equipped to the Campus Martius The king came to the breaker of the vase, and said to him, 'No one bears his arms so clumsily as thou,' and, seizing his axe, he cast it on the ground. And when the soldier had bent a little to pick it up the king raised his hands and crushed his head with his own axe. 'Thus,' he said, 'didst thou to the vase at Soissons'." Geoffrey of Tours, History of the Franks

751: Martel's son, Pépin the Short, elected first Carolingian king. Pépin's son, Charlemagne, becomes king in 768 A.D. and, running against the entire grain of French history, successfully invades Germany.

PÉPIN II ("PÉPIN THE SHORT"): *Little Man, Big Tool*
Frankish monarch, mayor (741-751) and king of the Franks (751–768). "Perhaps surprisingly, Pépin the Short (Charlemagne's father) was a mighty warrior. Though only 3'6" tall, Pepin carried a two-handed sword which measured six feet in length". Isaac Asimov's Book of Facts *(1985)*

800: France is raided by Vikings who burn Paris. Charles the Simple pays them off by giving them Normandy. Becoming Normans, they invade England, becoming English. The English reinvade France. Only when Richard I of England decides invading the Holy Land is more of a challenge than invading France does France's Philip II get his country back.

CHARLES THE SIMPLE: *Pays off the Normans*
"Rollo the Dane refused to kiss the foot of Charles when he received from him the duchy of Normandy. 'He who receives such a gift,' said the bishops to him, 'ought to kiss the foot of the king.' 'Never,' replied he, 'will I bend the knee to anyone, or kiss anybody's foot.' Nevertheless, impelled by the entreaties of the Franks, he ordered one of his warriors to perform the act in his stead. This man seized the foot of the king and lifted it to his lips, kissing it without bending and so causing the king to tumble over backwards. At that there was a loud burst of laughter and a great commotion in the crowd of onlookers". The Chronicle of St. Denis Based on Dudo and William of Jumièges (896)

1209: Pope Innocent III launches the Albigensian Crusade in southern France to destroy the heresy that the earth is just as bad as hell. 500,000 dead later, he wins, without necessarily proving his point.

1305-1378: Avignon Papacy. French King Philippe IV accuses Pope Boniface VIII of sodomy and goes to war with the Church until he gets a Frenchman, Clement V, elected. The papacy is moved from Rome to Avignon, and the next six popes are all French.

1337-1443: Hundred Years' War The English invade France, not having done it for a while. Humiliating French defeats follow at Crécy (1346), Poitiers (1356) and Agincourt (1415). France's bacon saved by the Lorraine teen proto-Goth Joan of Arc, who breaks the English siege of Orléans. The English leave, pausing only to burn Joan at the stake.

JOAN OF ARC: *Mother of Anglophobia*
"Of the love or hatred God has for the English, I know nothing, but I do know that they will all be thrown out of France, except those who die there."

1572-89: Wars of Religion between Catholic French (under Henry III) and Protestant French (under the Duc de Guise) triggered by the **St. Bartholomew's Day Massacre** of Parisian Protestants. Both Henry and the Duc de Guise get each other assassinated. The warring factions unite around a compromise candidate, Henry IV. He is assassinated in 1603.

1617: Louis XIII crowned at the age of 17. He starts a fashion for wearing wigs by using one himself to conceal his baldness.

1624: Cardinal Richelieu becomes principal minister.

CARDINAL RICHELIEU: *Minister of Death*
"If you give me six lines written by the hand of the most honest of men, I will find something in them which will hang him."

1643-1715: Aged 4, Louis XIV becomes king with Cardinal Mazarin, his mother's boyfriend, as principal minister.

LOUIS XIV: *The Sun King Unextinguished*
"How many baths did France's King Louis XIV take? Three: the first when baptized, the second when a mistress insisted, and the third when a doctor lanced a sore on his bottom and ordered him to soak the wound in a tub of water. Louis XIV also suffered from phimosis – an abnormal growth of foreskin – which made erections painful. After refusing to have an operation on religious grounds, Louis eventually consented to surgery and his marriage was consummated (after seven years) on his 23rd birthday." Wallechinsky and Wallace, The Book of Lists *(1993)*

1667-1714: Louis loses **the War of Devolution** (1667-1668) to the Spanish; **the Dutch War** (1672-1678) to the Spanish, the Austrians and the Dutch; **the War of the Grand Alliance** (1688-1697) to the Spanish, the Austrians, the Dutch, the English, the Portuguese, the Swedish and the German princes; and **the War of the Spanish Succession** (1701-1714) to the Austrians... etc. Overall, France loses most of its possessions in America, India, Italy and the Low Countries and is left bankrupt.

1682: Royal court moves to Versailles, which takes forty years and one billion livres to construct and costs 25% of France's annual income in upkeep.

LOUIS XIV: *Bigger than God?*
"In August, 1704, news was brought to Louis XIV of the French army's brutal defeat by Marlborough's forces in the Battle of Blenheim. 'How could God do this to me,' he cried, 'after all that I have done for him!?'" L. Norton, Saint-Simon at Versailles

---

1683: Louis demands that all women in France must give birth lying down on a table with "stirrups", changing obstetrics for the worst to the present day.

1685: Louis revokes the Edict of Nantes to please his pious mistress, Madame de Pompadour. 200,000 Huguenots leave the country.

1715: Louis XIV dies in bed of gangrene, fully dressed and in a three-foot long wig.

MAXIMILIEN ROBESPIERRE: *The Biter Bit*
"Pity is treason", said Maximilien Robespierre in a speech to the National Convention in February 1794 to justify the wave of executions he ordered during the Reign of Terror. The next time he heard the words were when they were repeated to him on the way to his own execution in July.

1789: French Revolution, storming of La Bastille. 40,000 die in a wave of massacres to enforce "Liberty, Equality and Fraternity" if necessary at the point of the guillotine.

1794: Robespierre overthrown and end of Reign of Terror.

1799-1815: The Revolution ends when Napoleon Bonaparte enters Paris and becomes First Consul. In 1804 he makes himself Emperor, creating a powerful central administration in France and extending his empire throughout Western Europe. Rebuffed in Russia, Napoleon is defeated at Leipzig in 1814.

THE WORSHIP OF NAPOLEONS
"So long as men worship the Caesars and Napoleons, Caesars and Napoleons will duly arise and make them miserable." Aldous Huxley, English writer.

1815: Escaping from imprisonment on Elba, Napoleon re-enters Paris, the beginning of the "100 Days". Defeated at Waterloo, he is exiled to Santa Helena, an island off the coast of Africa.

NAPOLEON: *Blind-sided: The curious incident of the shooting party*
Napoleon, who was a better hand with a field-gun than with a fowling-piece, accidentally shot Marshal Massena in the eye. With characteristic readiness, the emperor put the blame of the accident on Marshal Berthier, who, with characteristic readiness, accepted the blame, while Massena, who lost his eye, with characteristic tact accepted the transference of blame." A G Macdonnell, Napoleon and His Marshals, 1934

1852: Napoleon I's nephew crowned as Emperor Napoleon III.

1870: France declares war on Prussia to prevent the unification of Germany, and is crushed. The Prussians capture Paris and annex Alsace and Lorraine. Napoleon III abdicates and the Third Republic is inaugurated.

1914-18: World War I – Massive casualties in trench wars in North-Eastern France (1,350,000 killed). With British and American assistance, France fends off the German invasion.

1939-45: World War II – Germany occupies France. Vichy regime established. General de Gaulle, Under-Secretary of War, establishes government-in-exile in London.

1944: Allied forces land at Normandy leading to liberation of France. de Gaulle sets up provisional government. Purge against former collaborators.

1946-58: Fourth Republic – marked by economic reconstruction and potential civil war after France loses wars in both Indochina and Algeria.

1958: De Gaulle returns to power and founds the Fifth Republic.

1968: May – Parisian student protests escalate into national strike.

1981: Socialist candidate François Mitterrand is elected president.

1995: Jacques Chirac elected president, ending fourteen years of socialist presidency.

2002: January – Euro replaces Franc, first minted in 1360.

"VOTE FOR THE CROOK NOT THE RACIST", *unofficial campaign slogan of Jacques Chirac's 2002 election campaign in which he won over 80% of the popular vote.*

2002: May – Jacques Chirac re-elected president, trouncing National Front leader Jean-Marie Le Pen in the second round of voting. Le Pen's showing in the first round sends shockwaves across France and Europe and galvanises French voters into mass street demonstrations.

2005: *January* – France rejects the new European Constitution on the grounds that it will dilute France's dominance over the other twenty-four members of the European Union.

Un

French Charm

The World-Beating Rudeness of the French

The crassness of the French is as world-famous as their
cheeses – and as offensive. A deserved reputation?
It would be rude not to look further.

Begin with the Japanese. A people so well-mannered, their national language is the bow. The Japanese are famous for weird fads ranging from vertical pinball to David Beckham and now, the weirdest, the French. *Japan Times* reports that two million Japanese visit France every year. And it is driving them mad.

It is called "Paris Syndrome", a term coined by Dr. Hiroaki Ota, a Paris-based psychiatrist who practised in St. Anne's, the city's main mental hospital. The symptoms of this clinical depression usually appear after three months in France. A quarter of cases require hospitalisation.

He hears the same complaints over and over: "They [Parisians] laugh at my French", "They don't like me", "I feel ridiculous in front of them". The disorder has a progression: first, mild anxiety, then a growing persecution complex, fear of leaving home, despair and sometimes suicide. The cause is always the same: a bad social experience with the French, triggering a profound sense of cultural alienation.

Tadahiko Kondo, 59, a conference organiser, fell ill on arrival in Paris: "Everything was unpleasant. People were cold, rude and never smiled [People] who come to France think it is all about Louis Vuitton and gastronomy. They become depressed because France is not like that".

The ailment is dismissed as largely imaginary by Bernard Delage, the – French – president of *l'Association Jeunes Japon* (Young Japan), an organisation designed to help Japanese expatriates in France: "The problem is with a relatively small number of girls, spoiled types who come out with daddy's money to experience the freedom. But find they can't cope in France". He has the good grace to add: "Of course, Parisians are indeed unusually awful".

France's reputation for rudeness to visitors is legendary. Like most legends, it has a basis in reality. Recent surveys all confirm the belief that the French like nothing better than to flip off foreigners in a thousand subtle ways.

PARIS SYNDROME
"A Japanese woman in her twenties stopped a well-dressed Frenchman in the Opera Métro station yesterday and asked him in broken English for help with a public telephone. He replied with a finger in the air and walked on, leaving another potential candidate for 'Paris Syndrome'… a state of depression which hits [foreigners] who come to live in the 'City of Light'." Charles Bremner, London Times *newspaper,* 14 December 2004.

AND IT'S OFFICIAL
"The French are arrogant, rude and surly", says former Senator Bernard Plasait. "Our bad image in this area, the arrogance we are accused of, our refusal to speak foreign languages, the sense we give that it's a great honour to visit us are among the ugly facts of which we should not be proud". His official government report on tourism in France (November 2004).

The post-office clerk who won't give you change on a €10 note when you try to buy a stamp; the banker who won't take your traveller's cheques though the issuer's logo is pasted on the bank's door; the cafe waiters who ignore your flailing arms even though you've been waiting twenty minutes for the bill; the store assistants who watch fish-eyed as you struggle to make yourself understood in mangled French and then, only after the money has changed hands, reveal that they speak your own language perfectly. (That's an old trick. "In Paris they simply stared when I spoke to them in French; I never did succeed in making those idiots understand their language" – Mark Twain in 1879).

SURVEY SAYS DING!

Lonely Planet's *survey of independent travellers votes France "the least hospitable country in the world".*

Ipsos *survey of world travellers who were asked which European countries they most enjoy visiting, place France fourth.*

But... Reader's Digest *poll of 4,000 Europeans makes the French only the second rudest people on the Continent, runners-up to the world-beating Germans who, unlike the French, simply don't know they're being rude.*

To be fair, the French are equal opportunity insulters. French jokes focus on Belgians for stupidity, Occitans (southern French) and Corsicans for laziness, Bretons (from Brittany) for being poor, and Auvergnats (from the Auvergne) are supposed to be cheap.

In *The French* (1982), Theodore Zeldin records the misery of ordinary French people who have a French regional accent in France. He quotes historian Rémy Pech, who has become a fervent *Oc* separatist: "There will one day be a [France] in which people will be better What needs to be destroyed first is their contempt."

HISTORIC RUDENESS – YESTERDAY AND TODAY

"I do not dislike the French for the vulgar antipathy between neighbouring nations, but for their insolent and unfounded airs of superiority." Horace Walpole, English writer, 1787.

"An isolated and helpless young girl is perfectly safe from insult by a Frenchman, if he is dead." Mark Twain, U.S. humorist, 1883.

"It's said that Parisians don't like the rest of the people who live in France, and with that in mind, what chance would an out-of-town skateboarder have of receiving a welcome greeting? To tell the truth, very little. Parisians go out of their way to make you feel shitty. Taxi drivers rip you off for every penny they can, waitresses look at you like you've just farted as you explain how you are a vegetarian, and the hotel staff makes you feel about as welcome as diarrhoea on a chairlift." Transworld Skateboarding *magazine, Vol. 18 #2, 2004.*

Where does this contempt come from? Maybe self-protection. France is a relatively new country. Its boundaries in today's form date only from 1919 (or even from 1935 when the Saar region voted to join Nazi Germany rather than be French). It includes formerly independent states like Brittany, Languedoc and Navarre; Aquitaine once belonged to England; Nice and Savoy were annexed only in 1860.

The elites in "true France", Paris and its outlying territories making up the Ile-De-France, developed rudeness to emphasise their superiority over the regions; in turn, the regional populations developed their own forms of rudeness as a passive resistance to Paris.

The problem is real, according to the Plasait Report, a 2004 government investigation into the decline of tourism in France. The report criticised a lack of warmth and professionalism amongst service staff and a failure to treat customers, both foreign and domestic, as a friend. The report concluded with 81 proposals on how the French can become better hosts. Tourism Minister Leon Bertrand said, "Our aim is to let tourists know that France is trying to improve and the French that they have to do better".

RUDENESS DOESN'T PAY OFF

The 2004 Plasait Report reveals that the French Ministry of Tourism's proud boast that the country is the world's No. 1 travel destination is a sham, since "a considerable proportion of the [75 million visitors] are just passing through on their way somewhere else". Travellers are counted a second time on their way home. Europeans remain nine days on average (the Spaniards six), while Americans stay thirteen days and the Japanese only five. The government was particularly alarmed by the 21% or €4.85 billion ($6 billion) drop in spending by foreign visitors. The report concludes: "We have to learn that the tourist is not a nuisance but a benefit. Our welcome is not good enough. This is not a fantasy but a cruel reality".

BREAKING THE CODES: *"Hello", "Please", "Thank you" and speaking French don't guarantee a civil response. Here are six Codes of Conduct formulated by author and American expat Polly Platt to deal with the French:*

1. Don't smile. *To smile at a Frenchman suggests familiarity and that you assume you are their equal.*

2. Flirt. *The French set great store on their sexual value as individuals. Grit your teeth and play along.*

3. Use the Ten Magic Words! *They are "Excusez-moi de vous déranger, Monsieur (or Madame)," (Excuse me for disturbing you, Sir, or Madam) and "mais j'ai un problème," (but I have a problem).*

4. Add "Monsieur" or "Madame" after "bonjour","au revoir", etc. *Formality implies your deference.*

5. Shake hands. *The French are tactile. They have 102 physical contacts with each other every day (compared to an American's two). This is the least you can get away with.*

6. Watch out at the door. *The French have a highly defined sense of personal privacy even if they have offices in public or work areas. God knows what they're doing in there. But just knock before entering.*

The irony is that the French are acutely sensitive to incivility directed at them. In November 2004 a sign appeared in the visa section of the French Consulate in New York telling applicants that "rudeness will result in the denial of the application and denied entry into France".

When the *Washington Post* headlined the story, it got a snappy response from Natalie Loiseau, press attaché at the French Embassy: "A visa is a privilege, not a right. We are a sovereign nation, just like the United States, and we can decide who gets a visa and who does not".

No, since European Union law states that a visa refusal by one country means that all the other 24 E.U. states must also deny entry to the applicant. The other member countries thought that this was too harsh a penalty for ruffling the feathers of a French immigration clerk. The sign was removed.

Other French public officials, even the highest, are equally prickly. During a 2002 E.U. conference, one of them turned on mild-mannered, milk-and-water Tony Blair, Prime Minister of the U.K., during a discussion on E.U. subsidies to French farmers and told him: "You have been very rude and I have never been spoken to like this before". In a fury, he cancelled an Anglo-French Summit scheduled later in the year. The speaker was the man European Commission officials call "The World's Rudest Frenchman", President Jacques Chirac.

THE WORLD'S RUDEST FRENCHMAN

Early in his career, President Chirac's aggressiveness was already a national joke. French schoolchildren in the 1970s and 1980s who threw a fit were often taunted for "faire un Chirac" ("doing a Chirac").

When Prime Minister, in 1988, he swore at his British opposite number, Margaret Thatcher, during an official discussion. Helmut Kohl, then German Chancellor, directed him to apologise.

"These countries are very rude and rather reckless of the danger of aligning themselves too quickly with the Americans. If they wanted to diminish their chances of joining the E.U., they couldn't have chosen a better way". Jacques Chirac, 2003, lecturing Eastern European countries who backed the U.S. position on Iraq, rather than France's .

French journalists Henri Vernet and Thomas Cantaloube report a conversation by a senior White House aide in their 2004 book Chirac contre Bush – l'autre guerre *(Chirac versus Bush – the other war): "The relationship between your President and ours is irreparable on the personal level. You have to understand that President Bush knows exactly what President Chirac thinks of him." The journalists reveal that the U.S.A. regularly eavesdrops on the telephone conversations of President Chirac in the Elysée Palace and whilst they do not say what the notoriously blunt-spoken M Chirac says of Mr Bush, they quote the U.S. President as habitually referring to the Frenchman as "the Jackass".*

Continues overleaf

from overleaf

Monday 4 July 2005, reported by Reuters. "French President Jacques Chirac cracked jokes to Russian and German leaders about bad British food and mad cow disease. Chirac was overheard making a series of jokes at Britain's expense to Russian President Vladimir Putin and German Chancellor Gerhard Schröder on the sidelines of a meeting in Kaliningrad, Russia. "The only thing they (the English) have ever done for European agriculture is mad cow disease," Chirac quipped. He took the opportunity of a receptive audience to snipe at British food. "You can't trust people who cook as badly as that," he joked, the paper said. "After Finland, it's the country with the worst food."

The Tower of Psychobabble

The Point of the Eiffel Tower

Expensive toy, suicide magnet and spy base, few national monuments say more about France than la Tour d'Eiffel.

THE RIDICULOUS TOWER
"The Eiffel Tower which even money-grubbing Americans, we can be certain, would not want, is the dishonour of Paris. Everyone knows that, everyone says it, and everyone is profoundly upset – and we are only the weak echo of public opinion, which is rightly alarmed [about] this vertiginously ridiculous tower dominating Paris like a gigantic black factory chimney." Public petition signed by 300 French intellectuals, artists and "passionate lovers of beauty", 1887.

No one wanted it, everyone hated it. The only reason it was built was that the general manager of the 1889 Paris Exposition was bribed to select the design from seven hundred others by engineer Gustav Eiffel, who did not design it anyway but needed a major project to divert attention from certain charges pending against him, specifically the bribery of public officials. So the Eiffel Tower was born.

A public tender for the project was announced in May 1886 with a two-week time limit. Eiffel's design, actually drawn up by his associates Emile Nouguier and Maurice Koechlin a year before, was the only credible submission finished in time (others included a lighthouse, a "Temple of the Sun", a giant water sprinkler to assist Paris during drought and, since the exposition was supposed to commemorate the centenary of the 1789 French revolution, a towering guillotine). Eiffel won the contract along with 1.5 million francs of public funds.

In January 1887 three hundred workers began construction on the tower and completed it two years, two months and five days later. On 21 March 1889 it was inaugurated by a motley bunch of international celebrities including the Prince of Wales, Buffalo Bill and Thomas Edison. They had to walk a large proportion of the 1,665 steps to the top since the American Otis Elevator Company had refused to bribe French procurement officials and had its bid to build the elevator rejected (although no French company could meet the contract so the work went back to Otis which completed the job by mid-June, four months after the Exposition opened).

That day, Eiffel wrote on a woman's fan: "I have created a 300 metre-high flagpole for the French flag". He had reason to celebrate. During construction, it became clear that construction costs far exceeded the public money allocated. Eiffel's company, which had deliberately under-budgeted, offered to meet the short-fall on condition the City of Paris give it sole rights to manage the Tower for twenty years. In the first year, two million paying customers visited the Tower and Eiffel paid off his debt. After running costs, the next nineteen years were pure profit.

TOWERING ACHIEVEMENT:

Built:	1887-1889 for 1889 Universal Exhibition and Centennial of the French Revolution
Height:	300.51 metres (986 feet) (+/- 15 cm depending on temperature)
Height inc. T.V. antenna:	320.755 metres (1052 feet)
Maximum sway in wind:	12 cm
Rivets:	2,500,000
Steel pieces:	18,038
Weight:	7,300 tons (1,000 tons removed during 1990s renovation)
Steps to top:	1,665
Steps walkable by visitors	704 (ground to second floor)
Base:	412 feet square, although also noted as about 2.5 acres
Paint:	50 tons of "Eiffel Tower Brown" every 7 years (last paint job completed 2003)
Visibility:	42 miles
Cost:	7,800,000 gold francs (in 1889)

Eiffel, Alexandre Gustave, 1832-1923, French engineer. A noted constructor of bridges and viaducts, he also designed the Eiffel Tower and the internal structure of the Statue of Liberty. Initially charged with corruption in the 1888 scandal of Ferdinand de Lesseps' failed Panama Canal project, he was cleared of all wrong-doing by a French appeal court in 1893. Immensely rich, he spent the remainder of his years experimenting in aerodynamics by dropping objects out of the window of his own custom-built laboratory on the Tower's third level.

In 2004 the Tower welcomed 6,230,050 visitors. It is Europe's most popular tourist attraction. It was not always so popular. During construction, three hundred artists, writers, intellectuals and architects, one for each metre of the edifice, selected themselves on the basis of their world-wide reputation (admittedly, most were world-famous only in France) to issue a public condemnation of the project. One of them, the author Guy de Maupassant, was caught by the others having lunch in the Tower's restaurant, but saved his reputation with the defence: "Well, it's the only place in Paris where you can't see the thing".

It was meant to be temporary. Designed for demolition after the Paris Exposition, its life was extended for twenty years so Eiffel could pay off its costs. In 1909 there were serious proposals to turn it into scrap. The management company quickly found uses for it: a wireless antenna was erected in 1908 and television masts in 1958; Citroën used it as a giant advertising hoarding; and a meteorological station – unmanned – is installed on the third level. The French intelligence services have historically used the Tower as a vantage point for radio and telephone eavesdropping.

"A HOLE-RIDDLED SUPPOSITORY" – THE INTELLECTUALS' VERDICT (1)
"This belfry skeleton", Paul Verlaine, French poet and absinthe addict.

"This mast of iron gymnasium apparatus, incomplete, confused and deformed", François Coppée, French poet and anti-semite.

"This high and skinny pyramid of iron ladders, this giant ungainly skeleton upon a base that looks built to carry a colossal monument of Cyclops, but which just peters out into a ridiculous thin shape like a factory chimney", Guy de Maupassant, French writer and certified lunatic.

"A half-built factory pipe, a carcass waiting to be fleshed out with freestone or brick, a funnel-shaped grill, a hole-riddled suppository", Joris-Karl Huysmans, French writer and suppository fan.

DEATH FROM ABOVE (1) *The Eiffel Tower's official website (www.tour-eiffel.fr) claims that in 1914 its military radio-telegraphy station intercepted the transmission of a German spy. On the basis of this tip, the dancer Mata Hari was eventually arrested and shot. The story of the intercept was entirely invented to disguise the fact that Mata Hari had always been a double agent in the pay of the French themselves. Her execution was the result of internal rivalries between the country's counter-intelligence services and was a vicious miscarriage of justice.*

All of these uses, points out Colin Wright in his *Paris: Biography of a City* (2004), could have been achieved by other facilities just as cheaply. In fact, in terms of pure utility, the Eiffel Tower has traditionally had only one use: "suicide magnet".

After 350 fatal jumps (and two survived attempts), the French press campaigned for a long while to have suicide barriers built into what *Le Figaro* called "the cursed tower" but were opposed by the management company on the basis of cost.

In 1966, it bowed to pressure and built steel-wire fences around each of the tower's three platforms. "Now suicide candidates will just have to throw themselves into the Seine", said the official in charge of tower safety. A further twenty people have jumped since then with the last suicide in May 2004 gouging a 30 centimetre-deep trench in the tower's car park.

DEATH FROM ABOVE (2):
The World's Suicide Magnets
Mt. Mihara, Japan: *estimated 10,000 (more than six hundred suicides in 1936 alone)*
Golden Gate Bridge, San Francisco, U.S.: *1,200 (recorded) suicides since construction in 1937*
Beachy Head, U.K.: *1,100 (known) since 1890*
Bloor Street Viaduct, Toronto, Canada: *400 since construction in 1919*
Eiffel Tower, Paris, France: *370 suicides since construction in 1889 (making it Europe's largest man-made 'suicide magnet')*
Leaning Tower of Pisa, Italy: *87 suicides recorded since 1850*
Sydney Harbour Bridge, Australia: *40 since construction in 1932*
Empire State Building, New York: *31 suicides since construction in 1931*

Always there, looming but meaningless, the tower can bring out the darker side of humanity. It did in Victor Lustig. In 1925, he noted a newspaper article claiming that the government was exploring the idea of demolishing the tower rather than stump up for expensive repairs. So Lustig had stationery printed up and personally "appointed" himself to the position of Deputy Director General of the *Ministère des Postes et Télégraphes*. He then invited scrap iron dealers to tender for the job.

TOWER OF PSYCHOBABBLE: *The Intellectuals' Verdict (2).*
Roland Barthes, French semiologist, explains the Eiffel Tower: " Hence we might speak, among men, of a true Babel complex: Babel was supposed to communicate with God, and yet Babel is a dream which touches much greater depths than that of the theological project; and just as this great ascensional dream, released from its utilitarian prop, is finally what remains in the countless Babels represented by the painters, as if the function of art were to reveal the profound uselessness of objects, just so the (Eiffel) Tower, almost immediately disengaged from scientific considerations which had authorized its birth (it matters very little here that the Tower should be in fact useful) has reconquered the basic uselessness which makes it live in men's imagination." (1979).

His next step showed a masterly understanding of the dynamics of French business. He invited one of the tenderers with the improbable name of André Poisson to dinner at the Crillon Hotel. There, he described the life of a public servant such as himself, one in which he was expected to dress and entertain on a lavish scale, yet paid a small pittance. Poisson immediately handed over a large bribe and left, confidently expecting the arrival of the government contract. It never came. Yet Lustig made no effort to hide knowing full well that Poisson would be too embarrassed to reveal the fraud. He was so confident that he sold the tower a second time. The new mark went to the police, the matter exploded in the press and Lustig, with the gendarmes hot on his heels, had to hop aboard the *Queen Mary* and beat a swift retreat to the United States.

Perhaps the last word should go to one of the "money-grubbing Americans" whose tourist dollars the tower was designed to attract, the writer and lyricist Don Black: "Symbologists often remark that France – a country renowned for machismo, womanising, and diminutive insecure leaders like Napoleon and Pépin the Short – could not have chosen a more apt national emblem than a thousand-foot phallus".

THE FALL GUYS

The Eiffel Tower has always attracted "base jumpers", daredevils who jump off high buildings and, just at the last moment, release a parachute to land gracefully to the admiring applause of the spectators. Sometimes, not so gracefully. The first "base jumper" to try his luck was Franz Reichel, a mustachioed Austrian tailor, in 1912. He leapt from the first deck to test a tent-like parachute coat he had invented. The experiment failed and, so legend has it, he died of fright before bursting like a melon on the terrace 182 feet below. In May 2005 a 31-year old Norwegian with a parachute and a camera-fitted helmet jumped off the second deck, 380 feet above ground. The parachute opened successfully and he began to float to earth. However, the canopy caught on the first deck, the parachute was pulled from his body and he ended the fall more suddenly than he expected.

Trois

The Quasimodo of Pop

Serge Gainsbourg and French Rock

How revered French pop idol, songwriter, artist, actor and Gitane-powered sex maniac overcame personal ugliness to become a nation's heartthrob.

There is a wildly popular tradition in French music called the *chanson*, a high-syrup ballad or love-song. During its heyday, it would be crooned by one of France's middle-aged pop idols like Johnny Hallyday, Charles Aznavour or Sasha Distel, caught in all their embalmed glory in a single spot, the mic held close to the lips, eyes brimming with a far-away look as if the singer was receiving an unrequested barium enema. The king of the *chanson* was Serge Gainsbourg.

He was the definitive French pop star. Specifically, he was old, he looked like a prune and he wrote catchy little numbers with pretentious lyrics that he demanded were art.

"He had a typical French feel for rock; he was hopeless at it", wrote rock historian Caroline Sullivan in the *Guardian* newspaper at the time of his death.

FROM UNDER A ROCK
"Ugliness is in a way superior to beauty because it lasts", Serge Gainsbourg, toad-faced French "rock star" (1928-1991).

"He was only interested in two things – sex and money (in that order)". There was one other thing he was interested in: being a real rock star like his American equivalents. In a career lasting four decades, he was to fail hopelessly.

Born Lucien Ginzburg of Jewish musician parents in 1928, he was a young, trendy art teacher and amateur jazz pianist when he changed his name to Serge Gainsbourg. The old name was just "too Jewish" for France. (And why not? Charles Aznavour's original name was Shahnour Verengh Aznavourian).

What Gainsbourg was good at was writing the sentimental, plinkety-plonk tunes filling up the new French charts and giving them bizarre, sour lyrics. His first big hit in the mid-'50s was *Le Poinçonneur Des Lilas* about a Métro ticket clipper who goes so mad punching all those "*p'tits trous*" (little holes) that he punches "*un grand trou*" (a big hole) in his head with a gun. This was not a comedy number, mind, but the kind of thing that got the hip Parisian beatniks clicking their fingers.

Soon he was performing his own material in jazz clubs like *Milord L'Arsoille*. Singing in a voice that seemed filtered through an ashtray, his eyes screwed shut with passion and accompanied by vague and self-conscious hand-ballets, his act was so mannered that the in-crowd spectators, including president-to-be François Mitterrand, thought it was deliberate.

"His delivery", summed up his British biographer, Adam Clayson, "was a gravelly croak, bubbling with catarrh". Not surprising, since he sustained himself through his career with a bottle of

THE HISTORY OF FRENCH ROCK.
Why is there no French Rolling Stones? Why did no French performer appear at Live Aid? Why doesn't Madonna go and live in Paris (a question demanded by every Londoner)? The answers lie in the story of French Rock.

PRE-WAR: *In the early twentieth century, Paris was the counter-culture capital of Europe, teeming with avant garde painters, decadent poets, realist novelists, pioneering film-makers and folk singers. This artistic fertility contrasts with its absolute failure in the international pop scene during the second half of the century.*

POST-WAR: *At the end of World War II, the "chansonniers" fell in with the spirit of existentialism and working class angst against the "conformism" of everyone else. Stars included Georges Brassens with soupy but bitter albums such as* Le Parapluie *(1954) and Jacques Brel with* Quand On N'a Que L'Amour *(1957) and Ne Me Quitte Pas (1959). Bringing up the rear was the warbling Armenian shrimp Charles Aznavour whose still-continuing career includes 740 songs and over a hundred albums like* La Mamma *(1963).*

1960s: *The scene only had mopey proto-hippy Juliette Greco to contend against the rise of the "rockers" like Johnny Hallyday, still huge in France as a type of Gallic Zombie-Elvis, and "ye-ye" girls such as Sylvie Vartan of* Comme un Garçon *and Francoise Hardy.*

bourbon and five packs of unfiltered Gitanes a day. His record label tried hard to persuade him to concentrate on the writing of his sub-jazz tunes rather than singing them because, to put it simply, he was an ugloid. His eyes were heavily hooded, and his nose and ears lumpy. French teen magazine *Special Pop* found the kindest way to describe him was as "a drowsy turtle". One of the girls, the many girls, who fell for him despite or because of his looks, remembered him as "like a filthy uncle smelling of nicotine, whisky and socks". At the time, he was thirty-two.

PURE UGLY?

"He had a complex about his looks and the reception he got if he ever risked getting on stage didn't improve matters. I remember offensive remarks about his physical appearance coming from the front rows. They used to throw things." Michel Gaudry, double-bass player.

By the 1960s, it seemed all over for him. The day of the crooner was passing even in France, swept away by *le pop* from the U.S. "Here is a summary of the basic ingredients for French pop success in the Sixties", analyses U.S. biographer Angeline Morrison: "One – beautiful girl who is entirely unable to sing. Two – pure, bubble-gummy "yé-yé" pop melody. Three – brilliant 'ironic' lyrics".

Well, Gainsbourg could do all that. He latched on to the virginal, sixteen-year-old France Gall, a friend of the family, and began churning out hits for her like *Baby Pop*, *Teenie Weenie Boppie* and the one that won her the 1965 Eurovision Song Contest (for Luxembourg), *Poupée De Cire, Poupée De*

1970s: French pop is dominated by "symphonic rock" clone copies of early King Crimson and Yes. Ange's Le Cimetiere des Arlequins (1973) and Atoll's L'Araignee-Mal (1975) eventually evolve into Vangelis' thumping movie tracks and Jean-Michel Jarre's undanceable electronic dance albums, Oxygene *(1976) and* Equinoxe *(1978).*

1980s: The French (and Belgian) new wave is a freeway pile-up of styles, almost all originating in the U.K. or the U.S. It includes Telephone's pub-rock, Bijou's punk-rock, La Muerte's psychobilly, Les Thugs' punk-pop, Telex's synth-pop and culminates in Eric Debris' combo Metal Urbain which produced synthesizer and drum-machine tracks that were like Ultravox yet worse.

1990s: Giving up on domestic originality, French pop welcomes "world music" influences like Raksha Mancham's Phydair (1992) and The Gypsy Kings Allegria (1990). An apologetic Grunge influence seeps in with FFF's funk-metal Blast Culture (1991) along with DJ Cam's castrated trip-hop. By the end of the decade, the scene is flooded by sub-Moby pop electronica like Air's Moon Safari (1998) which jams together Pink Floyd's psychedelic ramblings, ambient jazz, random quotes from soul, funk and disco, and melodies Burt Bacharach and Ennio Morricone might have written for ready cash. Otherwise, the towering creative personality of mainstream French pop remains Vanessa Paradis.

BEYOND: *Nothing yet. Perhaps Stereolab. Perhaps not.*

Based on Piero Scaruffi's The History of Rock Music, *2002.*

Son (*Lonely, Singing Doll*). Gall was pretty if dim and only fathomed that Gainsbourg's interest in her was more than commercial with *Les Sucettes* (*The Lollipops*) which, it was explained to her, slowly, after its successful release, was about oral sex. She was so shocked she retired from performing, got bored, decided to make a come-back and was persuaded by her record company to partner again with Gainsbourg, who wrote for her *Les Petits Ballons* (*The Little Balloons*), a sincere tribute to her breasts. Gall retired again for twenty years.

By then Gainsbourg had moved on to bigger things, At the time there was no one bigger than Brigitte Bardot. Her movie career was not what it had been, as audiences had begun to recognise that her dramatic range did not extend much beyond her dramatic physique, so she had re-emerged as a singer of *le Rock and Roll*. She took on the unshaven, shambolic Gainsbourg as a writer for a 1967 T.V. special and, to the mesmerised fascination of the media, as her latest lover. Worse, she invited him back in front of the spotlights to sing with her.

PURE LUCK?
Gainsbourg may have been "the toad-faced godfather of French pop" but he was improbably successful in love. Amongst many others, his partners included Laura Betti (Italian film star of the '50s), Juliette Greco, Brigitte Bardot, Catherine Deneuve and Jane Birkin. His third wife, 25 years his junior, was "Bambou", the modelling name of Pauline von Paulus, niece of the Nazi Field Marshal who surrendered at Stalingrad.

The result was a series of songs slavishly *Américain* but so off the mark

SELECTED LYRICS

"*Annie likes the lollipops*
The lollipops with aniseed
That give her mouth the taste of aniseed
And when she's done
With just a little stick on her tongue
She goes shopping for another one"
Les Sucettes (The Lollipops), 1966

"*Harley David son of a bitch*
There you go, you are hard, you're in heat
Harley David son of a bitch
That vibration really affects you

Harley David son of a bitch
You shouldn't have fallen off
Harley David son of a bitch
You're dead, and I'm glad"
Harley David Son of a Bitch, 1967

"*Out of a painting by Francis Bacon*
I've come out
To make love to another man
Who said to me
Kiss me Hardy
Kiss me my love

In Frisco, not far from Sodom,
There as well
I met a handsome young man
Who said to me
Kiss me Hardy
Kiss me my love
Love on the Beat, 1984 (In French, "Beat" is a homonym for "bite", slang for "penis".)

"*Suck baby suck*
With the CD of
Chuck Berry Chuck
Suck baby suck
To the laserdisc of
Chuck Berry Chuck
Do you want me to give you a video?
Look
I have everything by Avery Tex
In Yankee in the original text
As well as Donald Duck"
Suck, Baby, Suck, 1987

they might have come from Uranus. Their first hit was a mangled version of *Bonnie and Clyde* and it was followed by *Comic Strip* (with Bardot breathily mouthing all the "Bangs!" and "Ka-Pows!") and then the enduringly hilarious *Harley David Son of a Bitch* which featured Bardot in leather hot pants astride a H.D. Sportster while Gainsbourg grunts at her: "Hey, what the hell you doing on my Harley!".

This was nothing to what was to come. As their affair reached its climax, they recorded the notorious, *Je T'Aime Moi, Non Plus* (*I Love You Me, Neither*) in a midnight session on December 1967. To an easy-listening tune, the pair simulated the grunts, whimpers and whispers of a couple making love. Bardot's moan of "You are the wave, I am the bare island. You go and you come between my loins" was matched by Gainsbourg's answering groan: "I see you, I want you, I come between your kidneys".

The song was to be a gigantic hit but not for Bardot. When the original recording was played back, the blonde bombshell lost her nerve and begged Gainsbourg not to release the track. Gainsbourg was happy to agree because he had already found a new sexual and musical partner in Jane Birkin.

....

FAMOUS ANGLO-SAXON ACTRESSES NOW OWNED BY THE FRENCH

JANE BIRKIN: *After her scandalous debut in* Blowup *(1966), went to France and married Gainsbourg. Became huge star in France appearing in such films as* If Don Juan Were A Woman *(1973) in which she played Brigitte Bardot's lesbian lover, and the film version of* Je T'Aime *(1976), directed by her husband Serge Gainsbourg, in which she suffered an unlubricated buggering.*

CHARLOTTE RAMPLING: *After her scandalous debut in* The Knack *(1965), went to France and married French musician Jean-Michel Jarre. Became huge star in France appearing in such films as* The Night Porter *(1974) in which she has sado-masochistic sex with Dirk Bogarde and* Max, Mon Amour *(1984) which sees her fall in love with a chimp.*

KRISTIN SCOTT-THOMAS: *After her charming debut in* Under The Cherry Moon *(1986), went to France and married French obstetrician, François Oliviennes. Became huge star in France but has not yet had bizarre sex with anyone on screen, especially not in* Four Weddings And A Funeral *(1994). Awarded* Legion d'Honneur *in January 2005, possibly to encourage her. In 2006, left her husband and returned to the U.K. "The One That Got Away".*

JOHNNY DEPP: *Resides in France. Vehemently opposes American intervention in Iraq. Co-owns Man Ray club / restaurant in Paris with Sean Penn and John Malkovich that serves vegetarian Tibetan cuisine in a free jazz environment. You couldn't make this up.*

PETULA CLARK: *Iron-permed, undying belter of up-beat popular international hits of the 1960s. With nearly 70 million recordings sold worldwide, the most successful British female recording artist ever. Married her French publicist, Claude Woolf, and now lives in France. In 2005, her CD* L'essentiel - 20 Succès Inoubliables *charted in France and Belgium. That year she was 73.*

Birkin is, in the words of Sam White, veteran correspondent in Paris, "one of those long-legged, horse-faced Anglo-Saxon actresses to whom the French are irresistibly drawn in the belief that under their cold Atlantic lid lies a seething cauldron of filthiness". Birkin had just appeared in the definitive Swinging Sixties film *Blowup*, which featured the first ever screening of pubic hair (hers). How could Gainsbourg resist? He re-recorded *Je T'Aime* with her and released it to massive commercial success.

BIRKIN ON GAINSBOURG ON BARDOT

"What did I, who have rivalled Raquel Welch as the media's most physically ideal woman, see in Serge Gainsbourg? Why, his monstrosity". Brigitte Bardot, 1970.

"Serge's affair [with Bardot] was a little fling. It was nothing that lasted very long, but when it was over, Serge's self-esteem was rather bruised. He tends to over-react when that happens." Jane Birkin, 1978.

"That woman has flattened me like a hot iron! I can never sing again!" Serge Gainsbourg, 1969.

Naturally it was banned by the Vatican but, to Gainsbourg's joy, it reached No.1 in the chart that really counted then, the U.K. (It was not immediately so popular in the U.S. where it reached No. 69).

Overnight Gainsbourg and Birkin became the French John and Yoko. While she became a spectacularly successful movie actress (in France), Gainsbourg revived his performing career with a vengeance, based on the two principles that had sustained his patchy record so far: sex and shock.

1971 saw the release of his concept album, *Histoire de Melody Nelson* (*The Story of Melody Nelson*), based on Nabokov's novel *Lolita*. (Gainsbourg gloried in his image as a dirty old man. One of his last publicity stills shows him, unshaven and drunk as ever, at a 1990s music awards ceremony, draped over a just-about-post-pubescent Vanessa Paradis. She looks like she is being smothered by a moth-eaten fur rug). He followed it up with his gesture to punk rock, 1975's amazingly crass *Rock around the Bunker*, a song-set entirely devoted to the Nazis that included tracks like *Tata teutonne*, *Eva* and *SS in Uruguay*. Radio stations gave it no airplay but it gained him a following amongst pre-Goth teenagers in France.

By the end of the decade, he discovered that U.K. and U.S. musicians had discovered reggae. He flew to Jamaica and recorded *Aux Armes et cetera*, a reggae version of the French national anthem, *La Marseillaise,* with Bob Marley's band, The Wailers, whom he referred to as

INCEST IN FRENCH ENTERTAINMENT.

Gainsbourg's bizarre love song to his daughter, Lemon Incest, *is emblematic of the professional inter-breeding in French entertainment. In 1973, Gainsbourg's then wife Jane Birkin appeared in* If Don Juan Was a Woman *as the lesbian girlfriend of Brigitte Bardot, Gainsbourg's former lover. Director Roger Vadim had once been married to Bardot and went on to have a child by Catherine Deneuve who later became Gainsbourg's lover after Birkin left him.*

"mes chimpanzees" (my monkeys). In a country as sensitive about its nationalism as France, *Aux Armes* caused an outrage and Gainsbourg's tour of the country was disrupted by bomb threats and demonstrations by far right and veterans' groups.

At one show in Strasbourg, a group of four hundred ex-paratroopers marched into the auditorium with the firm intention of smashing the place up. The Wailers refused to go on. Gainsbourg's response was legendary. He went on stage and sang *La Marseillaise* absolutely straight. The bullet-headed paras could only stand there saluting until, at the end, he flipped them off and zoomed out of the theatre into a waiting car. "A couple of minutes later", remembers Sly Dunbar, "we were fifty miles away". (The legend lost some lustre when it was revealed that the concert promoter had hired his own gang of ex-soldiers to form a tight wall in front of the stage in case the audience tried any tricks. Gainsbourg was never in any danger).

Aux Armes went to the top of the French charts but it was a rare commercial success. He was more famous for being infamous. Another album, *Ecce Homo*, toyed with the idea of a gay Gainsbourg, singing songs like *Bowie, Beau oui comme Bowie* (*As Pretty As David Bowie*), while his Lolita fixation reached its high point in the creepy video for *Un Zeste de Citron* (*Lemon Incest*) which showed him half-naked eyeing his thirteen-year old daughter, Charlotte, across a large bed. It caused barely a stir.

By this stage, his music was not important anyway. Listening to Gainsbourg was always more of a cultural duty than fun. He became a regular

---

OBITUARY FOR GAINSBOURG (1)

"Like Jonathan King and 'Weird' Al Yankovic, Gainsbourg could turn his hand to any kind of music, just as long as you didn't ask him to do it well. The clattery, clumsy rhythms of his sixties 'rock and roll' efforts were a pathetic, Pat Boone take on the music.

"Je T'Aime has the dishonour of sounding like twenty years of lame porno soundtracks – except, astonishingly, even less funky. The stinkiest hippie on the lowliest commune could have beaten Serge's '70s acoustic numbers into the ground.

"Your phone is a better synthesizer than the ones on his '80s records.

"And then he died. His influence is with us today, of course – France still turns up the odd snippet of paedo-pop in honour of the old bore (Latest example: 'Moi. Lolita') – though it's worth remarking that the only French music to have become remotely fashionable since Serge turned his toes up is House, the only kind of music he didn't get a chance to ruin.

"And Serge looms large in the memory of assorted neurotics desperate to convince themselves they're having filthier sex than the general public. That public ignores such people and gets on with shagging like rabbits – and whatever soundtrack they choose, you can bet your life it's not Serge Gainsbourg."
Tanya Headon, Name and Shame, 2002.

feature on French T.V., usually reeling into the studio drunken and unshaven but always capable of some outrage to delight the watching public. During one interview, he burned a 500 franc note to protest against high taxes while, in perhaps his most famous outburst on the Michel Drucker show, he informed Whitney Houston in a loud but not persuasive voice, "I want to fuck you".

On 2 March 1991, Gainsbourg died of a heart-attack and was buried in Montparnasse Cemetery in Paris. France went into something approaching national mourning. The impressive list of people who attended his funeral included Catherine Deneuve, Yves Saint Laurent, Claudia Cardinale, Jacques Chirac and Brigitte Bardot. Most impressive however was the fax from President Mitterrand who described Gainsbourg as "our Apollinaire". His home at 5bis rue de Verneuil is still covered by graffiti and poems. Gainsbourg's songs are now studied in French schools as part of the national curriculum.

OBITUARY FOR GAINSBOURG (2)
"If I make another album, it will be to prove that I am the best, writing in words of fire what is an art form. I don't wish to pass to posterity after my death. Fuck posterity." Serge Gainsbourg, 1989.

OBITUARY FOR GAINSBOURG (3)
"He was the most loved man in France when he died, which is just as well because he thought he was ugly and needed as much love as he could get." Jane Birkin, 2004.

Quatre

Asterix *vs.* Ronald McDonald

José Bové Trashes American food

How one middle-aged hippy beat the French army, trained in a Libyan terrorist camp, trashed a McDonald's – and became a national hero.

In a country where posturing and the dramatic gesture are highly rated, the saintly innocence on 51-year old José Bové's face as a police helicopter landed on his lawn and then whisked him off to jail made sensational photos across France.

"I am a sacrifice to the new totalitarianism!", he cried to the media crews swarming over his farm in Larzac. "There have been three totalitarian forces in our lifetime: the totalitarianism of Fascism, of Communism and now of American capitalism".

The human sacrifice went off to serve three months in a minimum-security prison where he began an immediate hunger strike. This lasted a couple of weeks (he allowed himself freshly squeezed orange juice) and then he was released, his term reduced by a presidential pardon.

"A country that allows this is not worthy of being the nation of human rights", he proclaimed to a crowd that included his wife, his girlfriend, celebrities, supporters and members of his union, *la Confédération Paysanne* (*la Conf*, the Peasant Confederation) greeting his triumphant release. Bové then flew to Yasser Arafat's compound in Ramallah to express his solidarity with the Palestinian people.

As far as the French public are concerned, Bové ascended to superstar status on 12 August 1999, when he turned up in his tractor at the head of a rag-tag procession of local protestors to destroy a half-built McDonald's restaurant in the town of Millau in the Tarn River Canyon.

In full view of the invited – naturally – media, Bové crashed his tractor through the fence surrounding the restaurant, broke through the door and then, assisted by his mates, stripped the place clean of roof tiles, panelling and pipes with crowbars and chainsaws. As four policemen watched disinterestedly from a safe distance, the protesters painted their slogan on the roof: "Out with *McDo*. Protect our Roquefort".

Roquefort, that was apparently Bové's beef. The previous year, the French had banned the import of American beef into their country, insisting that it be labelled "hormone

"I AM NOT A COMMODITY. I AM A REAL PERSON". THE LIFE OF JOSÉ BOVÉ. *Born 11 June 1953, son of two agricultural chemists from Luxembourg (his father was regional director of the National Institute of Agricultural Sciences Research, and member of the French Academy of Sciences). Brought up outside France, including in Berkeley, California. Expelled from Catholic school in Paris for atheism. Studied philosophy at Bordeaux University but dropped out after a month. Became a full-time protester, eventually occupying public lands in the Larzac region. Stayed, illegally building a sheep barn on a planned French military base. Became a sheep farmer, producing roquefort cheese within a "farming commune". His farming schedule allows plenty of time for his activism. In 1985, he trained in a Qadaffi-sponsored "direct action" training camp in Libya . In 1987, formed the* Confédération Paysanne, *an agricultural union to oppose genetically modified foodstuffs. In 1995, he joined* Greenpeace on their ship, the Rainbow Warrior, *to protest against nuclear weapons testing. In 1999, he led union members to destroy a McDonald's restaurant in a gesture against "American cultural imperialism". Sentenced to three months in prison but actually served 44 days. In 2001, helped destroy genetically modified crops in Brazil. In 2002, deported by Israeli police while protesting in Ramallah. Has also "intervened" to support the movements of the Tahitians, the Kanaks, the Sunni Iraqis and the Kurds. On 22 June 2003, Bové began a ten month-sentence for the destruction of GM crops. President Jacques Chirac reduced the sentence to end in December.*

treated". In fact, the *Ministère de l'Agriculture et de la Pêche* (the Ministry of Agriculture and Fishery) was not concerned in the least by additives but was much more interested in creating a closed home market for its own powerful beef farmers. A health scare was a useful opportunity to sidestep European Union rules on free trade (the same trick had been used successfully to close off France to British beef after the "Mad Cow" crisis of the 1990s). The United States responded by slapping a 100% import tax on a number of French agricultural products, including Roquefort cheese.

Enter José Bové. Twenty years before, as a student drop-out, he had joined a rolling caravan of protestors occupying some public land as a protest against the French army who had planned to set up a base there. Bové and his companions illegally built a sheep barn and, after the French army had retreated (as is its wont), decided to keep the land. To do that, they found they actually had to run the place as a farm. They set up a "peasant action committee on Maoist principles", brought in five hundred sheep and, thanks to subsidies from the French government and the European Union, began producing a rudimentary version of Roquefort, called *la Tomme*, selling it to local markets.

SOMETHING STINKS ABOUT ROQUEFORT. Roquefort cheese, made from aged sheep's milk, is an acquired taste. The texture is clammy, the colour is a corpse-like white with veins of blue mould running through it. The taste is strong, musky and salty. It crumbles in the mouth. Eating it is like sucking on the thigh of an elderly bag lady. Roquefort represents a €300 million ($370 million) a year business to the French. Nearly 80% of the 15,000 tones produced each year are consumed domestically. It can only be produced in the caves of Roquefort-sur-Soulzon because it is aged using bacteria specific to its damp, dark caverns. It was the first non-wine produce in France to be granted the A.O.C. label (Appellation d'Origine Contrôlée). AOCs are a type of immutable trademark that France has persuaded both the European Union and the World Trade Organisation to recognise. Any Roquefort that does not carry a French A.O.C. cannot be marketed anywhere as "Roquefort" and will be subject to legal action. As a result, a closed market has been created for this cheese which sells for the inflated price of €25 ($31) a pound.

While the American import tax on the cheese had precisely zero effect on Bové's sales, it was a good enough excuse to protest against what he really disliked, the United States and, specifically, the most convenient symbol of its success, Ronald McDonald. "We are peasants and citizens, not shareholders nor servile slaves at the service of American crap food (*malbouffe*)", he has proclaimed.

MCDONALD'S IN FRANCE. *In France, McDonald's does what it does everywhere: it sells hot food cheap. This is not good enough for some French people. Their objections are wrapped up in apparently altruistic concerns for the environmental implications of Mickey D's business, although these are heavily policed by the health and safety agencies of every country in which it operates. McD also defers to the cultural traditions of its markets (eg, in India it serves no beef products, out of respect for Hindu sensibilities). The chain operates to the same standards as francophone multinationals that trade in foodstuffs, from the hypermarket chain Carrefour to the food-and-drink giant Nestlé, which seem to escape the hostility of French activists. For all this, much of the French population is happy enough with McDonald's. France is McD's sixth largest market: it serves 1.6 million French customers every day through 800 French restaurants owned and run by French franchisees. 98% of all foodstuffs served by McDonald's in France are sourced in France . It invests heavily in the French environment and in 2005 won le prix Admical – Fondation de France for its charitable work.*

The story of the raid was splashed across French newspapers. The Paris media portrayed Bové as "the Asterix of the Larzac plateau", not only because of the Village People-style handlebar moustache he shares with the cartoon character but because of his cheery resistance to a foreign threat to France's treasured culture. *Libération* newspaper proudly ran the headline "Bové: France's No.1 Oppositionist".

It took four days before the French police realised that events were getting out of hand. They arrested four of the raiders on Bové's farm, though the leader himself had beaten a convenient retreat to Bordeaux. Only when he realised he was big news did he join his colleagues in the cells, driving his tractor to the police station to turn himself in. Over the next two weeks, eighteen members of the French parliament, from greens and communists to the extreme right, demanded Bové's release – including the then socialist Prime Minister, Lionel Jospin. (Naturally, the French had already tried to release the group, but Bové refused to pay his bail. "You just don't ask union members to post bail to get out of jail," he sniffed, so they were forced to keep him).

The trial was all he could have hoped for. Twenty thousand tie-died, spliff-puffing and undeodorised supporters packed the narrow streets of Millau to watch Bové turn up at the courthouse aboard a tractor-drawn trailer decorated like a tumbril. "*Non à la McDomination*," chanted one cluster of gonzos. "W.T.O. [World Trade Organisation] equals death," said another. The press polls showed 45% of the French population agreed with Bové smashing up the restaurant. He received 2,000 fan letters a day. President Chirac, always eager to stress his multi-polar credentials, issued a statement: "I am in complete solidarity with France's farm-workers, and I detest McDonald's food".

Inside the court, things seemed even better. Judge François Mallet, a one-time communist and popular local figure, was more than willing to convert the trial of Bové into a prosecution of *la mondialisation* (globalisation). Bové's demand that fourteen French and foreign celebrities of the new "Citizens' International" appear as witnesses was allowed and they were questioned benignly about politics and U.S. policy by a celebrated Parisian human rights lawyer.

Bové ran the court like a ringmaster, insisting that his McDonald's attack, which inflicted €150,000 ($185,000) of damage, was really caused by the Americans.

BOVÉ THE FRAUD?

"His critics describe an opportunist, a veteran activist with no real farming roots, who has 'not seen his sheep for a month'. They cite his Californian upbringing, and France's Elle Magazine *once called Bové 'the man who fooled us most, who perpetuated fraud'. And before he founded the* Confédération Paysanne, *a leftist peasant farmers' union, they asked why an authentic French farmer would really need to spend time at a Qaddafi-sponsored 'direct action' training camp in Libya."* B.B.C., April 2002.

"It was a provocation the moment that the Americans decided to tax Roquefort and there was no recourse for us through the W.T.O. It's an organisation above the law that no one can challenge," he said. McDonald's, he claimed, "was a legitimate symbol of bad American eating habits".

True, there were uncomfortable moments when the judge questioned

BOVÉ THE UNTOUCHABLE?

"It would astonish me greatly if the judge dares to order us to be arrested after the trial. If so, the state would be making a great mistake, triggering an unprecedented situation" – José Bové the day before the police chopper whisked him off to serve his three-month sentence.

Bové's description of his rampage as a "peaceful, non-violent dismantling" by asking how an attack using tractors, crowbars and chainsaws could be "non-violent". On the whole, it was going wonderfully until the jury returned its verdict of "Guilty" and gave Bové three months in jail.

No one was more surprised than Bové who immediately launched a string of appeals, demanded a pardon from President Chirac and proclaimed "This is the first time a union leader has been sentenced to such a long prison term in France for a legitimate action of civil disobedience". He added: "Last summer, I drove to prison in my tractor. This time, if the police want to throw me in the Bastille, they have to come and get me."

And so they did, avoiding all the high jinks with the tractor by landing on his lawn one fine dawn in June 2000 and taking him off to jail by helicopter.

BOVÉ THE MARTYR?

"Everything must be done to prevent José Bové being sent to prison. The struggle against the inegalitarian logic of liberal globalisation is a just one. Bové should be thanked, not jailed." Julien Dray, French Socialist Member of Parliament.

Bové claims to be a victim of "the conspirators of globalisation". Ironically, he may be right, but if there was a conspiracy it was hatched in France and not the U.S. Bové's jail sentence was unusual. Earlier that year, militant farming campaigners ransacked the offices of the former environment minister Dominique Voynet only to have the case against them dropped, while those who destroyed hundreds of thousands of euros' worth of goods at an agribusiness factory in Mayenne were not even pursued.

Bové's mistake was to carry out his action in the name of the upstart union he himself had started, *la Confédération Paysanne*. Small, militant and pretty much a fan club to himself, it competes directly with the larger *Fédération Nationale des Syndicats d'Exploitants Agricoles* (F.N.S.E.A., the National Federation of Agricultural Workers).

The F.N.S.E.A. does what it likes, from burning imports of British lamb in Calais or hijacking lorries carrying Spanish wine into France and emptying their cargo into the gutters. It gets away with this because the local *chambres départementales d'agriculture* (departmental farming committees) are swamped with its members who ruthlessly exercise the stranglehold this gives them on the policies (and subsidies) of the French Ministry of Agriculture. Highly influential, the F.N.S.E.A. intermeshes with police, state and regulatory authorities at all levels.

"It is never a good thing to see a trade unionist in jail," an F.N.S.E.A. vice-president, Dominique Barrau, observed of Bové's imprisonment, "but now he will have time to contemplate co-ordinating his actions with my union".

RONALD MCDONALD UNDER SIEGE

Inspired by Bové, McDonald's in France and its French employees are still subject to attack. "The McDonald's franchise located in Paris at Strasbourg St. Denis has been shut down by striking workers for the better part of a year. Now the strikers are occupying the McDonald's and using it as a storefront to sell t-shirts to fund striking French artists and anything that José Bové is up to at the moment. So here we have the confiscation of private property that has been turned into a squat, and illegal commerce, and nothing is done about it." National Review Online, *August 2003.*

Bové remains unrepentant. He continues his campaign, with much national support, against "American *malbouffe*". He still loathes McDonald's, a loathing underlined by the recent release of his police interviews regarding that incident in Millau. "That McDonald's will be destroyed as many times as necessary", runs one statement, "even if it takes a bomb".

There are plenty of others in France who share the same hatred of McDonald's and the globalisation it supposedly symbolises. On 19 April 2000 a bomb exploded at a McDonald's in Dinan, France. One employee was killed by the blast. The culprit was never traced.

Music with Menaces

France's Blood-Curdling Signature Tune

Almost every French government since the Revolution has hated its national anthem. Booed at French cup finals, mangled by Serge Gainsbourg and beloved by French racists, just what is wrong with *La Marseillaise*?

Everyone remembers that scene in *Casablanca*. A party of jack-booted Nazis gather around the piano in Rick's and begin singing *Die Wacht am Rhein*. At other tables, cowed huddles of Vichy French droop into their small cognacs. The corrupt chief of police raises an eyebrow. But, wait! A brave East European resistance hero is striding over to the band. "Play the *Marseillaise*!", he commands. "Play it!" The bandleader glances at the club's American owner, Humphrey Bogart, who nods. The band strikes up, everyone sings. Even the young French whore, who had been touting for business over at the Germans' table, belts out the anthem, tears and snot dribbling down her face. Overwhelmed, the Nazis beat a hasty retreat. The room erupts with liberty, equality and fraternity.

"To arms, citizens! Form into battalions! Let us march, let us march! And may their impure blood irrigate our fields!.."
Lines from La Marseillaise, *by Rouget de Lisle*

LA MARSEILLAISE

Arise children of the
 fatherland
The day of glory has
 arrived
Against us tyranny's
Bloody standard is raised
Listen to the sound in the
 fields
The howling of these
 fearsome soldiers
They are coming into your
 midst
To cut the throats of your
 sons and your friends

Chorus
To arms, citizens!
Form your battalions!
March, march
Let the impure blood (of
 our enemies)
Soak the furrows (of our
 fields)

What do they want this
 horde of slaves
Of traitors and
 conspiratorial kings?
For whom these vile chains
These long-prepared irons?
Frenchmen, for us, ah!
 What outrage
What methods must be
 taken?
It is us they dare plan
To return to the old
 slavery!

What! These foreign
 cohorts!
They would make laws in
 our courts!
What! These mercenary
 phalanxes
Would cut down our
 warrior sons
Good Lord! By chained
 hands
Our brow would yield
 under the yoke
The vile despots would
 have themselves be
The masters of destiny

Tremble, tyrants and
 traitors
The shame of all good men
Tremble! Your parricidal
 schemes
Will receive their just
 reward
Against you we are all
 soldiers
If they fall, our young
 heroes
France will bear new ones
Ready to fight against you

Frenchmen, as
 magnanimous warriors
Bear or hold back your
 blows
Spare these sad victims
That they regret taking up
 arms against us

But not these bloody
 despots
These accomplices of
 Bouillé
All these tigers who
 mercilessly
Ripped out their mothers'
 wombs

We shall enter into the
 career
When our elders will no
 longer be there
There we shall find their
 ashes
And the mark of their
 virtues
We are much less jealous
 of surviving them
Than of sharing their
 coffins
We shall have the sublime
 pride
Of avenging or joining
 them

Drive on sacred patriotism
Support our avenging
 arms
Liberty, cherished liberty
Join the struggle with your
 defenders
Under our flags, let
 victory
Hurry to your manly tone
So that in death your
 enemies
See your triumph and our
 glory!

Of course, sometimes *La Marseillaise* works in reverse. In October 2002 in Paris's *Stade de France*, Corsica's Bastia met Brittany's Lorient in the French soccer cup final. Played before the start of the match, the national anthem provoked a barrage of whistles and jeers by nationalist Corsican fans who began throwing bottles at two government ministers, both women, who had been greeting the players on the pitch,

NO ROYALTIES FOR THE ROYALIST
Claude-Joseph Rouget de Lisle (1760-1836), who wrote the words and music of the Marseillaise, *was horrified when it became a hit tune for the Revolution. He was a Royalist and refused to take the oath of allegiance to the new constitution. Cashiered, imprisoned and barely escaping the guillotine, he was set free after the Revolution only to find that the French government had claimed the copyright of the song for itself.*

The *Marseillaise* is maybe the most rollicking of all national anthems. The tune is bumptious and springy while the words of the seven long verses (with a chorus after each) combine blood-curdling threat, empty boasts and wheedling self-pity. Only the French could sing it with a straight face.

It was composed over a night in Strasbourg during the French Revolution (24 April 1792) as a propaganda exercise by amateur musician and captain of engineers Rouget de Lisle.

Printed up and distributed to the army, it was played at a patriotic banquet at Marseilles. Revolutionary soldiers from the town, the Provenal volunteers, entered Paris singing this song and, to its infectious beat, they stormed the Tuileries. The Convention accepted it as the French national anthem in a decree passed on 14 July 1795.

After that, with a few tweaks here and there (Hector Berlioz rearranged the tune in 1830) the future of the *Marseillaise* was assured. With its fist-shaking menaces against foreigners and tyrants alike, hardliners on both the right and the left all over France adopted it as their signature tune. (And not only in France. In 1917, after the collapse of the tsarist regime, the *Marseillaise* became the national anthem of Russia until it was replaced by the Bolsheviks with *the Internationale*, which is even bloodthirstier).

Not everyone is happy. In 1999, the 83-year-old charity campaigner Abbé Pierre and founder of the world famous *Emmaus* human rights organisation led a campaign condemning the "vile" lines of the *Marseillaise*, claiming it was an "incitement to racism" and should be rewritten to reflect the French "love of peace". After all, he wrote to President Chirac warning against its racist overtones, "it is regrettable that a country which claims to be peaceful can have a national anthem whose chorus concedes the existence on this Earth of 'impure blood'." Chirac made no reply.

The Abbé's warnings seem prophetic. Singing the *Marseillaise* has been adopted as a mainstay of any mass rally by the far-right party, Jean-Marie Le Pen's le Front National, and in 2002 it was Le Pen who made it through the first round of the presidential elections to face Chirac himself in the run-off, and all to the ominous chorus of "Marchons! Marchons!". Left-wing parties struck back by reclaiming the revolutionary anthem as their own. This leads to much confusion during traditional May Day street

VARIATIONS ON THE THEME. *Many musicians have sampled, stolen or written variations on the Marseillaise, ranging from Tchaikovsky's 1812 Overture (which uses its theme to symbolise pulverisation of Napoleon's army by Russian cannon) to Django Reinhardt's Echoes of France to the Beatles' All You Need Is Love. The most controversial version was Gainsbourg's cover so hated by music lovers and Franch fascists alike.*

demonstrations when stringy-bearded Trotskyite marchers find themselves accidentally mingling with thick-necked skinheads on a counter-demonstration, both chanting the same national anthem.

Caught somewhere in the middle, Chirac's notoriously trendy education minister Jack Lang once sent out 72,000 copies of a C.D. featuring the national anthem to schools all over France. "The *Marseillaise* is not just our national anthem, it is also an international hymn to liberty and deserves to be better known and understood by all our pupils," he said.

The C.D. includes the traditional version with orchestra and warbling sopranos but also fifteen other interpretations – from jazz, Arabic and house to, naturally, Serge Gainsbourg's much-hooted version.

It is ironic that the only reason the *Marseillaise* may be known to young people around the world anyway is that the Beatles sampled its bombastic opening bars for their 1967 hit *All You Need Is Love*. And the only reason John Lennon did that was so that he could contrast the militaristic violence it idealises with his own message of peace and toleration.

ANYTHING BUT!
Not every French government has been so enthusiastic about their militaristic and xenophobic anthem.
- *Napoleon (1800-15) preferred a song called "Let's Look after the Health of the Empire".*
- *The Bourbon kings (1815-30) chose* Où peut-on être mieux qu'au sein de sa famille *("Where can we feel better than in our family?").*
- *For Louis-Philippe (1830-48) the national anthem was* La Parisienne *("The Parisian") by Casimir Delvigne. The Second Republic's anthem was* Le Chant des Girondins *("The Song of the Girondists") by the famed writer Alexandre Dumas.*
- *Napoleon III (1852-70) chose* Partant pour la Syrie *("Going to Syria"), written by Hortense de Beauharnais, queen of the Netherlands and, incidentally, his mother.*
- *The Free French Government liked to lead with* Le Chant des Partisans *("The Song of the Fighters") by André Montagnard.*
- *The* Marseillaise *was finally made the official national anthem by the constitution of the Fourth Republic (Article 2 of the Constitution of 4 October 1958).*

Six

The Scent of a Nation

Vive Pepé LePew!

The French are stylish, urbane and sophisticated, their country is the home of *haute couture* and the laboratory of famous perfumes. So why are they held in such bad odour around the world?

In 1791 the royal family fled Paris pursued by revolutionary troopers. Disguised as commoners, their coach got as far as Varennes. Legend has it that they were betrayed by a female goose-seller in the marketplace who noticed that Marie Antoinette smelled of heavenly Houbigant scent rather than of dead meat, urine and tobacco like most of her customers.

A SCENT OF THE CLASSICS
"The old fellow has vanished; went on towards Arezzo the next morning; not liking the smell of the French, I suppose, after being their prisoner for so long." George Eliot, Romola, *1863.*

The French have always had an easy and even affectionate relationship with the gasses emerging from their various orifices. The writer Rabelais celebrated the winy farts of the priests in the sixteenth century while the Duke de Villeroi congratulated his men on the "strength of their goatish essences" before the battle of Ramillies (1706). Emile Zola, one of France's most pungent social commentators, declared on his deathbed that his greatest achievement was to

51

have captured the "complete smell of France". (Ironically, Zola died of accidental asphyxiation, though of coal gas rather than anyone he knew).

That same smell has often horrified France's more fastidious Anglo-Saxon and German neighbours. In 1798, readers of the *London Times* recoiled in disgust as they read a two line love-letter from Napoleon seized by the ships of Admiral Nelson on its way to Josephine. It read: "Returning in three days. Don't wash".

Today, unforgiving foreigners still wrinkle their noses at the olfactory tolerance of the French. The usually internationalist *Economist* magazine can still write without fear of contradiction that "the otherwise sophisticated French have long had a reputation for a certain blithe disregard for personal odours" while established travel and expat websites feel it necessary to warn travellers about "That Smell".

"My first impression of France was not the best", writes Kelby Carr, travel writer and journalist for Gofrance.com. "We had arrived at Charles de Gaulle, and hopped onto the shuttle bus into the city. And it hit me like a sledgehammer. That smell of body odour. Whoa! I don't know who sat in the seat before me (or when he or she last discovered the marvels of soap and water), but it almost made my eyes water. Fortunately, this situation seems to have improved. After all, the French have some of the best soap in the world. I guess they are starting to use it. But you will still run into some unpleasant smells."

It wasn't always like this. "In the Middle Ages in France, cleanliness was paramount", says Danièle Alexandre-Bidon, a specialist at the School for Higher Studies in Social Sciences in Paris. "Using water on the body was seen as a source of cleanliness and purity – literally as well as religiously."

BREATHE MY SECRET SUBSTANCE
"When we smell another's body, it is that body that we are breathing in through our mouth and nose, that we possess instantly, as it were in its most secret substance, its own nature. Once inhaled, the smell is the fusion of the other's body and my own." Jean-Paul Sartre, writer, philosopher, lover and notoriously smelly man.

AN AMERICAN IN PARIS
"Paris was cool 'cause I had never been to Europe. Me and my manager go to this club So I'm looking at the girls, and the girls are looking at me, but every time I step on the dance floor the odour burned my retina. It was singeing the hair out of my nose! It was the first time I went to a club and as a parting gift, they were giving out deodorant at the door – I cross my heart! And the street (outside of the club) was full of deodorant 'cause all the cats didn't know what to do (with it)." Anthony Mackie, actor, GQ magazine interview, 2004.

LOUIS XIV: THE SUN KING UNEXTINGUISHED
"How many baths did France's King Louis XIV take? Three: the first when baptized, the second when a mistress insisted, and the third when a doctor lanced a sore on his bottom and ordered him to soak the wound in a tub of water." Wallechinsky and Wallace, The Book of Lists, 1993.

Manuscripts at the Louvre bear witness to the multitude of recipes for shampoos, soaps, toothpastes and depilatory creams. All-over hair removal caught on – for both sexes – after returning Crusaders brought the idea back from the Middle East. The wife of one French king, Eleanor of Aquitaine, is credited with inventing dental floss, although she later defected to the English.

"It was only much later that a different mentality arrived which feared exposure to air and water, and believed the body's goodness had to be heavily protected from outside elements", adds Alexandre-Bidon.

By the time of Louis XIV, French high society had rejected bathing wholesale. This was not surprising given the unsanitary quality of *Grand Siécle* water supplies which were believed to propagate disease. The *Memoires* of the Duc de Saint-Simon recount the general filthiness of life at the giant palace of Versailles where the nobility, despite their three foot-high wigs and embroidered brocade, were crawling with lice and, rather than walk two miles to the nearest bathroom, would piss on the wall in one of the king's corridors. Instead of a bath to remove bodily odours, it became common practice to disguise them with perfume. It was around this time that France established its world-leading scent industries.

SPECIFICALLY FRENCH:
"In the court of Louis XIV, people doused themselves with perfume to chase away bad smells but they didn't wash themselves, while in other European courts of the same period, baths were raised to the status of an institution. In this, there is a certain national continuity, not to say a certain French specificity." Edouard Zarifian, professor of psychiatry, University of Caen.

Following the Sun King's example, the French became legendarily open-minded regarding personal cleanliness. This tradition has lasted for centuries and, on the verge of the millennium, *Le Figaro* newspaper sensationally published a double-page report on the nation's personal hygiene, drawing on sources ranging from the Federation of Perfume Industries to the government-supported Health Education Committee. The report found:

- 40% of French men, and 25% of women, do not change their underwear daily.

- Fully 50% of men, and 30% of women, do not use deodorant.

- 96% of the French live in homes equipped with showers or baths, even more than those with bidets. But only 47% bathe every day (compared to 80% of those squeaky clean Dutch and even 70% of the British).

- The average Frenchman uses 1.3 pounds of soap a year compared to 3 pounds used by the average Briton and 2 pounds by the average German.

- 85% of Frenchmen wash their hands before a meal but only 60% after using the bathroom. 6% never wash their hands at all. (*Le Figaro* suggested respondents were lying since, if their claims were true, France's annual soap consumption should be at least 2 lb per person).

- 67% of French respondents said they brushed their teeth twice a day. (*Le Figaro* did the maths there too. If the figure were true, sales of toothpaste should be more than 240 million tubes a year, not the current 198.5 million).

- The report featured many anecdotes about the basic realities of French hygiene. "One is shaken to observe that even in the higher classes, bodily hygiene leaves a great deal to be desired," a French doctor told the newspaper. "When I discuss this with my colleagues, they all report daily incidences of dubious underwear and powerful odours."

Le Figaro cited experts who concluded that "more than one French person in two does not respect elementary rules of body hygiene".

That survey was concluded five years ago, the same year that the U.S. cable channel Cartoon Network banned the showing of any more of the old Warner Brothers' Pepé LePew cartoons in case the amorous but odorous skunk caused offence in its francophone markets. And yet in 2005 the magazine *Le Point* revisited the subject of French hygiene and found to its nose-wrinkling horror:

"Only one in 10 of the population regularly uses soap, while almost one in 25 admit that they never shower or bath, and one in 33 say they never brush their teeth. No wonder, perhaps, that nine out of 10 French women and half of all French men apply perfume and cosmetics every day, spending €17 7 million ($21.8 million) between them. The French do spend long periods in the bathroom: between 48 and 56 minutes each day, according to the figures. Yet much of this is apparently devoted to pursuits other than cleanliness. While in there, one third say they read and one quarter that they daydream. A further 14% make telephone calls, eight per cent sing, six per cent smoke – and one in 100 eats."

As Pepé would have said: "Le sigh".

VIVE PEPÉ LEPEW

"He's great. He's a romantic. He's a wit. He's misunderstood. He's imperturbable. He's persistent. He's the world's greatest lover. What else could he be but French? So, of course, he had to be a skunk." Chuck Jones, creator of Warner Bros' much loved but visibly odorous cartoon character, Pepé LePew.

The Pain in the Neck

De Gaulle and the Strategy of Ingratitude

General de Gaulle saved France, or so he often said. But who saved de Gaulle and why did he repay them with spite, obstinacy and ultimately betrayal?

P resident Charles de Gaulle, a six-foot-four-inch humourless Frenchman with "a head like a banana and hips like a woman" (as one British official remarked), did not hit it off with Winston Churchill, the man who during the Second World War was his chief protector, paymaster

THE GALL OF DE GAULLE
"We shall stun you with our ingratitude", General de Gaulle to Winston Churchill 1945, referring to the military aid that the Allies provided to France to defeat Germany.

and propagandist. Once, during dinner at Chequers, Churchill was informed by his butler that de Gaulle wished to speak to him on the phone. Churchill, in the middle of soup, refused to take the call and others that immediately followed. Eventually he stomped off to the phone, returning ten minutes later, crimson with rage. "Bloody de Gaulle! After all we've done for him, he had the impertinence to tell me that the French regard him as the reincarnation of Joan of Arc." Pause. "I found it necessary to remind him we had to burn the first one".

A LONG STORY SHORT

De Gaulle, Charles André Joseph Marie (1890-1970), French "general" (promotion never confirmed) and President of France (1945-6, 1958-69). Born second son into conservative teaching family. Became professional soldier, early career hindered by accusations of arrogance. Known inaccurately as advocate of mechanised warfare. Wounded during World War I and taken prisoner, taken into the French cabinet during World War II. Opposing surrender to Germany, fled to London and "assumed" total control of the Free French Forces which, though contributing little to actual victory, ensured he received a hero's welcome in Paris after liberation. After brief period leading a post-war government, unsuccessfully attempted to form his own political party and retired from politics in 1953. As France descended into chaos over the Algerian War, de Gaulle became president again in a semi-official coup d'état. To the consternation of right-wing supporters, he withdrew France from Algeria but pursued a hyper-nationalist foreign policy, characterised by "anti-Anglo" actions such as leaving N.A.T.O. (1966) in protest against "American hegemonism" and vetoing the U.K.'s entry into the European Economic Community. Despite a policy of state intervention in the economy ("dirigisme"), labour and student unrest made his position untenable and he resigned in 1969, dying a year later at his home in Colombey-les-Deux-Eglises and bequeathing to France a legacy of anti-Americanism in foreign affairs and government interference in social and economic matters.

To a man as colossally vain as General de Gaulle, the fact that he is barely remembered now outside France except as the butt of Churchill anecdotes – and a rather ramshackle airport – would have been infuriating. And, as his life and history show, there was nothing de Gaulle liked more than paying off scores against old friends. If France and the French are sometimes called ungrateful, it was "*le grand Charles*" who made ingratitude into enduring national policy.

THE EARLY YEARS: "THE MONSTER OF AMBITION"

If he was anything, de Gaulle was lucky. He graduated from military college just in time for the Great War which killed 1,375,000 French soldiers. De Gaulle missed most of it. Two weeks after the outbreak of war, he was wounded in the leg and out of action for three months. Wounded again in March 1915, he convalesced for eight months. Fit at last, he was sent to Verdun where he was captured and spent the last thirty-two months of the war in German prison camps.

On his return, his luck really paid off. He found that the colonel of his old unit, Phillipe Pétain, was now Marshal Pétain, the hero of the defence of Verdun and France's most venerated commander. De Gaulle latched onto Petain's boots like chewing gum.

PÉTAIN'S HELPING HAND
De Gaulle wrote an embellished account of how he had been captured by the Germans and sent it to Marshal Pétain who signed it and passed it on to the approval committee of the Legion of Honour who made de Gaulle a Chevalier. Letters reveal that de Gaulle knew well that "my citation much exaggerates the facts".

It was Pétain who got him into the elite army staff college, the *Ecole Supérieure de Guerre*, generally a fast-track to the top but de Gaulle's sour, cocky attitude alienated his commanding officers. He left with only an average grade (and Pétain had to intervene to get him that). General Chauvin, one of his then classmates, described him as "a monster of ambition who would sell his own mother to get ahead".

De Gaulle got ahead in the years before the Second World War because the way was cleared for him by Pétain, who became Minister for War in 1934. De Gaulle named his son Phillipe after him and almost every one of his books on his pet theories of war has a dedication to the old man so oily the ink nearly runs off the page. Once, when he was threatened with close arrest for forcing troops on a double forced march in deliberate defiance of orders, de Gaulle was able to say smugly: "You will see. Everything will die down, because I belong to the *maison* Pétain".

ECOLE SUPERIEURE DE GUERRE'S REPORT ON DE GAULLE: *"An intelligent, well-read officer, keen on his job; brilliant and resourceful qualities. Unfortunately, he spoils his undoubted talents by his excessive assurance, his contempt for other people's point of view, and his attitude as a king in exile." Colonel Moyran, Staff College.*

In 1939, at the outbreak of war, de Gaulle was a full colonel, commander of the French Fourth Armoured Division and about to be appointed to the Cabinet as Under-Secretary of State for National Defence – all thanks to Pétain.

"The old man is a traitor", de Gaulle pronounced of his old friend and mentor within two years. "I will have him shot. I alone represent France."

THE WAR YEARS: "THE OBSTRUCTIONIST SABOTEUR"

Pétain's mistake, a mistake shared by the entire French army, was to think that the Germans had won the war.

In May 1940, as the Germans swept over the border, de Gaulle's tanks at Caumont forced a large formation of Panzers to retreat. As a reward for being the first and only French commanding officer to check any German advance during the invasion, he was given the provisional – never confirmed – rank of Brigadier General (thus his title of *Général* de Gaulle).

With no one wanting to take the blame, the elderly and feeble Marshal assumed France's government and sought peace with the Germans.

De Gaulle was not in Paris but in Bordeaux, the right place at the right time. The British

EXCESS BAGGAGE: *"What is equally beyond doubt is that, if he had not pulled de Gaulle into that aeroplane at Bordeaux, de Gaulle would never have been heard of. Spears, and Spears alone, created de Gaulle; and in so doing made history. de Gaulle knew it, and resented it. When Spears took him to see Churchill, the latter said: "Why have you brought this lanky, gloomy Brigadier?" Spears replied: "Because no one else would come". Robert Boothby, British politician, Boothby: Portrait of a Rebel, 1978.*

liaison officer, General Louis Spears, who was about to embark for England, bundled him onto a plane and took him to London where, as the only French officer available, he proclaimed himself head of the "Free French Forces" in a broadcast over the B.B.C. put at his disposal by Churchill. As an afterthought, he also proclaimed Pétain a traitor and ordered anyone who cared to shoot him.

De Gaulle had no resources at all beyond 100,000 francs (about £500). The British government gave de Gaulle a plush headquarters in Carlton Gardens and provided all his funds. In the first year alone he received $40 million, de Gaulle insisting on dollars since, as he told Jean Monnet, his economic adviser, he had "no faith in sterling".

Churchill gave de Gaulle continued access to the B.B.C. and his broadcasts drew an increasing number of French to his cause whom the British then armed and trained. De Gaulle responded with a policy of obstruction all the way down the line.

As soon as British troops liberated Syria, the Free French administration Churchill allowed to take over control of the Vichy colony were instructed not to co-operate with British soldiers (commanded, incidentally, by Major General Spears, the same man who had saved de Gaulle at Bordeaux).

When American troops sailed for the islands of Miquelon and Saint-Pierre in the Atlantic, which Roosevelt wished to reinforce during the Battle of the Atlantic, de Gaulle gave orders that if they attempted a landing, they were to be fired upon by his garrison. When British and American troops finally landed in North Africa as part of Operation Torch, de Gaulle snapped: "Well, I hope the people of Vichy throw them into the sea. You can't break into France and get away with it".

Churchill was confounded by this paranoia. At one point, driven beyond endurance, he shouted at a visibly delighted de Gaulle: "*Si vous*

GENERAL WITHOUT SOLDIERS

Of 338,000 troops rescued at Dunkirk, 120,000 were French and nearly all preferred to return to occupied France. There were also more than two hundred French naval ships lying in Portsmouth and Plymouth harbours, including two battleships, four cruisers, several submarines and eight destroyers. In the end, Royal Marines had to board them by force and the French crews resisted with violence. They were interned and later repatriated. Only 50 officers and 200 men, out of a total of 18,000 sailors, stayed in England to serve under the self-appointed de Gaulle.

NO GOOD DEED GOES UNPUNISHED.
"I shall never get on with les Anglais. You are all the same, exclusively concentrated on your own interests and business. You think I am interested in England winning the war? I am not. I am only interested in France's victory."
De Gaulle to General Spears, British Officer Commanding, Syria, and the man who saved him at Bordeaux, 1941.

m'obstaclerez, je vous liquiderai!" ("If you get in my way, I'll destroy you!"). Contingency plans were laid to have the man who had become "this obstructionist saboteur" interned on the Isle of Wight.

During D-Day, de Gaulle refused permission for 170 French liaison officers in Britain to embark with the Allied invasion forces. He became more co-operative as American forces approached Paris but only because he needed Eisenhower's agreement to pause the advance and allow a Free French division under General Leclerc (one of nine divisions equipped and paid for by the Americans) to take Paris on 25 August 1944.

WITH FRIENDS LIKE THESE
"De Gaulle is out to achieve one-man government in France. I can't imagine a man I would distrust more. His whole Free French movement is honeycombed with police spies, he has agents spying on his own people. To him, freedom of action means freedom from criticism. Why should anyone trust the force backing de Gaulle?" President Roosevelt to his son, Casablanca, 1941.

De Gaulle himself then proceeded to the Hôtel de Ville where he made a speech, proclaiming himself head of the government and underlining "the essential role played by the French in their own liberation". The effect was rather spoiled when he was forced to request Eisenhower to loan him two U.S. Army divisions to return to Paris and march down the Champs Elysées in order to secure the city properly.

PRESIDENT DE GAULLE: "THE MOST UNGRATEFUL MAN SINCE JUDAS ISCARIOT".

Ironically, but characteristically, the people of France did not show themselves adequately grateful to de Gaulle after the war. When they rejected the constitution he drew up centring power on himself, de Gaulle resigned, retiring to Colombey-les-deux-Eglises to sulk and write his *Mémoires de Guerre (War Memoirs)*, called by George Pompidou, his successor as president, "a three-volume love letter to himself".

NO FRIEND OF THE PEOPLE.
"In politics it is necessary either to betray one's country or the electorate. I prefer to betray the electorate." De Gaulle, 1961, on his decision to abandon the French-Algerians who had helped sweep him to power.

In the late 1950s, the conflict between native Algerians struggling for independence and French settlers threatened to spill over into France itself. In 1958 a senior army commander, General Jacques Massu rebelled against Paris, proclaiming "Vive de Gaulle!" from the balcony of the Algiers Government-General building. De Gaulle answered two days later that he was ready to *"assumer les pouvoirs de la République"* (take on the powers of the Republic).

His first acts as President involved selling out the people who put him in power. He quickly conceded Algeria its independence and disowned the French-

Algerians. (Right-wing elements of the French army never forgave him and tried to assassinate him throughout the 1960s, failing hopelessly).

At home, grandeur meant a heavily state-directed economic strategy. As American investment from the Marshall Plan ebbed away, de Gaulle was able to replace it with German investment after the Franco-German Friendship treaty he signed with Chancellor Adenauer in 1963.

Friendship, as the Germans soon found out, did not necessarily mean "friendliness". When German ministers dared to criticise the amount of money that the new European Economic Community was ploughing into French agriculture, de Gaulle refused to negotiate and his "empty chair" policy meant that all EEC business between July 1965 and January 1966 was frozen.

Naturally, he did not forget his old friends. At a time of industrial depression for the U.K., de Gaulle vetoed British entry – twice – into the new European Common Market. At the same time, he was anti-American. In 1968, he made a state visit to Phnom Penh where he made an aggressively pro-Vietminh speech, forgetting that the only reason U.S. troops were in Vietnam was because of French failure in its former colony.

"France is violently opposed to blatant American imperialism now rampant in the world. France will continue to attack and oppose the United States in Latin America, in Asia and in Africa", he told Gloria Emerson of *The New York Times* in 1967.

His intention was to establish France, a medium-weight, not very rich, not very powerful nation, as a kind of "third force" in foreign affairs and so establish her independence of the economic and military alliances that grew up in the Free World after the war.

Finally, he announced that France could no longer tolerate an "American protectorate" masquerading "under the cover of N.A.T.O.". He withdrew from N.A.T.O.'s military integration but, to ensure his country remained within the American nuclear umbrella, not the organisation as a whole. 60,000 U.S. troops were ordered to leave the country and thirty bases were shut down. The Americans were shocked. "The most ungrateful man since Judas Iscariot

NO FRIEND OF THE GERMANS
"Treaties are like roses and young girls. They last while they last." De Gaulle, 1963, after signing the Franco-German Friendship Treaty.

NO FRIEND OF THE AMERICANS (1)
"You may be sure that the Americans will commit all the stupidities they can think of, plus some that are beyond imagination." De Gaulle, Phnom Penh, 1968.

NO FRIEND OF THE AMERICANS (2)
In 1966, upon being told that President Charles de Gaulle had taken France out of N.A.T.O. and that all U.S. troops must leave French soil, US Secretary of State Dean Rusk asked him: "Does that include the 60,000 American dead in military cemeteries as well?" De Gaulle made no reply.

betrayed his Christ", he was called by one congressman in the US.

He was equally troublesome beyond the Atlantic Alliance. Having encouraged Israel to become a major client of the French arms industry, he cut off supplies and supported its numerous (and oil-rich) Arab enemies during the Six Day War. "The Jews", he sneered, "are an elite people, sure of itself and domineering". During a state visit to Canada, a country beset by a wave of separatist terrorism, he made a speech from a balcony on Montreal city hall and ended it shouting "Vive le Québec libre" ("long live free Quebec"). The tour was immediately cut short by the Canadian government who reminded him of the thousands of Canadian soldiers who twice fought and died for the freedom of France.

NO FRIEND TO THE CANADIANS
"The people of Canada are free. Every province of Canada is free. Canadians do not need to be liberated. Indeed, many thousands of Canadians gave their lives in two world wars in the liberation of France. Canada will remain united and will reject any effort to destroy her unity." Lester B. Pearson, Canadian Prime Minister, Nobel Prize winner and former Canadian soldier in France responding to de Gaulle's "Vive Québec libre" speech.

His come-uppance came not from outside but inside France. During May 1968 Paris erupted in a wave of student protests against the dull, oppressive and corrupt system that he represented. De Gaulle responded true to form when confronted by real trouble. He fled the country.

He flew to French army bases in Germany where General Massu, the soldier who put him in power in the first place, gave him a stiff talking to and sent him back. His bluff was called and he became a joke in the streets. He lost a national referendum and resigned.

A year later, while writing yet more memoirs at Colombey-les-deux-Eglises, he suddenly said "I feel a pain here", pointing to his neck, just seconds before he fell unconscious due to an aneurismal rupture. Within minutes he was dead.

Harold Macmillan, a former British Prime Minister and someone who had dealt with de Gaulle during his time in London provided the best epitaph: "How odd he should die of a pain in the neck. We always thought he was a carrier, not a sufferer."

NO FRIEND TO HIS FRIENDS
General de Gaulle: "Alors Massu, toujours aussi con?" *("So, Massu, still a twat?") General Massu answered :* "Toujours aussi gaulliste, mon Général?" *("Still a Gaullist, General?"). Generals de Gaulle and Massu in conversation at a French army base during 1968.*

CHIRAC AND DE GAULLE.

In November 2004 President Chirac, heading the main Gaullist party in France, made a speech at the unveiling of a bronze statute to de Gaulle. "I take great joy in this moment", said Chirac. "The heritage of General de Gaulle was a very special idea of France, but one resolutely open, open to Europe, open to the world. It was a dream, above all, of independence". The statue stands at the bottom of a street dedicated to the man who really created de Gaulle and guaranteed the independence of modern France. It is the Avenue Winston Churchill.

Huit

Mean Time

France Is Retarded By Nine Minutes And Twenty One Seconds

"Time has a different meaning here. It certainly doesn't mean money", said one U.S. executive doing business in France. So, why are the French so unpunctual?

In 2004 the British and French governments commemorated the *Entente Cordiale*, the old alliance by which the French agreed to recognise Britain's claim to some Sudanese desert in return, as it turned out, for the British saving them during the First World War. The centrepiece of the celebrations was a state dinner hosted at Windsor Castle by the Queen for President Jacques Chirac. Every detail was painstakingly planned and timed. The Waterloo Room, in which the meal was to be served, was even renamed the "The Music Room" to soothe French sensibilities.

LATE FOR HIS OWN FUNERAL
"L'exactitude est la politesse des rois" *("Punctuality is the politeness of kings") Louis XVIII (1755–1824). His brother, Louis XVI, was executed at 10:15 am on 21 January 1793, fifteen minutes behind schedule.*

The evening arrived, the Queen was standing outside the gates, the band played but – no president. It began to rain. After twenty minutes hanging about, the Queen went back inside for a quick G&T, deciding to let Chirac greet himself. He turned up thirty minutes behind schedule. (Revenge was swift. After dinner came a two-hour, full-cast performance of *Les Miserables*, a searing portrait of how depressing it was to be French in the nineteenth century).

TIME OUT OF JOINT
"I can't get my French colleagues to understand that time is an important element in the functioning of a company. There is a great negligence about time in France." Gunther Lorenz, M.D., France.

Anyone who has ever sat in a Montparnasse bistro watching the waiter ring his girlfriend, gel his hair, watch football on the big screen T.V. and only then get the *café filtre* ordered twenty-five minutes ago will not be surprised that Samuel Beckett wrote *Waiting for Godot* in France. The French take their own sweet time.

If you can't trust the French to do anything on time, their tardiness is something others have always counted on. With war approaching in 1913, German diplomat Prinz von Donnersmarck told the French ambassador: "I am convinced that you will be beaten and for this reason. In spite of the brilliant qualities which I recognise are possessed by the French and which I admire, you are not sufficiently punctual. In the coming war that nation will be victorious whose servants from the top of the ladder to the bottom will do their duty with absolute exactitude, however important or small it may be."

WAR DELAYED BY LUNCH
"The French, in spite of their gallantry, were often unreliable and unpunctual. It may be their methods were different from ours. They came and went like autumn leaves. Where we would hold a position they would abandon it and retake it with a brilliant counter-attack, and l'heure militaire, *lunch hour, was meaningless in operations."*
Sir Tom Bridges, Toy Drum and Tin-Whistle, *1914.*

Even today, foreigners are exasperated by the French refusal to "do their duty with absolute exactitude". Polly Platt, author of the useful *French or Foe* (third edition 2004), a manual on how not to go mad while working with the French, tells the tale of an American executive arriving for a job interview with two French managers of the B.N.P. bank:

"One of them received me on the dot of the appointed meeting, and the other kept both of us waiting for forty minutes. He didn't say he was sorry – and didn't give an excuse. And the one who was on time didn't seem at all bothered. It was as if this was perfectly normal."

Another of Platt's interviewees works at the French telecommunications company, Alcatel: "I'm meeting this French colleague for lunch – he finally arrives, half an hour late and doesn't even say he's sorry. He is wrong to waste my time like that!"

WORKING LATE
*Proudfoot Consulting analysing international firms found Japanese C.E.O.s were
most punctual – 60% said they were hardly ever late. French C.E.O.s were worst
with just 36% saying they were usually punctual when it comes to meetings.*

Their stories are far from unusual. Foreigners tend to be astonished by the casual French attitude, not to say plain rudeness, in the way they deal with other people's time. The shop assistant who won't finish her phone call to take your order. The taxi driver who must finish reading his paper before he can drive you anywhere. The help line that can't take your call because all the staff are having lunch. You might experience any of this anywhere in the world. In France such experiences are the rule, not the exception.

The French approach to time is blamed by some outside observers on "the Latin temperament". This fuzzy generalisation falls apart beside the punctuality (and courtesy) of the Belgians and that of the ethnic French who make up 20% of the most clock-ridden nation on earth, the Swiss.

If the racial theory is bunk then what about cultural differences? In his books, *The Silent Language* (1959) and *The Hidden Dimension* (1969), anthropologist Edward T. Hall argues that national cultures really divide into two types when it comes to time: "monochronic" and "polychronic".

Some cultures, mostly Protestant, northern and heavily industrialised, are "monochronic". In the U.S., the U.K., Holland, Germany, Switzerland, Canada and Scandinavia, time is an absolute. Being late or abusing someone else's time is taboo. Other culures, says Hall, are "polychronic" and the value given to time is more elastic and indulgent. Most of the world is "polychronic" apparently, taking in Asia, Africa, the Middle East, the Mediterranean, Latin Americans and, no surprise, France.

Then again, the French train system is famous for punctuality (so it should be with a €10 billion, $12 billion) annual subsidy from the French taxpayer). And while their shops sometimes open on time, they all close absolutely on the dot for the two-hour lunch break. Those mealtimes are important. Harriet Welty, an expert on French "etiquette", points out in her book *French Toast* (2001) that while it is actually rude for a French couple to turn up *less* than half an hour late to dinner with friends, if they turn up to lunch *more* than two minutes

CLASH OF THE CHRONICS
The classic example of a "monochronic" versus "polychronic" clash is the battle of Waterloo (1815). Napoleon chose not to attack at dawn because the ground was wet and he wanted his breakfast. Instead, he waited until noon. This was fine with the Duke of Wellington because he had arranged to meet up with the Prussians in the afternoon. The British, facing devastating barrages, might have broken except that General von Blucher, with true German punctuality, turned up right on time. The two hours Boney whiled away eating devilled kidneys at the breakfast table and lecturing his marshals on the importance of timing lost him the battle, the crown and France.

late, they will apologise profusely and with apparent sincerity.

So it seems that the French can keep time if they want to. They just don't want to. Almost every book and source recognises this fact without daring to say it – or say why. Very simply, in a country as clannish and competitive as France, time – and its use or misuse – is an excellent way of enforcing their superiority over the stranger, the subordinate, the "other guy". In other words, *you*.

Polly Platt, who has to live and work in France, diplomatically sums it up: "The French are punctual whenever necessary Most have an inner alarm about when to be on time. They also know when it doesn't matter. In business, it also makes a difference if they are *demandeur* (soliciting someone for something) or *demandé* (being solicited) It's part of their *liberté*, like smoking or letting their dogs mess up the sidewalk."

THE FRENCH ARE RETARDED

The French may not keep time but when someone else has it, they want it bad. At an international conference in 1884, twenty-five countries met to fix a standard world meridian. Despite furious French lobbying for Paris, the Royal Observatory at Greenwich in the U.K. won the prize to be the world's longitude 0°. Only San Domingo voted against, with abstentions from France and Brazil. Until 1978, all French maps and official documents by law had to express the time not as "Greenwich Mean Time" but as "Paris Mean Time retarded by 9 mins 21 secs".

Even today, the French campaign to have Paris reclassified as the starting point for time has not quite died. In the run-up to the 2000 Millennium, it was proposed to plant a line of poplars all the way across France along the line of a theoretical "Paris Mean Time" which would be visible from space so that aliens, at least, would recognise whose time was most important on earth.

Cutting the Cheese

The Favourite Nibble of the Surrender Monkeys

France boasts of having a cheese for every day of the year. Even Frenchmen sometimes wonder why this is a boast: "How can one be expected to govern a country with 246 cheeses?", General de Gaulle once moaned.

HARD CHEESE ON THE MOORS. It is generally accepted that the Arabs first discovered cheese when desert nomads stored milk in sheep stomachs for long treks, found it solidifed and then ate the resultant evil-smelling paste. Cheese arrived in France with successive waves of Moorish immigration. One band halted in the Poitou region to herd their goats ("Chabli" in Arab, whence the names of two sorts of cheese derive : "chabis and "chabichou") and introduced cheese to the region. The French word "fromage" has been used since 1180, to replace the word "formage" (from the slang Latin "formaticus", ie "made in a mould"). In 1267, in the Doubs region, the first "fruitieres" (the ancestor of dairy co-operatives) produced big wheels of cheese (Beaufort, Emmental, Comté) None of this helped the Moors of Poitou who had all been impaled, burned at the stake or exiled by Charles Martel after the battle of Tours back in 732.

CHEESED OFF
"Well, what's cheese then? Corpse of milk!" James Joyce, ulcerated Irish writer and long-time French resident.

SLICES OF FRANCE

1. France manufactures around 500 different cheeses.

2. The French consume 1,207,000 tonnes of cheese a year (compared with 1,012,000 tonnes in Germany and 615,000 tonnes in the U.K.).

3. Invidually, a Frenchman eats 22.5kg of cheese a year (compared with 14kg for the average American).

4. In 2000, France produced 1,605,000 tonnes of cheese (making it the world's second largest producer of cheese after the U.S. with 3,830,000).

5. In 2003, France exported €1.9 billion ($2.3 billion)-worth of its cheeses around the world.

6. 60% of the cost of cheese production in France is subsidised by the European taxpayer. The E.U. also provides an export subsidy of 25c for every pound of French cheese exported.

7. France suffers around 750,000 cases of food poisoning every year with 70,000 hospitalisations and 400 deaths. Many of these relate to salmonella and listeria infections from the consumption of unpasteurised cheeses.

THE MCDONALD'S OF CHEESE

The French deride McDonald's hamburgers as "malbouffe" (crap food) or "McMerde", something cheap, nasty and industrially produced. So why, asks Pierre Broisard in *Camembert: A National Myth* (2003) are the French not making a stink about the best-known of all their cheeses? Presented as a white, flat wheel, Camembert's aroma, in which sophisticates think they can detect vague tonalities of wild mushrooms, is like having a cowpat rubbed in your face. Like most famous cheeses, it carries the French appellation contrôlée. However, the powerful Camembert producers have twisted the otherwise stringent A.O.C. rules so that cheese produced anywhere, even outside France (for cheaper production costs), can call itself Camembert. By the 1980s, the manufacturing process was automated in industrial plants. Robots with twenty arms now mimic traditional human actions. Today Camembert factories in Normandy, the five largest of which turn out about 1.5m Camemberts a day, employ a workforce of fewer than five hundred. "No cheese here has been touched by human hands", Boisard quotes one factory manager as saying. Today 90% of all Camembert is now produced industrially – 30% of it outside France (including in China). The French eat 800 tonnes a year and though it is, as Boisard says, "Pasteurised, homogeonised crap", José Bové has yet to trash a single cheese shop.

THE DEATH OF CHEESE? *France's cheeses are slowly dying out, nibbled away by the industrial brands and E.U. hygiene laws but also because paranoid peasant cheesemakers refuse to pass on their pungent secrets. "In thirty years, more than fifty cheeses have been struck off the menus because of this. The Mont-d'Or galette, which had been produced for four hundred years, disappeared this summer following the death of the last producer who knew the secret of how to make it," said Véronique Richez-Lerouge, President of the Association Fromages de Terroirs (Regional Cheese Association). "Fifteen years ago, there were two producers of Bergues left. Now there's one. He's eighty and won't tell anyone else his recipe."*

WHO CUT THE CHEESE? *A team from Cranfield University, U.K. used an electronic nose, a device used in the food and drinks industry for quality control, and a panel of blind-folded judges, to rate France's most malodorous cheeses. "However, I'm amazed that anyone would want to promote cheeses on their pungency", said one of the British scientists on the project, sponsored by the trade association Fine Cheese from France. "Most people in this country are more interested in what they taste like. The French must have a thing about smells."*

FRANCE'S SMELLIEST CHEESES – OFFICIAL!

1. *Vieux Boulogne: cows' milk cheese from Pas de Calais.*
2. *Pont l'Evêque: cows' milk cheese from Normandy.*
3. *Camembert de Normandie: cows' milk cheese.*
4. *Munster: cows' milk cheese from Alsace-Lorraine.*
5. *Brie de Meaux: cows' milk cheese from Ile de France.*
6. *Roquefort: sheep's milk cheese from near Toulouse.*
7. *Reblochon: cows' milk cheese from the Savoie region.*
8. *Livarot: cows' milk cheese from Normandy.*
9. *Banon: goats' milk cheese from Provence.*

CHEESE WARS

France and the United States are currently locked in a cheese war. In 2001 the European Union, prompted by heavy French lobbying, unilaterally slapped an import ban on U.S. beef. The U.S. responded with 100% import tariffs on luxury goods from Europe, including Roquefort cheese. Before the punitive tariff was imposed, 460 tonnes of Roquefort was sold there. Sales have fallen by 30% after the higher taxes doubled the price in U.S. stores. Perhaps more damaging to the French cheese industry is that Americans, angered by the opposition of President Chirac to the removal of Saddam Hussein, are boycotting French goods – including cheese. One French Internet cheesemonger who sells most of his Camembert and Roquefort to Americans has become the first victim of the fast-ripening stink over Iraq currently souring Franco-U.S. relations. Marc Refabert, the co-founder of fromages.com, which does more than 80% of its business with America, said his company's sales had fallen "substantially". "I'm getting inundated with emails from people saying they're not going to buy my products until France changes it's position," he said. "They're showing their patriotism, I guess – you can't argue with them. What good would it do?" The International Cheese Intelligence Unit (yes, there is such a thing), estimates that French cheese sales in the U.S. have fallen by 23% since 2004.

THE LIE OF THE LABEL

The Academy Award for cheese is the Appellation d'Origine Contrôlée (A.O.C.). It should mean that the name, labelling and traditional quality of the cheese are controlled by the government. French cheesemakers use the A.O.C. to protect their closed market. In reality, the government allows a lot of leeway. Take Camembert, which got its A.O.C. in 1983 – or, rather, three versions: one for any cheese that wanted to use the designation Camembert, allowing the raw material to come from anywhere; another was for "Camembert de Normandie", setting rules of production but not specifying the precise origin or quality of the milk; and the third designation marks out the tiny proportion of modern Camemberts made from unpasteurised milk and hand-ladled (even here the designation is not reliable since industrial manufacturers use this label on their packaging).

FRENCH CHEESE IS *MERDE*

Anyone stuck on a crowded métro in high summer can justifiably suspect that the French have a strange yearning for the earthy, not to say musky, aromas given off by the human body and its various leavings. But their coprophiliac tendencies, as food journalists Denise Thatcher and Malcolm Scott have noted, come to the fore when it comes to their cheeses. Here are their reviews:

Crottins de Charigol – *tiny, hard, goat's milk cheeses with black or grey-brown rinds. Horribly sharp and salty when fully aged and intimidating The name means "horse droppings".*

Selles de Cher – *a sweet, nutty goats' milk cheese which is covered with salt and charcoal, giving it a black coating. Selle means stool (in the lavatorial sense).*

Bouton de Culotte – *extra-small goat's milk cheeses, dried for winter use; extra sharp with a dark grey rind. Its name, "trouser button", comes from its unmistakable stench, very like that of urine.*

Pouligny St. Pierre – *a small, pyramid-shaped goat's milk cheese with a tangy flavour. To augment its natural flavour, like compost, it is ripened in rotting leaves.*

Dix

Old Wells of Hatred

Anti-Semitism in France

France is home to the largest Jewish population in Europe.
Just how welcome does it make them feel?

FEAR AND LOATHING
"France has the largest Jewish community in Western Europe but this does not make relationships as easy as they should be. Anti-Semitism has a long and often virulent history here, and still crops up in casual conversation in a way that would be rare in England or America. In the 1970s, my son was once warned by a hotel-owner in deepest France that he should not admit to being half-Jewish for fear of what might befall him. Brown and black immigrants are the main target for the far right today but Jews represent a more deeply rooted source of fear and loathing which draws on much older wells of hatred." Jonathan Fenby, British author and chevalier of the French Order of Merit, On the Brink, *2000.*

In 2001, a Frenchman, attending an up-market party in London, blurted out a few anti-Semitic remarks concluding that Israel was a "shitty little country" and asking expansively: "Why should the world be in danger of World War III because of *those people?*".

So far, so ordinary. France's history of anti-Semitism is long and ugly, and more than a few smart, modern Frenchmen have no qualms voicing it in cocktail chitchat. What makes this anecdote more significant was the speaker: His

Excellency M. Daniel Bernard, the Ambassador of the French Republic to the United Kingdom.

It so happened that his host owned a newspaper and, next day, the headlines were full of the Ambassador's gaffe. Rather than apologising, Bernard claimed he could not remember making the remark. The French Foreign Ministry stood by him, blaming the story on vague "malevolent insinuations". Two months later he was quietly removed from his post. A month after that, he was appointed French ambassador to Algeria.

MIDDLE AGES

France's relationship with its Jewish population has never been easy. Like other European countries, its Middle Ages were marked by racial and religious persecution of any group the majority hadn't previously expelled, impaled or burned at the stake. Any excuse would do. Jews were blamed for spreading the Black Death by deliberately contaminating wells. In 1349, such suspicions were enough to trigger a massacre in the town of Strasbourg. On St. Valentine's Day, in a carnival atmosphere, the two thousand Jews of the town were brought together on a huge platform and burned alive. The good townsfolk were not motivated only by religious hatred. All debts owed to Jews were cancelled as part of the festivities.

The lucky ones were those who got – or were pushed – out of France. Jews were expelled from Paris by Philip Augustus in 1182 and from France entirely by Louis IX in 1254, by Charles IV in 1322, by Charles V in 1359 and by Charles VI in 1394.

RELIGIOUS HATRED OR COMMERCIAL REALITIES?

"The Jews had already been settled in France for over a thousand years when Philip Augustus came to power in 1179. Four months after taking over the reins of government he imprisoned all the Jews in his lands and released them only after a heavy ransom had been paid (1180). The next year (1181) he annulled all loans made to Christians by Jews, taking instead a comfortable twenty per cent for himself. A year later (1182) he confiscated all the lands and buildings of the Jews and drove them out of the lands governed by himself directly Several years later (1198) Philip Augustus readmitted the Jews and carefully regulated their banking business so as to reserve large profits to himself through a variety of taxes and duties. He made of this taxation a lucrative income for himself." Jacob R Marcus, The Jew in the Medieval World, 1960.

REVOLUTION AND NAPOLEON

The dawning of the Enlightenment in the 1700s brought an easing of Jewish persecution almost everywhere except France. Famous *philosophes* like Voltaire and Diderot, now acclaimed by the French for championing the civil and moral liberties of man, did not oppose intellectual anti-Semitism, they *led* it.

Come the Revolution, Jews who had somehow survived French history only found themselves covered by the *Declaration of the Rights of Man* after frenzied argument in the National Assembly quite out of proportion to the minuscule role they played in national life. Even then, observing Jews were not considered to be protected under the law. One issue used by a prefect in Lorraine to avoid relaxing the harsh conditions of Jewish communities in his own district was circumcision: "It is the inhumane law of these people that the new-born male infant is to be bloodily operated upon as if nature herself were imperfect".

"THE RACE OF BRIGANDS"
"It is but with regret that I cite that wretched little Jewish people, who should not serve as a rule for anyone, and who (putting religion aside) was never anything but a race of ignorant and fanatic brigands", Voltaire, French Enlightenment philosopher, writer and toady to tyrants, Dictionnaire philosophique *(Philosophical Dictionary), 1764.*

A brief period of toleration followed under the Emperor Napoleon. He did not know much about Judaism (the first question he asked a rabbi presenting him with a petition was how many wives he had) but he did know that he needed manpower for his armies rampaging across Europe and that included Jews who, because they were excluded from so many other laws, had also been excluded from the draft. After Waterloo, the situation in France returned to grim normality.

THE NINETEENTH CENTURY

The "Damascus Incident" is typical of the Jewish-French experience. In February 1840 the Jews of Damascus in Syria, where France had an overwhelming colonial interest, were accused of murdering Father Thomas, the superior of the Capuchins, a Catholic monastic order, slaughtering him and his acolyte to obtain blood for a Passover ceremony (he had been robbed and killed by some renegade Turkish soldiers). The French consul, Comte Ratti-Menton, rounded up the nearest Jews, tortured them to extract confessions and eventually accused one of them, Isaac Picciotto, of the murder almost at random.

UNDIPLOMATIC LETTERS
In official correspondence to Paris during 1840, the French consul, the Comte de Ratti-Menton alleged that the murder of Father Thomas was based on "fiendish sacrifices by the Israelites", an "outrage to human society" and "a deliberate challenge by the Jews to the tutelary action of the French Government It is therefore advisable to impose a salutary terror upon the Jews".

He was only prevented from ordering French troops to conduct a general massacre of the Jewish ghetto in Damascus by a strong note from the British Foreign Office reminding Paris that such actions would not win over the natives to France's "civilising presence" in the area. To this day, the French government has always refused to declassify the files bearing on the incident, specifically, those entitled *Affaire du Père Thomas assasiné par les Israélites indigènes (The Affair of Father Thomas Murdered by the Jews)*. Perhaps the title says why.

During the nineteenth century, a horrible evolution of anti-Semitism occurred in France. Traditionally a prejudice of the Catholic right, it became a key theme of the Socialist left who taught that hating Jews for being successful business people and bankers was a class duty.

The two kinds of anti-Semitism came together during the "Dreyfus Affair" of the 1890s, in which an innocent Jewish officer was accused of treason and sentenced to life in solitary confinement on Devil's Island. The cheerleader for the violent riots and social persecution was Edouard Drumont, whose 1886 book *La France Juive (Jewish France)* was a smash best-seller, going through 114 editions in one year. He became a leading light in the newly organised *Ligue Antisémitique Française* (French Anti-Semitic League) which attracted 15,000 people to its opening meeting and 30,000 new members in its first month.

THE JEWS ARE TO BLAME FOR EVERYTHING

"The only one who has benefited from the Revolution [of 1789] is the Jew. Everything comes from the Jew; everything returns to the Jew. We have here a veritable conquest, an entire nation returned to serfdom by a minute but cohesive minority, just as the Saxons were forced into serfdom by William the Conqueror's 60,000 Normans. The methods are different, the result is the same. Immense Jewish fortunes, castles, Jewish townhouses, are not the fruit of any actual labour, of any production: they are the booty taken from an enslaved race by a dominant race." Edouard Drumont, Jew-hating maniac, journalist and author of La France Juive (Jewish France), 1886.

The long-lived League's stock-in-trade was to find the newest scandal rocking France's endemically corrupt public life, ranging from the Panama Canal bribery case of the 1880s all the way to the Stavisky Affair of the 1930s, and then accuse a shadowy conspiracy of Jewish capitalists as being its cause. Its legacy was a suspicion of all things Jewish amounting to a brooding hatred that erupted during the Second World War.

THE SECOND WORLD WAR

Of the 120,000 French Jews enthusiastically deported by France to Nazi death camps during the Occupation, only 3,000 ever returned.

The intellectuals caved in immediately after the invasion. In September 1940 the Association of French Publishers signed an agreement with the German ambassador to suppress works by Jews. To show the "decadence" of Semitic art, an exhibition of Jewish painters was mounted in the Palais Berlitz entitled *Le juif et la France (The Jew and France)*. Not one of the 200,000 visitors murmured a word of protest.

Much worse was to come. Without German prompting, the Vichy government passed the *Statut des Juifs,* (Jewish Law) banning Jews from public

MADEMOISELLE B.

"Consider the case of a woman know to history as 'Mlle. B', who arrived at Drancy [a French assembly point for deportees to the Nazi camps]. She was twenty-two years old. The French police told her to bring her valuables with her. On arrival, the camp staff noted her possessions in their ledger – three gold bracelets, diamond rings, a strand of pearls, stock certificates, bonds and a collection of seventy-five English books. Mlle. B. died in Birkenau concentration camp on 27 January 1945. By then her jewels had been stolen by the French staff at Drancy and her stocks and bonds lodged with the French state. None were ever returned to her family." Jonathan Fenby, On the Brink, 2000.

---

office and professions, and forbidding them even to stand in the food queues or use public telephones. By 1942, the yellow armbands were issued and the deportations began. "The enterprise would have been impossible to carry on without the assistance of the French administration", admitted native writer Jean-Paul Cointier.

As the war progressed, the repression slid from the hands of the Germans, who needed their own troops to fight in the east, and into those of *le Milice* (the Militia), the purely French-run police under the command of people like René Bousquet, the General Secretary of the Police, and Maurice Papon, who commanded the police in the Gironde. They relied on *délations* (denunciations) of Jews in hiding by their French neighbours to make up their quotas. One of thousands betrayed in this manner was a young woman arrested in her apartment after a tip-off by the concierge who had known her family for years. She was Madeleine Dreyfus, grand-daughter of Alfred Dreyfus, and she died in Auschwitz in 1944 weighing just 70 lbs.

After the war, many of the Frenchmen most guilty of crimes against Jews were not prosecuted. Bousquet became a director of the Indo-China banking company and U.T.A. airline while Papon began a thirty-year ministerial career in politics. Paul Touvier was head of the Milice in Lyons. Among his crimes were the kidnap and murder of an elderly Jewish couple;

PLUCKY LITTLE ITALY?

"The number of [Jewish] dead would have been far higher if the Italian Fascist leader, Benito Mussolini, had not ordered troops in France to defy German-French plans for mass round-ups in Italian-occupied south-eastern France. Thousands were smuggled into Italy after Italian generals said that "no country can ask Italy, cradle of Christianity and law, to be associated with these (Nazi) acts". Paul Webster, The Vichy Policy on Jewish Deportation, www.bbc.co.uk/history.

THOUGHTS OF A FUTURE PRESIDENT

"If France doesn't want to die in the mud, the last French people worthy of this name must declare a merciless war against all who, here or abroad, are preparing to open floodgates against it: Jews, Freemasons, Communists always the same." François Mitterrand, minister in the Vichy government and later President of France, writing in Revue de l'Etat nouveau, 1942.

a grenade attack on Jews as they left a synagogue; and the murder of seven Jews on Nazi orders in retaliation for the Resistance's killing of a Vichy official (the eighth of his captives was allowed to escape because he was a gentile). After the war, he was hidden by an order of Catholic monks for thirty years until 1971 when he received a presidential pardon. After an international outcry, he was arrested again in 1989 and this time sentenced to life in prison where he died in 1996. A Gaullist Member of Parliament was among those attending his funeral.

It was suspected that men like these were protected by figures high up in the new French establishment who did not want their own collaboration revealed, including François Mitterrand, himself a high-level member of the Vichy government. Between 1981 and 1995, Mitterrand was also the two-term Socialist President of France.

NEVER AGAIN?

"The continuing attacks on Jews in France, which have been more numerous than in any other western country, are carried out with citizens and government leaders turning a blind eye. This indifference, coupled with the threat of anti-Semitism and verifiably documented acts of violence, are prompting a continued feeling of utter abandonment within France's Jewish community." Communiqué by the Simon Wiesenthal Center, 10 June 2002.

NOW

Is anti-Semitism alive and well in France today? Ariel Sharon, the pugnacious former Prime Minister of Israel, thought so. In 2004, he commented on the spreading rash of anti-Semitic incidents in France and encouraged French Jews to come to Israel "immediately". The French government responded by withdrawing a previously-issued invitation for Sharon to make a state visit.

Today, there are only 600,000 Jews living in France (before the war there had been 1,500,000), less than 1% of the population. Since January 2004, they have filed over 600 complaints of "serious" attacks against Jewish persons and property. Even the government recognises a newly resurgent anti-Semitism. After the repeated vandalisation of Jewish cemeteries, the Interior Minister (now Prime Minister) Dominique de Villepin was forced to acknowledge that "the increase in racist and anti-Semitic acts is a reality in France".

To tell the truth, anti-Jewish violence did not die with the war. It has erupted regularly over the last fifty years. In 1980, a motorbike parked outside the synagogue on the Rue Copernic in an up-market section of Paris blew up, killing four passers-by and wounding eleven. It was the sixth and most serious attack on a Jewish target inside a week. Four years later, gunmen attacked the patrons of Jo Goldberg's restaurant in a Jewish neighbourhood in the heart of Paris. After throwing a grenade through the window, the gunmen opened fire with automatic weapons, killing four and wounding another thirty, many of them seriously.

What is new is that the attackers did not come from either the left or the right of French politics. They were drawn apparently from the five million-strong community of French Muslims, the largest in Europe, the legacy of France's colonial empire. While almost the entire majority are decent and law-abiding, strong hostility to Israel has turned to pure hatred of their Jewish neighbours in some of them. In the autumn of 2002, for instance, two hundred *Maghrebins* attacked Jews in the Champs Elysées during the religious festival of Rosh Hashanah.

Despite the almost systematic disregard of growing anti-Semitism in the French press (in 2002, not a single one of the 510 officially listed attacks on Jews were reported in any of the national newspapers), the French government does recognise that something is going seriously wrong within the country. When French President Jacques Chirac learned that a Jewish school had been set ablaze in the Paris suburb of Gagny, he flew to the scene of the fire announcing a new set of security measures for Jewish schools and businesses. "When one attacks a Jew in France, it's France in its entirety that is attacked," he told reporters. "Anti-Semitism is contrary to all the values of France."

Not only France's history but its present make that claim seem very hollow.

IN THE NEWS
"The French government angrily rejects charges of widespread anti-Semitism among French people. President Chirac has said that an attack on French Jews is an attack on France, but several recent incidents have highlighted the scale of the problem. The Jewish singer Shirel was subjected to a torrent of anti-Semitic abuse on stage from young people in the audience, while the well-known comedian Dieudonne gave a Nazi salute on state television to illustrate his attack on Israeli policy. Late last year, a Jewish school in a Paris suburb was burned, and the organiser of a demonstration against the ban on headscarves in schools used the occasion to attack Zionism. The visit of the Israeli president to Paris this week – the first for 60 years – shows how keen France is to reassure Jewish people. But it's clear that tensions are high in a country that contains the world's third largest Jewish community and Europe's largest number of Muslims." Alistair Sandford, B.B.C. news report, Paris, 2004.

RETURN OF THE OLD SCHOOL RACIST

Modern anti-Semitism is not an exclusively Muslim phenomenon in France. Jean Marie Le Pen of the Front National (National Front) provides anti-Semitism with real political credibility. His extremist right wing party is not a fringe group as it would be in any other western country; in 2002 he took 18% of the national vote in the presidential election. Le Pen is fond of making remarks with a bitter, Jew-baiting nuance. In 1987 he referred to the Nazi gas chambers as "a point of detail of the Second World War" and started calling the then Interior Minister, Michel Durafour (whose name means "oven"), "Durafour-crématoire" ("crematorium oven"). In February 1997, Le Pen accused President Chirac in a wide-ranging and especially mad attack of being "in the pay of Jewish organisations, and particularly of the notorious B'nai B'rith".

Onze

Thin Ice

The 2002 Winter Olympics and the Biggest Scandal Ever to Hit... Figure Skating?

In the grand scale of things, amateur figure skating must rate pretty low. But not so low that it can't be reached by some good old French vote-rigging, blackmail and corruption – as the world found out at the 2002 Salt Lake City Winter Olympics.

T he French usually do pretty well at the Winter Olympics, and so they should with the Alps in their back garden. Every four years they appear high in the various skiing, sledding and skating medal tables. The scandal that broke out over the 2002 Pairs Figure Skating showed just what some of them are prepared to do to get there.

On 11 February, Russian skaters Elena Berezhnaya and Anton Sikharulidze swished into the arena at Salt Lake City's Delta Centre and performed their routine, *Méditation*. Television commentators applauded the artistry but carped that the tip of Sikharulidze's left skate touched the ice during his side-by-side jumps with his partner (this represents a performance-shattering technical error in this essentially made-up "sport").

The competition progressed and the highly favoured Canadians, Jamie Sale and David Pelletier, took the ice with their own programme, *Jealousy*, a flawless performance. Pelletier was so sure of victory, he sank to his knees and kissed the ice as the crowd chanted: "Six, six", expecting maximum marks.

They were to be disappointed as the nine I.S.U. (International Skating Union) judges, all picked from different skating bodies around the world, cast their votes to deliver a five-four split in favour of the Russians.

"I am angry. It is tough tonight. It is the toughest day of my life," said Pelletier, bursting into tears (he is the male of the partnership). The final decision, it transpired, turned on the votes of a French judge, Marie-Reine Le Gougne, who favoured the Russians by 0.1 of a point in the technical scoring, enough to get them the gold. In the overheated world of middle-aged, leathery blondes and unmarried elderly gentlemen representing the big cheeses of figure skating, something smelled ripe.

WHAT LIES BENEATH
"In my heart it was clear. There should have been a majority – or even unanimity [in favour of Canada]. I'd really thought they won. When I glanced at the ranking listing the Canadians in second place, I said, 'My God. . . is there something I didn't see?'". Bernard Lavoie, judge on the Pairs Figure Skating jury, Salt Lake City Winter Olympics 2002.

Bickering broke out amongst the judges on the shuttle bus after the event. At the hotel, it escalated with sniffy comments, huffy looks and Bette Davis-style denunciations aplenty.

Eventually, Le Gougne cracked. She tearfully admitted in the lobby to a British judge, Sally Stapleford, and three of her colleagues that she had been pressured to vote for the Russians. She fingered Didier Gailhaguet, President of the French Figure Skating Federation and head of the French Olympic Winter Sports Committee. In return, Gailhaguet told her, the Russians would back the French in the Ice Dance competition.

TEARS OF AN OLYMPIC ATHLETE
"When I turn 50, I am sure I will look at the medal and say 'well, it seems like it does not shine enough. It should be gold.' I'm not saying our hearts our broken but they're broken a bit." David Pelletier, Canadian winner of silver medal (later upgraded to gold) in the Pairs Figure Skating competition, Salt Lake City Winter Olympics 2002.

Triumphantly, the witnesses to Le Gougne's outburst took the story to the world media who pronounced "Skategate" and put the heat on the International Olympic Committee to investigate. An Executive Council of the International Skating Union, the grand inquisition of world skating, was scheduled.

The French participants wiggled furiously. Le Gougne back-tracked. "M. Gailhaguet did not put any pressure on me. I judged in my soul and conscience", Le Gougne told the French sports daily *L'Equipe*. "I considered that the Russians were the best. I never made a deal with an official or a Russian judge."

In his own media interviews, Gailhaguet began cutting her loose. "We cannot continue to let our judge be lambasted in this way", he sympathised broadly. "Some people close to the judge have acted badly and have put someone who is honest and upright but emotionally fragile under pressure." He did not quite wink and circle his finger round his temple.

As the media dug, the story became more bizarre as allegations emerged that Gailhaguet had connections to a mysterious Russian mobster who was fixing the results behind the scenes.

Three days after the competition, Le Gougne flew quietly out of Salt Lake City. The I.O.C. suspended her as a judge and, in an extraordinary move, awarded a second set of gold medals to the Canadian pair. "It was a band-aid solution", said I.O.C. member Dick Pound, "that allowed the I.S.U. to get out of town alive".

THE FRENCH HIT BACK

"The North American press is very powerful. There were 1,750 journalists covering this matter. The Federation and its judge were dirtied in a media campaign without precedent. It was total nonsense to award two gold medals." Didier Gailhaguet, President of the French Figure Skating Federation and head of the French Olympic Winter Sports Committee.

It wasn't over. A week after the Pairs competition, the Ice Dancing competition took place. It was won by Marina Anissina and Gwendal Peizerat of France, who took the country's first gold in the event since 1932. Irina Lobacheva and Ilia Averbukh of Russia were awarded the silver. The Italian pair who were the world champions came a surprising third.

By winning the Ice Dancing competition thanks to another 5-4 vote, the judges ended Russian domination of the event. Russians had won four straight and six of the previous seven Olympic Ice Dancing events.

After the games, Italian authorities working in concert with the F.B.I. did actually arrest a Russian mobster, Alimzhan Tokhtakhounov, a native of Uzbekistan living in Venice, on charges of conspiracy to commit wire fraud and bribery. By fixing the competition, Tokhtakhounov had hoped to get a visa allowing him to return to France where he had lived in the 1990s before being deported on suspicion of racketeering. Transcripts of recorded phone conversations revealed him ringing an un-named male French skating official in Salt Lake City as the competition was under way:

A LITTLE GOLD FOR ME

"[Tokhtakhounov] arranged a classic quid pro quo: 'You'll line up support for the Russian pair, we'll line up support for the French pair and everybody will go away with the gold, and perhaps there'll be a little gold for me,'." U.S. Attorney James Comey, leading the investigation into Alimzhan Tokhtakhounov's alleged fixing of the 2002 Winter Olympics.

"Everything will go well now because you French, with the vote, have made them champions," he chortled. "It happened, it happened. Even if the Canadians are ten times better, the French vote has given them first place."

An I.S.U. investigation held in Lausanne did not find the affair so humorous. Both Gailhaguet and Le Gougne were found guilty of colluding to fix the outcome of the Pairs Figure Skating event in favour of the Russian pair. They were banned from participating in the sport at any level for three years. Critics who had been expecting at least a lifetime ban and a possible recommendation of criminal proceedings were dumbfounded.

Transparency International, a Berlin-based non-governmental organization which monitors official and institutional corruption around the world, described the three-year sanction as "scandalous and an insult to sport, not to mention a gross violation of the Olympic oath".

Le Gougne remains unrepentant. "It was clear that I judged correctly," she said. "Today, if I had to do it again, I would do the same thing. I would put the Russians first for sure. I will prove my innocence They won't stop me now. I have nothing more to lose. I will fight this to the end."

An I.S.U. official at Lausanne, asked if and indeed when Le Gougne would be able to establish her innocence, replied with a vivid skating metaphor: "When hell freezes over".

ACCEPTING THE VERDICT WITH QUIET DIGNITY AND GRACE
"It was a masquerade. It is scandalous. My most basic rights of defence were denied. They have decapitated me from the start. It was a political assassination. This hearing was arranged in a totally biased way. It was totally unfair. The I.S.U. only wanted to justify the awarding of the second gold medals. I've been the scapegoat from the beginning. I want my honour and dignity back. I've been dragged through the mud for months. I've been through hell." Marie-Reine Le Gougne, I.S.U. Olympic judge, receives news of her three-year suspension.

Paris When It Sizzles

The 2003 Heatwave and France's State Health Service

France is proud of its social pact, a combination of state intervention from above and the proudly vaunted idea of the French family from below. So why did so many of the poor, the sick and the elderly die in August 2003?

In the first two weeks of August 2003 a heat wave struck France. It was hot, not uniquely hot, but hot enough. In Paris, temperatures reached 37°C (98.6°F), high above the summer average of 24°C (75°F). And 14,800 people died.

This was no natural disaster but an epidemic caused by a set of social breakdowns and political failures as peculiar to France as the "*pacte sociale*" (social pact) on every French politician's lips during elections. The pact is shorthand for heavy state spending on welfare in line with social, and especially family, values apparently unlike those in any other country.

IT BURNS, IT BURNS
"The French social model rests at the heart of the European social model. People from other continents expect that France will maintain the burning flame of this [great] social model." Nicole Notat, Secretary-General of the CDFT trade union, 2003.

Temperatures began to climb on 1 August. Four days later, the average high across France had reached record levels and remained that way for a week.

Forecasters for the national weather service, *Météo France*, had expressed concern about the health implications, but it was only when *Pompes Funèbres Générales* (France's largest funeral parlour) announced that its morgues were full of heat-related fatalities that the press picked up the story on 10 August. Officials responded with an emergency *Plan Blanc* (White Plan) on 13 August but by that time the dead were in their thousands and temperatures had fallen.

> "You are ready for new and workable solutions to the problems of violence and insecurity, determined to re-establish social opportunity, and anxious to strengthen the foundations of our social pact – employment, healthcare, the retired and the poor." Jacques Chirac, Presidential Election Address, 2002.

Hospitals and cemeteries overflowed. News programmes showed mask-wearing firemen retrieving decomposed bodies from apartment buildings and stacking them in refrigerated warehouses. In Paris, an agricultural showroom was turned into a temporary morgue. In Chartres, emergency services left one body in the flat where it had dropped for ten days since there was nowhere else to put it.

It was the vulnerable that died. The Institute of Health Surveillance estimated that 80% of victims were 75 years or older. Its analysis noted a high proportion of deaths in state retirement homes. The problem was that in August, France shuts down and everyone heads south on holiday, leaving their elderly relatives without, as events showed, visits or telephone contact.

"Is it normal that last night there are three hundred people who can't be buried because the family hasn't turned up to claim the body. Is that

WHO'S TO BLAME?
On 19 August 2003 a commentary headed "French barbarity" appeared in Le Figaro *newspaper attacking the French habit of abandoning elderly relatives and dependants to go on holiday: "It's not up to the State to take care of our elderly. It's up to us."*

the government's fault?", demanded the State Secretary for the elderly, Hubert Falco, two weeks after the crisis when his own handling of the emergency was under fire. "There are three hundred families who haven't yet realised that they have a granny or a mother who is dead."

On paper, French healthcare had been rated the best in the world – specifically, a 2000 report by the World Health Organisation (W.H.O.) placed France first amongst 191 countries rated. (Then again, it also ranked San Marino second, well above the U.S. at thirty-seventh). And yet, compared with other countries, France had suffered disproportionately.

ESTIMATED DEAD, SUMMER 2003

France	14,800
Italy	4,200
Netherlands	1,400
Portugal	1,300
U.K.	900
Spain	100

(National Institute for Health and Medical Research)

In practice, as a further 2003 W.H.O. Report reported, the French health service displayed systemic faults from top to bottom including "lack of anticipation, organisation and co-ordination". It criticised the service for closing hospital wards during August rather than providing cover for the doctors and nurses on holiday which, the report noted, would have been artificially expensive because of France's laws regarding temporary employment.

The W.H.O. also referred to certain "government officials, who [showed] reluctance to cut short their own holidays to deal with the crisis". Though casualties were soon recognised to be more than seven times those of 9/11, Health Minister Jean-François Mattei did not leave his villa in the south of France until 17 August while President Chirac, vacationing in Canada, chose not to cut short his salmon-fishing at all.

"If they [the government] had acted sooner, many lives could have been saved," Patrick Pelloux, head of the Association for French Emergency Physicians, told *Le Parisien* newspaper.

Dr Muriel Chaillet, who worked round the clock at Paris' Saint Antoine hospital during the height of the heat wave had welcomed the *Plan Blanc* that now allowed her to open closed wards, use volunteer staff and order life-saving equipment. But, as she said on 22 August when the heat wave was over, "the ventilators we ordered four days ago only arrived today – it's all too late".

The heatwave exposed not just the cracks in France's health system but also a gigantic hole that politicians and public alike seek to cover up. For each of the last five years, the system has been overspending its budget by €10 billion ($12 billion). One British man went to Paris for a hip operation and was astonished to find that the package he was given included a private room with a second bed for his wife, two weeks post-op physiotherapy, and – of course – wine with lunch and dinner. As a citizen of the E.U., all this was free. The whole service is suffering from poor accounting and endemic over-prescription. One fifth of the country's health spending goes on pharmaceuticals.

HELP THE AGED

In 2005, with all proposals for any kind of health reform coming under fire from the public and unions, the French Prime Minister suggested helping the elderly sections of the population, so vulnerable during the 2003 heatwave, by abolishing one of France's – eleven – national holidays. He asked for the nation to turn it into a "day of solidarity" to generate funds for geriatric healthcare and "demonstrate the reality of our social pact". The reality was a little more real than he imagined. Millions of workers in the public and private sectors went on strike in protest at giving up their day off for a load of old grannies too feeble to turn on the air conditioning. "Once the nation's guilty conscience for the heatwave deaths eased off", noted a reporter in Le Monde, "wage-earners were amazed to find themselves selected as the main source of the funding for the elderly. It seems they will refuse to be so. So who is going to pay for health in the future? No one knows. Perhaps we will win the lottery."

85

Government economists warned last year that the health system's annual deficit could rise to €29 billion ($36 billion) by 2010 without a major overhaul.

After the heatwave, the Health Minister announced a reform package, *Hospital 2007*. It was met by a wave of strikes by healthcare workers. One group of surgeons protested at any suggestion of a wage cut by driving their Mercedes *en masse* to an English seaside resort for a "holiday of protest" during a union-called day of stoppages and demonstrations across the country. The government announced that turn-out was low and that most public-sector workers and doctors had turned up for work.

"When a Ministry is unable to count the dead from a heatwave over the summer, it's hard to see how it can count strikers on a single day," replied Patrick Pelloux, President of the Association of Emergency Hospital Doctors.

Treize

Sade But True

Whipping France's Intellectuals Into A Frenzy

How France managed to turn the violent, boring, sexually bizarre Marquis de Sade into a hero.

I t's not just that he was French, it's that he could only have been French, and only the French could have made him a hero. His works are now seen as an exploration of sexual and political freedom. On the other hand, he was a serial rapist, torturer and, the probability is convincing, a murderer. He was the Marquis de Sade.

DE SADE, THE UNSMOOTH OPERATOR
"Imperious, choleric, irascible, extreme in everything, with a dissolute imagination the like of which has never been seen, atheistic to the point of fanaticism, there you have me in a nutshell, and kill me again or take me as I am, for I shall not change."
Marquis de Sade, author, psychopath, bore and hero of French culture.

THE PAINFUL TRUTH

Born Donatien-Alphonse-François de Sade in Paris, the only son of small-time nobility. "The Marquis", formally only ever a "comte" (a count), was educated by his uncle, the Abbé de Sade, and then a strict Jesuit school. Joined the army at 14 and served in the Seven Years War. Returned to Paris and, in May 1763, married the daughter of a rich magistrate. His private life became a public scandal involving repeated torture of young prostitutes and employees of both sexes, sometimes with help of his wife. Sentenced to death in 1772 but reprieved. His mother-in-law obtained a lettre de cachet *(a royal warrant) against him and in 1777 he was imprisoned, beginning a twenty-seven year stretch at a variety of prisons and asylums during which he wrote his disturbing fantasies – including sexual mutilation, paedophilia, sodomy, rape and incest – into novels like* The 120 Days of Sodom, Justine *and* Juliette. *During his stay at the notorious Bastille, he caused a riot that may have contributed to the beginning of the French Revolution. Released himself in 1790, became a judge on the Revolutionary Tribunals. Arrested and sentenced to death by the Jacobins for molesting prisoners in his charge, escaped during a mix-up over names. In 1801, imprisoned again, this time by Napoleon, disgusted at the publication of* Justine, *and wound up back at the asylum at Charenton where he wrote the 10-volume novel,* Crimes of Passion. *Died there in 1814, aged 74. His works have proved to be a continuing source of business for the symbolist poets, surrealist artists, existential and structuralist intellectuals of France.*

His cup of tea was something more than a bit of slap and tickle. His tastes ran towards sexual mutilation, among many other twisting directions. On Easter Sunday 1768 de Sade met a young widow called Rose Keller in the street and offered her a position as a maid. Keller went with him to his small house in Arcueil where, according to her, de Sade threatened to kill her before tying her to a bed and whipping her with a birch branch. He then sliced her buttocks open with a hunting knife and poured wax into the wounds. The resourceful woman finally escaped by tying sheets together and climbing out of a bedroom window, running directly to the authorities. De Sade's defence, which was accepted, was the same one sexual predators give the world over: "She was asking for it". This is one of the milder episodes of his life.

"SADISM"

"The term for the obtaining of sexual satisfaction through the infliction of pain or humiliation on another person or even an animal; also the morbid pleasure those in certain psychological states experience in being cruel or watching acts of cruelty. The name derives from the Marquis de Sade (1740-1814), a vicious pervert and writer of plays and obscene novels, notably Justine *(1791),* Philosophie dans le boudoir *(1783) and* Les Crimes d'amour *(1800)."* Brewer's Dictionary of Phrase and Fable, *Fourteenth Edition, 1991.*

This was a life almost exclusively devoted to violence masquerading as sex. If he could not actually do it in practice (and, to be fair, the French tried to keep him behind bars as much as possible) then de Sade wrote about it in principle, as he did in *The 120 Days of Sodom*.

This book lists six hundred perversions in an order of complexity. He begins with something simple, a priest who likes sucking the snot out of a girl's runny nose, and ends with fetishistic mass-slaughter. The book was never completed. He got so excited writing it that, halfway through, the prose dwindles into sketch-notes of all the atrocities that came to mind, some of them listed in increasingly shaky handwriting. Was it all just fantasy?

He was never actually convicted of anything. This is not quite true. In 1777, he was sentenced to death for "sodomy" but this verdict was overturned after his mother-in-law bribed the judge. More serious charges never stuck. When he inherited the Chateau la Coste in the Vaucluse valley from his father, the Marquis hired six young servant women and a boy (for variety). Eventually, four got away,

NOTES FROM "120 DAYS OF SODOM"

"No. 137: A notorious sodomist, in order to combine that crime with those of incest, murder, rape, sacrilege, and adultery, first inserts a Host in his ass, then has himself embuggered by his own son, rapes his married daughter, and kills his niece." Marquis de Sade, listing perversions for his novel.

MY WIFE'S MOTHER, MY NEMESIS

A mother-in-law is rarely a heroine of any story. Despite the best efforts of de Sade's many fans and biographers, Marie de Montreuil is the exception. When her eldest daughter, Renée-Pélagie, married the Marquis in 1763 she adored the educated aristocrat. For ten years, she devoted formidable energy to hushing up his bizarre scandals (she even got him off a death sentence, the result of an orgy in which de Sade and his gay valet, Latour, accidentally poisoned four prostitutes with a home-made aphrodisiac and then tried to revive them through anal intercourse). But then de Sade crossed her. He involved his wife's devout, virginal younger sister, Anne-Prospre, in an orgy at his castle, deflowered her and then abandoned her. Marie went to work. She packed Anne-Prospre off to a convent and took out a lettre de cachet (a royal warrant allowing the holder to have individuals jailed without charge so long as their living costs were met) against de Sade in 1777. From jail, de Sade assailed her with a stream of mail, denouncing her as a middle-class hag unfit to lay hands upon a nobleman of his calibre. In 1790, the tables were turned. De Sade became a Revolutionary Tribunal judge, sentencing old school aristocrats to death. The Montreuil family were in danger of the guillotine until Marie reminded de Sade that his jail letters might be of interest to the Jacobin death squads. He released them but, with a single-mindedness that will appeal to all mothers-in-law everywhere, she passed on the letters anyway to Marat, head of the Committee of Public Surveillance. It was not her fault that Marat could not read her hand-writing and had the perfectly harmless Marquis de la Salle executed instead. Pausing only to get a divorce for her daughter, Mme de Montreuil, not being, sexy, radical or a sadist, then disappears from history.

BLUE MOVER

De Sade found the porn of his time "that one finds on sale in those shoddy stalls by the banks of the Seine" too bland for his taste. So he began writing his own, which was sold from the same stalls but bound in blue covers. These "blue books" provide the origin of the term "blue" to describe pornography.

telling a magistrate stories of violent orgies in which the other servants had been strangled or suffocated. When questioned, de Sade said they had simply run off. Because he was a nobleman and they were peasants, the servants were flogged for perjury, which must have pleased de Sade more than the authorities could have guessed.

There is no real use in speculating why he was the way he was. His father was a notorious bisexual playboy, his mother became a nun. The uncle to whom he was sent to be educated at the age of five

---

FOR DE SADE *While ordinary people might think praising de Sade for his social thought is about as credible as praising Hitler for his motorways, this has not stopped France's many, many intellectuals trying to turn this sexually violent, loudmouth bore into some a kind of saint.*

Guillaume Apollinaire *(1880-1918) Symbolist poet, severely brain-damaged in World War I and suspect in 1911 theft of the Mona Lisa: "de Sade is the most liberated spirit of all time" and "his teaching will dominate the twentieth century".*

André Breton *(1896-1966) "Leader" of Surrealist movement: "De Sade would understand that the simplest Surrealist act consists in going down into the street, revolver in one's hands, and firing at random, wilfully, into the crowd."*

Simone de Beauvoir *(1908-86) Feminist author of many unintelligible works, including Must We Burn de Sade? (1955): "[de Sade] posed the problem of the Other in its extremist terms; in his excesses, man-as-transcendence and man-as-object achieve a dramatic confrontation." Hnunk?*

Georges Bataille *(1867-1962) Father of post-modernism. Became so post-modernist, he tried to set up his own religion with his lover as first human sacrifice. Author of The Use Value of D.A.F. de Sade (1930): "Since it is true that erotic pleasure is not only the negation of agony that takes place at the same instant, but also a lubricious pleasure in that agony, it is time to choose between cowards afraid of their own joyful excesses and the conduct of those who judge that any given man need not cower like a hunted animal but instead can see all the moralistic buffoons as so many dogs."*

Jacques Lacan *(1901-81). Deconstructionist, radical psychoanalyst and, until his students revolted en masse at the gibberish of his seminars, university lecturer. Author of Kant with Sade seminar 1973: "As emphasised by the kind of Kantian that Sade was, one can only enjoy a part of the Other's body, for the simple reason that one has never seen a body completely wrap itself around the Other's body to the point of surrounding and phagocytising it. All this is admirably clear. Do we not agree?."*

was a priest of an unconventional sort in that he reportedly ran a brothel on the side. So what? Families can be difficult.

He was violently anti-religious; then again, so were many French intellectuals of the time, although few went as far as de Sade who, according to police testimony given by one child prostitute, reported: "He [de Sade, said that he had] once had sexual union with a girl with whom he had taken Communion, that he had made off with the two Communion wafers, had shoved them into that girl's sexual parts, and that he had sexual congress with her, all the while saying: 'If you are God, avenge yourself'. He then asked me to take an enema and empty my bowel onto a statuette of Jesus Christ. I declined."

His atheism is one reason that a later class of French intellectuals led by symbolist poet (and pornographer) Guillaume Appollinaire resurrected his writings in the early 1900s. Another reason was de Sade's ideas about political and, above all, personal freedom. A brief scan of his social works reveals that he was most ardent for man's freedom to do whatever his nature inclined, even if that includes a little rape and torture. He was most coherent in his arguments against the imprisonment of law-breakers, not surprising for a sex criminal who spent twenty-seven years in various jails and asylums.

His spells behind bars in no way make him a martyr. Life in a royal prison for a nobleman was not too strenuous. He had his own food sent in and his own clothes. His correspondence to his long-suffering wife consists mostly of demands for money so that he can attend soirées hosted by other prisoners. Not only was he allowed to write what he liked but, on 2 July 1789, he somehow got hold of a megaphone, and spent a happy afternoon shouting "They are cutting the throats of the prisoners in here!" through the window of his cell in the Bastille. This inflamed the brooding Parisian crowd so much that, a few days later, a huge mob stormed the fortress, marking the beginning of the French Revolution.

De Sade would have been sorry to miss the fun. He had been transferred to the insane asylum at Charenton where he was permitted to stage his own plays using the inmates as actors. This was hardly a high security institution since, boring of the place in 1790, he waddled to the gates (he had grown morbidly obese on a diet of rich prison food), announced "I am the Marquis de Sade" and released himself on his own recognisances. When he was eventually brought back to Charenton, after a brief career as a Revolutionary Tribunal judge dishing out death sentences galore, he was allowed to bring a 12-year old mistress with him who, perversely, was not allowed to leave until his death in 1814.

AND AGAINST. *"But if there seems little reason for literary people to concern themselves with Sade, he has found a new lease of life among French philosophers and anthropologists. Bored and uneasy with our little lives we resort to the greater amplitude of symbols. Bardot, Byron, Hitler, Hemingway, Monroe, Sade: we do not require our heroes to be subtle, just to be big. Then we can depend on someone to make them subtle."* D J Enright in "The Marquis and the Madame", Conspirators and Poets, 1966.

Quatorze

French Women Don't Get Fat

No, They're Addicted, Anorexic and Anxious

Some European and U.S. women are convinced that their French counterparts are naturally slimmer than they are. The French put it down to their "appreciation of food". But from other perspectives, that explanation is very thin indeed.

I t is unusual for a French attribute to induce a feeling of inadequacy in other nations. What causes women the world over to get their Bridget Jones-style big pants in a twist on the way to their compensatory barrel of fudge is that, well, "French Women Don't Get Fat".

This is accepted as holy writ by even the hard-boiled harpies editing magazines and presenting lifestyle programmes who gush about "the French Paradox" (Florence Fabricant, cookery expert, *New York Times*) and marvel how "French women don't get fat, but they do eat bread and pastry, drink wine, and regularly enjoy three-course meals" (Oprah Winfrey). Apparently, "the ability to eat good food, drink fine wine and remain slim" is all "a matter of

A JOURNALIST WEIGHS IN
"They don't diet and they don't spend hours panting round the gym. So how can French women put away as much ice-cream, rich pastries and steak frites *as they want and yet stay so slim?".* Mimi Spencer, The Observer newspaper, 2004.

attitude, with a smidgen of wisdom and a pinch of common sense thrown in" (Jana Kraus, Top 100 Reviewer, amazon.com).

And it's all true, isn't it? Visions appear of pixie Audrey Tautou buzzing about a picture-book Paris on a moped, just as light as a puff of Gauloise. Or of Sophie Marceau in *The World Is Not Enough*, so slinky, so svelte, so French, right up until the moment Bond has to blow her head off. Or of Catherine Deneuve, still slim and gorgeous even though she's about 97. Now why can't you be more like them, fat-arse?

If you buy that rubbish, then you'll also want to buy *French Women Don't Get Fat* (2004) by Mireille Guiliano or *Chic and Slim: How Those French Women Eat all that Rich Food and Still Stay Slim* (2004) by Anne Barone. Both books surrender to the idea that French women are always thin because they are somehow just better than anyone else.

"Forget diets. They are no fun and don't work", says Barone. "What I learned from French women is that ultimately staying slim is not about counting calories or fat grams. It is not about exercise exhaustion. It is really about personal style."

What gives these claims a spurious believability is the widely circulated statistic that while a hefty 22% of Americans are obese, only 11.3% of the French weigh in at the same level (these figures, quoted by Mireille Guiliano, come from the French health authorities). According to Guiliano, this is all because the French *appreciate* food more.

THE REAL REASON WHY MIREILLE GUILIANO DOESN'T GET FAT: ABUSE AND MEDICAL ATTENTION
"On an educational séjour to the United States long ago, Guiliano ballooned up on a shameless Yankee diet of brownies and bagels and became an anomaly: A fat French girl. When she returned to France a year later her father took one look at her and said, 'You look like a sack of potatoes'. But Guiliano met Doctor Miracle, a discreet doctor and armchair psychologist who weaned her back to Gallic slimness. His programme – rich in pleasure, savoir-faire, and age-old French secrets – is the backbone of French Women Don't Get Fat." Debra Ollivier, journalist for Salon and author of the nauseatingly entitled Entre Nous: A Woman's Guide to Finding Her Inner French Girl *(2003).*

They have elaborate food rituals. They go to the market several times a week and eat only what is in season. Unlike Americans, who buy processed, flavourless food and therefore need to eat a lot of it to feel gratified, the French, by eating better-tasting food and savouring it more consciously, "fool themselves" into being satisfied with less. That is, French women do, since, in Guiliano's book, it is specifically the women who must master "the useful art of self-deception, mentally balancing the pleasures of food against the competing desires to fit into the latest fashions and to be attractive to French men", who she says like their wives to be "very elegant, very thin".

But statistics work both ways. There are other facts and figures that suggest *French Women Don't Get Fat But...*

1. FRENCH WOMEN WILL DO SOON

For every thin, angle-poise Frenchwoman along the lines of Charlotte Rampling, there's another like Brigitte Bardot who seems to be all carpet-skimming parabolas now. True, only 11.3% of the French are clinically obese but in 1990 the figure was only 6% (if the rate of obesity increases at the same rate, the French will overtake the U.S. in 2020). Other studies indicate that French women have gained about 2 kilograms (4.5 pounds) since 1970, men twice as much. Childhood obesity in France now runs at around 16-19% and, to counteract this trend, the French government has just banned 8,000 soft drink vending machines in its schools.

THE SHAPE OF THINGS TO COME "

French women don't get fat yet. France once thought it was protected from obesity. But in reality, the epidemic is now spreading at about the same rate as in the United States. The problem has just been delayed by five, ten years compared with over there," says Jean-Marie Le Guen, a doctor and Socialist opposition deputy who has tabled a law in Parliament to help in the fight against obesity.

Ironically, obesity is in a way a measure of France's success since it implies that more of the population now have easier access to the cheap, plentiful foods that Americans had thirty years ago. (A more positive side-effect is that while French people may be growing wider they are also growing taller, about three centimetres since the 1970s).

2. FRENCH WOMEN ARE DOPED-UP

One reason that French women may eat less than their counterparts in other countries is that they prefer to shovel pills down their throats rather than calories, including vast quantities of tranquillizers, sleeping pills and anti-depressants, all of which are notorious appetite suppressants. A 2003 survey by the *Observatoire Français des Drogues et des Toxicomanies* (French Observatory of Drugs and Addictions) found that almost one in five of French adults –

HOW DEPRESSING.

"The French are the world's leading consumers of medicine: three billion boxes a year. It's absolutely incredible! Our prescriptions are the longest of all the industrialised countries surrounding us." Jean-François Mattei, Health Minister of a country where 1.5 million people take anti-depressants daily.

including a quarter of all women – take mood-altering medicines. Almost one in ten women said they had taken sleeping pills or tranquillizers in the previous week. On average, a French person buys more than 40 boxes of medicines from chemists every year, a total of 2.6 billion pills and potions, according to government figures – more medicine per head than any other country in Europe. While an American woman might hunker down with a carton of Ben & Jerry's to cure their blues, her French equivalent deals with her own body shape anxiety with a fistful of pills.

3. FRENCH WOMEN ARE ILL

According to nutrition journalist Kate Taylor of the *New Yorker* magazine, somewhere between 0.5% and 3.7% of American women suffer some kind of eating disorder in their lifetimes. Among young French women, an estimated 1% to 3% are anorexic; 5% are bulimic, and 11% have compulsive eating behaviours. French women may be slimmer than those in the U.S. but, according to such statistics, more of them are unhappier about their bodily health and many of them are just plain unhealthier.

IT'S ENOUGH TO MAKE YOU THROW UP
"The problem is that, while they may be admirably successful at staying thin, French women are not necessarily more balanced in their attitudes about food. While many people think of eating disorders like anorexia and bulimia as an American problem, they are, as far as can be measured, far more prevalent in France". Kate Taylor, New Yorker *journalist*

4. FRENCH WOMEN ARE MORE LIKELY TO DIE OF LUNG CANCER

Cigarettes are a notorious appetite-suppressant. According to major surveys from both nations, the percentage of French women who smoke is five points higher than the percentage of American women. More significantly, in America, where cigarettes now have a loser image, only 10% of those with college and graduate degrees smoke (compared to about 40% of high-school drop-outs). But in France, nearly 33% of upper-income earners smoke. These categories are important since they are the ones that worry most about their bodily appearance. It seems that, in France, they have a lot to be worried about. The French national public health body, the *Institut National de Veille Sanitaire* (I.N.V.S.) now estimates that 12,000 French women will die from lung cancer each year from 2015, six times as many as in 1980. "It's hard to get across the danger", says Sylviane Ratte, of the French National Anti-Cancer League, "because for decades cigarettes have been associated with images of beautiful, thin women".

CIGARETTES: 0 CALORIES
"Smoking cessation is invariably associated with short term weight gain, at a range of 6-9 pounds. And over the long term, with the absence of nicotine to curb one's appetite and the use of food instead of cigarettes to satisfy oral fixations, weight can keep climbing. Tobacco contributes to many thousands of deaths per year from cardiovascular disease and cancer. But we need to be truthful about the role that cigarettes have had in our society. And we don't need to feel that the French are thinner because they are better than we are. They just inhale more." Stuart Henochowicz, Medviews.

5. BUT ONLY BECAUSE OTHERWISE FRENCHMEN WILL CHEAT ON THEM.

In the late 1990s, 67% of French divorce actions were for fault (including adultery). 95% were brought by French women against cheating husbands. "In a recent review of Guiliano's book, *Vogue* magazine contributor Julia Reed touched again and again on the fact that French women keep their bodies trim for their husbands. Hmmmm. Here's another thing I know about French women from those of my acquaintance: their lives revolve around their husbands Perhaps – just perhaps – French women don't get fat because they have a great deal invested in remaining married and pleasing a man in this way." Bethanne Patrick, Book Maven, Editor at A.O.L. Books.

THE FRENCH ARE THIN? FAT CHANCE!

"Actually, I saw a book on a bookshelf here called French Women Don't Get Fat. *That's so stupid. French women do get fat. All French women are not so thin. French women are famous for having form, just like Italian and Mediterranean women."* Marilou Berry, *uncharacteristically curvaceous French actress, interviewed by the* Sydney Morning Herald *newspaper.*

OUT OF SHAPE

7 January 2005 was National Weighing Day for the country's children, a strange ritual in France in which an army of hundreds of state-employed paediatricians fan out to more than 80 cities to weigh, measure, and interrogate children. What they found was not encouraging to style-conscious France. The French are getting fatter. While adult obesity is rising about 6% annually, among children the national rate of growth is 17%. An estimated 55,000 people in France already die of obesity-related illnesses every year. At the current rate, the French could be – quelle horreur – as fat as Americans by 2020 .

Quinze

The Permanent War

Milestones of an Anti-American Chronology

France is one of the United States' closest allies – on paper. In truth, over nearly a quarter of a millennium, France's relations with the United States have been characterised by a persistent hostility towards the country it considers its political, economic and cultural rival.

Hatred of America and Americans is nothing new, and it's never been localised. Walk into a sports bar in downtown Tehran, if there is such a thing, wearing a Stars and Stripes, and you can expect to find it draped on the coffin mailed to your mom minutes later. But, what the hell, that's an occupational risk of being the modern world's biggest economic, political and cultural success. The pygmies of Skull Island probably had mixed feelings about the great god Kong too.

AT WAR WITH AMERICA
"We are at war with America. Yes, a permanent war, a vital war, a war without death. Yes, they are very hard, the Americans, they are voracious, they want undivided power over the world." President François Mitterrand.

That success is highly visible in France. Go into any Carrefour supermarket in France and you'll find bakery shelves stacked with "Harry's American Sandwich" bread. McDonald's sells 585 million meals to the French every year, including such treats as *Le New York* burger and *Le Texas*. "Britney Spears" was the term most searched for on Google France in 2005. The all-time top box-office film in France is the American blockbuster, *Titanic*. While President Chirac sneers at American cultural imperialism, he can't resist inviting Steven Spielberg to the Elysée Palace to give him the *légion d'honneur*. Like it or not, America is an integer in French life.

Many French don't like it – and never have. The myth of Franco-American friendship begins with French assistance in the American Revolution and continues with the United States preserving French liberty – twice – in the twentieth century. The reality, pointed out most recently by John L. Miller and Mark Molesky in *Our Oldest Enemy* (2004), is hostility, bloodshed, sabotage, envy and, on the French side, over two centuries of knee-jerk anti-Americanism, that in the words of a diplomat from another nation, "represents a neurosis". Here are just a few milestones:

1704   During **Queen Anne's War (1702-13)**, 300 French and Indian marauders attack Deerfield in Massachusetts, massacring forty-four residents including twenty-five children. More captives die on a forced death march including the pregnant Mary Brooks who miscarries after slipping by the road and is summarily killed.

> THE OLDEST ENEMY
> *"The French presume they may with impunity kill, seize and imprison our traders, and confiscate their effects at pleasure, as they have done for several years past, [and], murder and scalp our farmers, with their wives and children." Benjamin Franklin, Albany Conference, 1754.*

1754   French invaders overwhelm George Washington's small force at Fort Necessity, Ohio, beginning the **French and Indian War (1754-60)**. Highlights include the massacre of American prisoners at Fort Oswego, Ontario and Fort William Henry, New York. Less successful against soldiers who haven't surrendered, the war ends with France's expulsion from all of North America.

1777   During the **War of Independence (1775-83)**, France gives little help to American colonists until their victory at Saratoga in 1777. Eventually a fleet is sent under Admiral Charles-Hector d'Estaing who bickers with the American commanders. As his allies attack the British in New York by land, d'Estaing abandons them and sails off to Boston. Angry rebels lynch a French officer unwise enough to go ashore. (D'Estaing also tries to arrest the Marquis de Lafayette, one of the few Frenchmen not ordered or paid to assist the Americans, for being there without official permission).

1779   D'Estaing's forces combine with those of General Benjamin Lincoln outside British-held Savannah, Georgia. D'Estaing insists on attacking before preparations are complete and suffers 800 casualties to 150 British. Despite American pleas, D'Estaing takes his fleet back to France in a sulk.

FOR OURSELVES, ALONE
"We do not desire that a new republic should arise and become exclusive mistress of this great continent." The Comte de Vergennes, French Foreign Minister, 1777.

1779   **August:** French ships join the American privateer *Bonhomme Richard* under John Paul Jones as it fights the bigger British ship, *H.M.S. Serapis*, off Flamborough Head. At one point, the French vessel *Alliance* actually fires on Jones' ship, its captain later confiding to one of his officers that his intention had been to sink the vessel and take credit for victory.

1781   After victory at Yorktown beside their French allies, the resurgent Americans beg that the new French fleet under Admiral de Grasse transport its troops to finish off the British at Charleston. Seeking a victory he doesn't have to share, de Grasse instead leaves for the West Indies and is promptly crushed by the British at the Battle of the Saints.

1793   With peace declared, President Washington issues the Neutrality Proclamation to keep the young republic out of European wars. Edmond-Charles Genet, minister to the United States of the new revolutionary government in France, has different ideas. He commissions privateers to attack British ships, hires private armies to attack Florida and

A REVOLUTIONARY ON REVOLUTIONS
"The affairs of [France] seem to me to be in the highest paroxysm of disorder because those in whose hands the government is entrusted are ready to tear each other to pieces and will more than probably prove the worst foes the country has." George Washington on the French Revolution, 1794.

Louisiana and, when the U.S. government complains, tries to affect the elections through bribery. The U.S. government demands his recall. Rather than return and face the guillotine, Genet asks the Americans for political asylum, becoming the country's first political defector.

1796   The French government presents President Washington with the gift of a new tricolour flag. When he declines to hang it in Congress,

French minister Pierre Ader complains it will be "hidden away in an attic and destined to become the fodder of the rodents and the insects that live there".

DETESTABLE

"These proceedings are rapidly rendering the name of Frenchmen as detestable as once it was dear to Americans." Secretary of State Timothy Pickering on French privateers operating from U.S. ports, 1796.

1797   When the federal government refuses to declare war on Britain, the French order the new U.S. ambassador to France off its soil or face arrest. In the **XYZ Affair**, a three-man commission arrives from America to normalise relations but French foreign minister, Talleyrand, declines to see them without a $250,000 bribe paid up-front.

1798   France and the U.S. fight an undeclared war at sea, beginning when a French privateer attacks a merchant ship and finds, too late, it's the *Delaware*, an armed vessel with 24 guns and a 180-man crew. With a navy of only 16 ships, the U.S. captures 86 French vessels during the **Quasi-War** (1798-1800).

A ONE-SIDED AFFAIR

"France is at war with us but we are not at war with her." President John Adams, 1798.

1800   Having denied publicly that his country has any interest in American territory, Talleyrand bulldozes Spain into transferring its Louisiana territories to France. He then reinforces New Orleans with 3,500 soldiers, closing the city to American commerce. Outraged, the Americans threaten war until Napoleon, busy fighting wars in Europe, writes off the whole affair by selling all 828,000 acres to the U.S. for $15 million.

1808   France tries to prevent the U.S. trading with Britain, its enemy. In April 1808, Napoleon seizes all American ships in French ports, confiscating goods worth $10 million. Over the next seven years, the French grab 558 American ships.

JEFFERSON ON NAPOLEON

"This ruthless destroyer of tens of millions of the human race, whose thirst for blood appear[s] unquenchable; the great oppressor of the right and liberties of the world." President Thomas Jefferson, 1810.

1831 After twenty years of negotiations, President Andrew Jackson finally manages to get France to agree to pay $4.6m for the illegal seizure of shipping under Napoleon but only on condition the Americans stump up $270,000 as compensation for French help during the U.S. War of Independence. After the

WARM APOLOGY
"Apologise! I'd see the whole race roasting in hell first." Andrew Jackson on the prospect of having to apologise to the French for his harsh words spoken in Congress, 1833.

Americans make this payment, the French refuse to fulfil their side of the deal. In Congress Jackson warns that the U.S. might take "hostile actions". The French pay up but now demand an apology for the warning.

1861 During the **American Civil War** (1861-65), the French manoeuvre to weaken the U.S. as a geopolitical rival by granting the Confederacy "belligerent rights", the next thing to full diplomatic recognition. The South is encouraged to purchase goods and raise loans in France. Napoleon III lobbies Britain to intervene on the side of the Confederates by sending ships to break the Northern

HERE'S GRATITUDE
"The government at Washington is the last to have a right to complain of the recognition of a revolutionary government." French Foreign Minister Edouard Thouvenal, responding to U.S. protests at French support for the Confederacy, 1863.

blockade. Four cruisers and two ironclad rams are constructed for the Confederacy in the French port of Bordeaux and only when it is obvious the North is going to win does France finally block their hand-over.

1861 Under the pretext of a "debt-collecting" exercise, the French land 30,000 troops in Mexico and install a puppet emperor under their control. After a string of military disasters, including a disastrous assault against smaller numbers in Pueblo, now celebrated by the Mexicans as a national holiday, *El Cinco de Mayo*, the French secure a tenuous hold over the country. As the Civil War ends, Washington threatens action unless the French quit Mexico – which they do with bad grace in 1867, leaving their puppet behind to be shot.

NOT TO BE TAKEN FOR GRANTED
"I, myself, regarded this as a direct war against the United States." General Ulysses S. Grant, commander of the U.S. Forces on hearing of the French invasion of Mexico.

1886 After defeat in the **Franco-Prussian War** (1869-71), the Third French Republic decides on some international bridge-building and commissions sculptor Frédéric Auguste Bartholdi to build a 305-foot structure, the Statue of Liberty, as a gift from France to the American people. The French government do not pay for this gift; it is financed by public subscription (Americans actually raise $390,000 of the $740,000 cost). Bartholdi initially plans to model the face on that of his girlfriend but considers her too beautiful for the Americans so he uses his mother instead.

1917   America enters **World War I** (1914-18) helping to prop up an exhausted France. Four million Americans mobilise to help France, and 120,000 die.

1918   President Woodrow Wilson, the first president ever to leave the United States, comes to France to help negotiate a just settlement. His proposals are sabotaged at every step by French Prime Minister Georges Clemenceau determined to cripple Germany as a potential rival forever. When Wilson has a stroke, Clemenceau jokes: "Oh, he's getting better is he? Couldn't we bribe his doctors?" The Versailles Peace Treaty, bulldozed through by the French, guarantees a new war twenty years later.

CALL US IN TWENTY YEARS
"America is the only nation in history which miraculously has gone directly from barbarism to degeneration without the usual interval of civilisation."
Georges Clemenceau, French Prime Minister and chief architect of the disastrous Versailles Peace Treaty, 1918.

1941   The U.S. enters **World War II** (1939-45). Relations with de Gaulle and the Free French Forces start badly when he threatens to fire on U.S. troops attempting to secure the French islands of Miquelon and St. Pierre.

1942   Vichy French forces attack American troops landing in French Morocco for "Operation Torch". At Oran, U.S. troops are machine-gunned in the water, suffering 90% casualties. Admiral Darlan, commanding French forces in North Africa, orders a ceasefire and commands

WELCOME TO FRANCE
"Well, I hope the people of Vichy throw them into the sea. You can't break into France and get away with it."
General Charles de Gaulle on Operation Torch.

the French ships at Toulon to steam for Africa. "Merde", replies Admiral de Laborde and scuttles the fleet rather than have it serve the Allies.

1944   **June:** the run up to D-Day and de Gaulle refuses to record a radio message about the invasion since it was going to be broadcast after one by General

Eisenhower. Pressured by Churchill, who reminds him that it isn't going to be Frenchmen shot at on the beaches of Normandy, de Gaulle sulkily agrees but doesn't mention the Allies at all nor the requirement that, during the fighting, French citizens should take directions from them. "He's a nut", decides President Roosevelt. The Americans take 100,000 casualties in the advance on Paris which de Gaulle demands is carried out by Free French General, Jacques Leclerc (nicknamed by Hemingway, "Lejerk") though his forces are a hundred miles away and the Americans are in the city outskirts.

1945   As the Allies mop up, de Gaulle sends troops into Italy to grab frontier land and orders them to resist any U.S. attempts to remove them. "Psychopathic" is how new U.S. president, Truman, characterises him. When he threatens to cut aid to France, the only thing keeping the economy going, French troops withdraw.

> **BELIEVE IT OR NOT**
> *"The almost unbelievable threat that French soldiers, bearing American arms, will combat American soldiers whose sacrifices contributed to the liberation of France itself."* President Truman, as France threatens U.S. forces, 1945.

1947   U.S. Secretary of State George Marshall oversees the donation of $13 billion in U.S. aid to rebuild Europe's economies. Over the next eight years, France receives $5.5 billion.

1949   French communists combine with wine growers to pressure the government to ban Coca-Cola for "health reasons". The Roman Catholic newspaper *Témoignage chrétien*, calls it "the advance guard of a tremendous offensive aiming at the economic colonisation of France". When it becomes clear that the U.S. will respond by blocking all imports of wine and perfume from France the government blocks the bill's final enactment.

MAD DOG
"America has rabies. Let us sever all our links with her, or else we shall get bitten and become rabid." Jean-Paul Sartre, moralist, lover and crazed Stalin fan, 1953.

1954   As the Free World struggles to contain communism, the French beg the U.S. for bombers, fighters and transports to help in their war in Indochina, all of which are provided. The U.S. ends up paying 80% of French war expenses.

1960   De Gaulle returns to power as President of France, ushering in a long period of knee-jerk anti-Americanism. Eventually he announces that although

France considers N.A.T.O. useful to her security, it is in fact an "American protectorate". He demands that the thirty U.S. military bases and 60,000 U.S. troops based in France be withdrawn.

1967   General Charles Ailleret, French Chief of Staff, announces that France's small nuclear arsenal will not only be targeted at the Soviet Union but also the U.S.A.

THE HEIGHT OF HYPOCRISY
"France is violently opposed to blatant American imperialism now rampant in the world. France will continue to attack and oppose the United States in Latin America, in Asia and in Africa." President Charles de Gaulle, forgetting the millions of Vietnamese and Algerian dead at French hands, 1967.

1968   The French government officially complains about the disparaging wise-cracks against de Gaulle on Johnny Carson's late night T.V. show. Carson replies that blaming him for de Gaulle's lack of popularity was "like Sophia Loren saying Twiggy stretched out one of her jumpers".

1979   When the Soviet Union invades Afghanistan in 1979, France refuses to join Jimmy Carter in imposing sanctions on the communist superpower. It also spurns an American-sponsored embargo on Iran after Islamic revolutionaries seize the U.S. embassy and hold 66 American hostages at gunpoint for a year.

1980   President Mitterrand takes office and sets the tone for continuing French foreign policy by denouncing the U.S.'s "jungle capitalism".

1986   Ronald Reagan orders a bombing raid on targets in Libya in response to Muammar al-Qaddafi's attacks on U.S. personnel in Europe. While the U.K. and Germany provide support, the French flatly refuse to allow U.S. planes to fly over French airspace.

THE GIPPER GYPPED
"Their refusal upset me because I believed all civilised nations were in the same boat when it came to resisting terrorism." President Reagan, remembering French obstinacy in his memoirs, 1990.

1990   When Iraq invades Kuwait, the U.N. Security Council unanimously approves a trade and financial embargo on Iraq. When the U.S. and the U.K. argue to turn this embargo into an armed blockade, Mitterrand declares his country cannot possibly support such a drastic action and his defence minister pointedly goes on holiday rather than get involved with Coalition efforts.

CRISIS? WHAT CRISIS?
"No legal basis exists for armed intervention against Iraq or even to liberate Kuwait. They don't need me to carry out Bush's policies; I'm going back to Tuscany." French Defence Minister Jean-Pierre Chevènement going on holiday to block Coalition efforts to isolate Saddam Hussein.

1991 Grudgingly, the French join the Coalition, sending 10,000 men to the Gulf (the carrier *Clemenceau* also goes but its jet fighters are taken off and replaced with trucks). It refuses to work under U.S. command, making unified strategic planning difficult. Then Mitterrand announces that French forces will neither fly over Iraqi territory nor march into it "for safety reasons". After complaints by his own army, he lifts the ban eleven days later.

REHEATING THE COLD WAR
"Their [American] weight tends towards hegemonism, and the idea they have of their mission is unilateralism. And that is not acceptable." French Foreign Minister Hubert Védrine, 1999, at the World Trade Organisation talks explains why France is blocking a general global free trade deal until it gets special protection for French films; to punish America for winning the Cold War, apparently.

2000 After 9/11, Jacques Chirac proclaims his support for the U.S. but his government soon reverts to form. One minister dismissed the Bush administration's attempt to isolate terrorist countries in the world as "Texas-style diplomacy", French code for what it apparently sees as simple-minded pig-headedness. As the U.S. and its allies target Iraq, the French run interference in the United Nations and its diplomats tour the world to block action against Saddam Hussein.

"WE ARE ALL ANTI-AMERICANS NOW."
12 September: Americans are touched by an editorial in France's newspaper of record, Le Monde headlined Nous sommes tous Américains (We are all Americans now). However, only the headline ever seemed to be read. The article that followed implied that Americans were to blame for 9/11 because, in the words of its author, the newspaper's publisher Jean-Marie Colombani, of their "ridiculous, if not downright odious" support for Israel. Less nuanced is a new magazine, l'Anti-Américain, a journal devoted to that special hectoring kind of humour the French take for satire. Its masthead carries the legend Nous sommes tous Anti-Américains.

During the actual invasion, Chirac's Foreign Minister (and now Prime Minister) Dominique de Villepin is asked if he wants the U.S. forces actually to win in Iraq. "I'm not going to answer", he replies. Newspaper polls answer for him: a quarter of the French population wanted the U.S. to be defeated militarily by the mass-murdering dictator.

2003 In one of the saddest symptoms of anti-Americanism in France, a statue in Bordeaux was covered in red paint and gasoline and set on fire by unknown vandals. This was the Bordeaux Statue of Liberty, a 2.5 metre (8 foot) replica of the real thing. Just a year earlier, a plaque had been added to commemorate the victims of the 9/11 attacks.

So, is France really riddled with hatred of Americans? Well, yes and no. As far as the ordinary French people in the street are concerned, puffing their Salems and drinking their Coors, *les Yanquis* are basically OK according to most opinion polls. Then again, according to a Taylor Nelson Sofres survey released in 2003, the five traits the French public most associate with the U.S. are: power, violence, inequality, wealth and racism.

Real, long-term anti-Americanism though is bred into the bone of French governments, both of the Left and the Right. From de Gaulle to Mitterrand, anti-Americanism is their way of stressing France's independence – and a safe way too because they know full well that the United States will never come down hard against a fellow member of N.A.T.O., of the W.T.O. and the United Nations Security Council. It's like flipping off your dad; he might withdraw T.V. privileges for a week but he's not likely to nuke you.

France's intellectual groupies too understand that there's no comeback for anti-Americanism in France, however vacuous or vicious. Post-modernist philosopher, Jean Baudrillard, wrote after 9/11: "All the world without exception dreamt of this event: It is they who acted but we who wanted the deed."

The invasion of Iraq heralded many new books from thinkers like Baudrillard vivisecting the policy, personality and culture – or lack of it – of the United States, like Emmanuel Todd's *Après l'empire* (*After the Empire*, 2003) or Philippe Roger's *L'Ennemi Américain* (*The American Enemy*, 2004). None of this is new. Fifty years ago, the French bestseller lists included titles like *L'Abomination Américaine* (1930) and *Le Cancer Américain* (1931) and pamphlets railed against American life. "Out with the Yankees!", wrote one more than usually berserk author. "Out with the people and their products, their methods and their lessons, their dances and their jazz! Let them take back their Fords and their chewing gum."

And yet a few French intellectuals, only a few, are beginning to wonder if the anti-Americanism in France's upper circles isn't – how to put this? – *wrong*? Bernard-Henri Lévy is another French philosopher, even more contrary and publicity-seeking than Baudrillard. So willing is he to go against the flow that now he is beginning to think (as far as the French are concerned) the unthinkable:

"Is anti-Americanism a horror?..", he asked haltingly in 2004. "It is a magnet of the worst. In the entire world and in France in particular, everything that is the worst in people's heads comes together around anti-Americanism: racism, nationalism, chauvinism and anti-Semitism."

Perhaps then, France's hatred of Americans provides it with a twisted proxy to hate what is hateful in itself.

90 Minutes Silence

The Meaningless Films of Jean-Luc Godard

Jean-Luc Godard is one of France's most respected – and typical – film-makers, academic, intellectual and political. So why is he box office poison around the world?

T he classic French "art film" that so many trendy flea-pits and state broadcasting channels still play wall-to-wall is the invention of one man. Almost single-handedly, he created all its conventions from clumsy jump-cut collages to moodily anorexic heroines to brain-ache dialogue composed mostly of *non sequiturs*. That man is Jean-Luc Godard. What he invented were films that deliberately cut out the audience. As a result, he got himself a Chevalier of the French National Order of Merit, a *César* Award (the French equivalent of the Oscars) and a place on Entertainment Weekly's list of The Greatest Directors Of All Time (he's No. 31).

WELCOME SILENCE
"Since Godard's films have nothing to say, perhaps we could have ninety minutes silence instead of each of them." John Simon, film critic, New York *magazine.*

A SNAPSHOT OF JEAN-LUC GODARD

Born Paris, 1930, to a Franco-Swiss family with interests in banking. Educated at the Lycée Rohmer and the Sorbonne. After working on short films in the 1950s, his parents finally stop his allowance. Starts writing super-theoretical cinema criticism for Les cahiers du cinéma *(Film Notebook), a magazine run by young film-makers who later become known as the* Nouvelle Vague *(New Wave) of French film-making. Directs his first feature,* Breathless *(1960), his only – comparative – hit. Its jump-cuts and hand-held shots delight film academics but its unfinished, meandering quality bewilders mainstream audiences. His influence spreads during the 1960s with films whose subjects are as controversial as their cinematography –* his The Little Soldier *(1960) is banned in France because of its stance towards the Algerian war. In 1965, he brings out* Pierrot le Fou, *a portrait of a drop-out rejecting bourgeois society, based on himself but played by the handsomer Jean-Paul Belmondo. His films became more argumentatively political.* La Chinoise *(1967), focuses in its entirety on Parisian students discussing "the revolution" while* Weekend *(1968) attacks consumer culture and what Godard sees as its most oppressive features, the supermarket and traffic jams. Organises his film unit along Maoist principles in the 1970s, filming tributes to the PLO and a portrait of Jane Fonda being politically re-educated by striking sausage-makers. Godard experiments with video before returning to "commercial" film with* Every Man for Himself *(1980) which features a character named Godard who says, "I have nothing to say. I make movies to keep myself busy. If I had the strength, I'd do nothing." Achieves latter-day notoriety for* Hail Mary *(1985), a typically chaotic modern nativity story condemned by the Vatican. He continues to make confusing film and video pieces, mostly in Europe.*

Most ordinary film-goers will never have heard of Godard or the extraordinarily influential school of filmmaking, *la Nouvelle Vague* (*the New Wave*), that he and like-minded French directors invented in the Sixties. This is because, of his hundred or so films, only one, *A bout de souffle* (*Breathless*, 1960), ever came close to being a popular success (grossing just over $200,000 in its US run; by comparison, *Psycho*, which came out in the same year, made $32 million).

In a career spanning nearly fifty years, Godard has become the Yoko Ono of cinema, building a career out of his "anti-image" films. His movies, he pronounces, are "truth twenty-four times per second". What this means is an extreme kind of naturalistic film-making, formless in terms of story and crude, even amateurish, in cinematic technique. What the viewer gets on screen are long, very long, home movies, shot clumsily. Because Godard has a reputation for not using scripts, ordering actors to tear up screenplays and ad-lib on the day of shooting, the films are endlessly talky. Because he is "political" (Godard, like many French intellectuals of his time, has dallied with hard-line Maoism), most of the talk is about the political aspects of everything from love to the workings of sausage factories.

A bout de souffle (Breathless, 1960)

THE PLOT

Michel (Jean-Paul Belmondo), a thug modelling himself on Humphrey Bogart, steals a car and shoots a policeman. On the run, he turns to his American girlfriend Patricia (Jean Seberg), a student and tries to persuade her to run away to Italy. After long discussions, she refuses and causes his "tragic" death.

THE CRITICS

"What can I say about a French film known as a classic to many without offending them? Quite a lot: but I would prefer to keep it limited. This film has neither a sense of filmic style so as to be art nor a narrative which is just as much owed to the audience who are sat waiting for a plot to appear." *The Guardian.*

"A film", he has been quoted as saying, "should have a beginning, a middle and an end but not necessarily in that order". His *Éloge de l'amour (In Praise of Love,* 2001) is a good example. The first section deals with an author discussing a forthcoming work on love while the second part, set three years earlier, focuses on an elderly couple discussing a contract to sell their wartime experiences to an American film company. "It is divided into two parts," Anthony Lane, the *New Yorker* film critic, observed. "How they fit together, Godard only knows."

Le Mépris (Contempt, 1963)

THE PLOT

In Rome, a mopey screenwriter depresses his wife (Brigitte Bardot) as he tries to "fix" a film of the Odyssey with a monstrously philistine American producer (Jack Palance).

THE CRITICS

"Portentous without having anything to say, improvisatory without imagination, full of esoteric references without relevance and in group allusions without interest". John Simon, *New York* magazine.

His visual motif is shaky hand-held photography, a signature he originated in *A bout de souffle* when he placed his cameraman in a wheelchair and pushed him along Paris streets behind Jean-Paul Belmondo and Jean Seberg. "Tracking shots are a question of morality", he has said. He perfected his style in *Week End* (1967), the story of a couple driving into the countryside to collect a dead grandparent's legacy, whose crowning visual is a ten-minute tracking shot of a traffic jam.

Often, and in fact usually, Godard's crew gets itself into these shots by mistake. In *Le Mépris* (*Contempt*, 1963), a searing attack on soulless Hollywood film-makers, the American critic Pauline Kael counted thirteen instances in which camera equipment or operators appear in shot, reflected against a mirror or as wall shadows. Godard describes such goofs as illustrating his work's "essential honesty".

Week End (1967)

THE PLOT
A couple (Mireille Darc and Jean Yanne) drive into the country, get caught in a traffic jam. Tempers rise, fights break out, motorists fight, riot and descend into cannibalism.

THE CRITICS
"Godard pushes his Brechtian didactics to the limit, his exhilarating modernism giving him free rein to draw on Freud, Marx, Lewis Carroll and James Bond." Thomas Delapa, *Boulder Weekly* film critic and teacher of undergraduate film at the University of Colorado at Boulder and Denver.

For all this, stars ranging from Brigitte Bardot to Gérard Depardieu eagerly volunteer to work in his films, not always to critical advantage. Depardieu's role in *Hélas pour moi* (*Alas for Me*, 1993), as a man who find that parts of his body are becoming possessed by God, was written-off with the comment "*Hélas pour nous*" ("Alas for us") by the film reviewer of *Le Figaro*. He is "a teacher, an artist", remembered famous French actor Yves Montand "and a very angry god all in one".

Naturally, Godard despises the stars with whom he is "forced" to work. Montand appeared opposite Jane Fonda in *Tout va bien* (*Everything's OK*, 1972), in which a professional couple become radicalised after being trapped overnight in a sausage factory on strike. Godard obviously did not consider "Hanoi Jane" radicalised enough because he then released another film which contains a single shot, a photograph of Fonda with some Vietnamese peasants, and nothing else except ninety-seven minutes of Godard and a buddy talking in voice-over about what a hypocrite she is. The *avant-garde* feminist film critic, Laura Mulvey, judges that the film is a classic of Godard's "always interesting" misogyny.

Godard attracted these big names because of the cachet his name has in the world of underground (ie non-commercial or, to be more precise, non-money-making) filmmaking. His work, according to the *Economist*, is the subject in courses at over 500 film schools in the USA alone. His success lies in the

Vladimir et Rosa (1970)

THE PLOT
Godard's free interpretation of the Chicago Eight trial, Judge Hoffman becomes Judge Himmler (who doodles notes on *Playboy* centrefolds), the Chicago Eight become a microcosm of French revolutionary society and Godard himself plays Lenin, discussing politics and how to show them through the cinema.

THE CRITICS
"What is not untrue is dull; what is not dull is clumsy; what is not clumsy is irrelevant."
Le Monde.

intellectual verbiage with which he surrounds – and stuffs – his films. Just as the films are very dense, Godard's writing about film – and he started as a very highbrow critic indeed at the magazine he helped found, *Cahiers du cinéma* (*Film Notes*) – is nearly impermeable to human intelligence.

This is where Godard's uniquely French touch comes in. France was the birthplace of conceptual art (which many date from 1917, when Marcel Duchamp exhibited a ready-made porcelain urinal under the title *Fountain*; the "piece", currently housed in Paris' Pompidou Centre, is now valued at some $3.5 million). Before Godard, many directors could have been called artists of the cinema; Godard was the first *conceptual* artist of the cinema. In other words, art is whatever the artist calls art, not what the viewer might think. As such, he has become the patron saint of deadly serious goatee-sprouting, beret-sporting student film-makers everywhere.

Forever Mozart (1996)

THE PLOT
A French theatre troupe attempt to put on a play in Sarajevo but are captured and held in a POW camp. They call for help from their friends and relations in France. Godard seems to be asking how one can make art while atrocities like those in Bosnia are taking place. Includes, somewhat disjointedly, a strong critique of the European Union.

THE CRITICS
"Its stories sometimes seem to form a whole and at other times the links among them are unclear. One gets the impression that in each episode Godard attempts to start a film only to come to the conclusion that it is impossible to continue. It features some of the most beautiful shots of tanks in the cinema." Louis Schwartz, *All Movie Guide.*

Fair to say, some excellent cinema did come out of France's *Nouvelle Vague*. Directors Francis Truffaut (an eventual Oscar winner for Best Foreign Film) and Bernardo Bertolucci, director of the sumptuous *Last Emperor* (1987), both started off alongside Godard. However, their technical and stylistic skills developed and they soon left their mentor far behind. Godard responded naturally by denouncing them for selling out in every magazine and lecture hall he could get into. (Truffaut suggests that working relationships with Godard were never easy. When asked in a press interview what might be a good title for Godard's biography, he suggested *Once A Shit, Always A Shit*. Bertolucci obviously felt even more strongly. In his film, *The Conformist* (1970), an assassin is given the contact details of a target he is supposed to murder. The address and phone number given out on-screen are of Godard's flat in Paris).

King Lear (1987)

THE PLOT

After Chernobyl, most of the world's great works of art have been lost. It is up to people like William Shakespeare Junior the Fifth (Peter Sellars) to restore them. He finds enough odd goings-on at a resort to remind him of all the lines of the play, including mob boss Don Learo (Burgess Meredith) and his daughter Cordelia (Molly Ringwald), a strange professor, named "Jean Luc-Godard', who repeatedly photocopies his hand for no particular reason, and four humanoid goblins. Then the film is sent off to New York for Mr. Alien (Woody Allen) to edit.

THE CRITICS

"Sheer nonsense doodled by the director with someone else's money." Leslie Halliwell, *Halliwell's Film & Video Guide*.

Godard himself never did sell out because it was rare that people would buy what he was selling. That is not to say he did not try. "I once told Godard that he had something I wanted – freedom", Hollywood producer Don Siegel once recalled. "He said, 'You have something I want – money!'." He snapped up contracts for commercial projects when they were offered. Trendy young execs at French and Italian T.V. station have all commissioned his work and then rejected what was turned in. Even the B.B.C., which will screen just about anything, rejected the "anti-image" film *British Sounds* (*See You At Mao*) (1969), as "unbroadcastable".

L'Origine du XXIème siècle
(The Origin of the 21st Century, 2000)

THE PLOT
Commissioned by the 2000 Cannes Film Festival to make an opening-night short commemorating cinema as it enters its second full century, Godard offered up a 17-minute montage of re-edited footage of wars and Nazi atrocities, interspersed with clips of Maurice Chevalier in *Gigi* and Godard's own *A bout de souffle*.

THE CRITICS
"He's nuts." Anonymous Cannes Grand Jury Member quoted in *Empire* magazine.

Today he is France's most highly respected and influential film-maker never to trouble the box office. Perhaps that has begun to mean something to him. In a recent visit to New York, he was asked at customs whether he was visiting the country for "Business or pleasure". "Neither", he replied, becoming at last his own best critic. "I make unsuccessful films."

Dix-Sept

The Way To Rusty Death

The 2CV and French Drivers.

Why is the unsafe, unreliable and environmentally unfriendly Citroën 2CV held in such esteem by the French? Is it because they are such bad drivers they are not qualified to notice?

The 2CV (*deux chevaux* – literally "two horses" from the French tax on horsepower rating, *cheval vapeur*) is the most popular French car made. Over forty years of production, it became as much a national icon as Edith Piaf. Like her, it was small, noisy and prone to breakdown.

The car was conceived in the early 1930s by Pierre Boulanger, then head of Citroën, as a low-priced, rugged "umbrella on wheels" that would let two French peasants in clogs drive 50 kilos of potatoes to market at 30 kilometres an hour on unpaved roads and use no more than three litres of petrol per 100 kilometres. Boulanger also insisted that the roof be raised to allow him to drive while wearing a hat.

SURVIVING THE FRENCH
"The secret of the 2CV's success? Mechanically, they're designed to survive the French." Quentin Wilson, Top Gear *magazine, 1996.*

Development was delayed by the Second World War. While Renault, the other giant French car manufacturer, eagerly put its plants in France at the service of the Third Reich (and, as a result, got itself confiscated by the state after the war), Citroën hid its five 2CV prototypes from the Germans by burying them in pits of pig manure.

Finally dug up and hosed down, the bug-eyed, hump-backed car was unveiled at 1948 Paris Auto Salon to ridicule by the press (one chippy reporter asking "Does it come with a can opener?"). The joke was on them since Citroën sold five million of the 2CV and its variants till it stopped making them in 1990.

THE MAKING OF A MONSTER

3,872,583 2CV sedans, 1,246,306 utility models and 30 more derivatives were produced from 1948 to 1990. In 1966, its peak year of production, 168,000 were made in factories in France, Britain, Cambodia and Chile. Manufacture was difficult to adapt to mass-production techniques. The 2CV's engine, for example, was always assembled by one man sitting at a bench. In 1988 production transferred from strike-ridden France, where break-even output was 250 cars daily, to Portugal, where production of 80 cars could reportedly provide a profit.

THE CAR THEY LOVE TO HATE.

"This mangy little goat from the outskirts of Paris is powered (and I use the word lightly) by a two-cylinder box of springs, iron, rods, cans and fire. It has more innovations and saloon talking pieces than a three-eyed girl in a beauty parlour. One of these is the hinged front windows, something like a barn shutter. If you're an elbow-out-the-window driver, you may get an unfunny whack on your funny bone. On the good side, it will get close to 55 miles to a gallon on regular fuel, which is not to be sneered at." Tom McCahill, Mechanics Illustrated, 1965.

"What does this minimalist car, an invention as French as the beret and the baguette, look like? Some have said it is a cross between a frog and a camel. A tin croissant. A hump-backed bug. An umbrella on wheels. A rag-topped rubbish bin. As aerodynamic as an aardvark. The epithets go on. It is so ugly, it's beautiful." William G. Miller, Boston Globe, 1988

"The 2CV became a cult car in the 1970s, a fashion icon bought by those who eschewed fashion. It was almost an anti-car, its temporary bolted-together look and roll-back fabric top appealing to those who scorned conspicuous material consumption. I used to believe the 'Nuclear Power? No Thanks' bumper stickers came as standard." Lesley Hazleton, New York Times, 1990.

The French are proud of this accomplishment but the truth of the 2CV's success is best summed up by journalist Jonathan Fenby: "it was not just plug ugly, it was dirt cheap". After the war, the European economy was in chaos and petrol was rationed. In France, the 2CV was the only car the majority of the population could afford and, thanks to generous state subsidy, "cost not much more than a box of cigars" (according to *Mechanics Illustrated* in 1965).

Mechanically, it was not as advanced as the VW Beetle with its air-cooled, flat-four, rear-mounted engine which sold 21 million world-wide. By comparison, the 2CV's first engine was a notoriously under-powered 375 cc design that its creator, Walter Becchia, had copied from a BMW boxer motorcycle.

Within months of its launch, there was a three-year waiting list – not because it was very popular but because the Paris factory could only make four a day (in the same year, Chrysler's Warren Avenue plant was churning out 750 cars every week).

Even today, the 2CV is held in peculiar affection, and not just by bearded geography teachers and anti-nuclear protesters who seem to make up its core market. In 2002 L'Automobile, the highly respected French motoring magazine, voted it "Car of the Century", praising "its safety, reliability and environmental friendliness". In reality, the 2CV was none of these things.

SAFETY. Much is made of the car's lightweight structure (the first models weighed only 600 pounds, less than half a Model T Ford) as its prime safety feature. On impact with heavier vehicles, the 2CV should simply be pushed away. In 1976, crash tests conducted by German car magazine *Auto Motor und Sport* showed that in most head-on collisions the car's hood compresses, protecting the passenger cabin. However, the 2CV's unique fixed steering column also pushes towards the driver with the risk of impaling him like a bug. In side-on impacts (the most common sort of impact), the flimsy 2CV fared worse. The U.S. National Highway Traffic Safety Administration gave the 2CV a one star rating for side-impact protection (ie, a driver and passengers had a 26% chance or greater of requiring hospitalisation after a side-impact).

SAFETY RATING
In 1996, the U.K.'s Department of Transport, working with the European Commission, issued a report rating car safety by make and model: in any collision with another car, the 2CV was estimated to provide a 10% chance of death to driver and/or passengers (only the Toyota Starlet offered a higher risk of 11% in the small car category) and an 80% risk of injury of any severity.

BURNING ISSUE
"But the most terrifying 2CV malady is potentially disastrous. Inside the engine there are two cardboard pipes funelling warm air from the exhaust manifold into the car's interior. They elongate with age, detach and catch fire. Many a 2CV has gone up in smoke without notice." Top Gear magazine, 1996.

RELIABILITY. The most impressive legend of the 2CV is its reliability. Impressive, because it isn't. While competitors cars like the Mini and the VW Beetle are rated by *Top Gear* magazine as requiring repairs only every 100,000 miles, something goes wrong with the 2CV every 20,000 miles, with the most serious problems due to rust. 2CVsRus, a

U.S. dealer specialising in the make, has to warn potential customers: "The frame gets its strength from the structure of folded sheet metal. The rust always starts from the inside. Once rust holes appear on the outside, the frame is unsafe to use! Remember: The frame is the backbone of the car. When this part is rusted away, you are an endangered species driving this car!" Corrosion is a problem because of the recurrent strike action at Citroën's strike-prone Paris plant which led to slapdash finishing on its production line (during the '80s, an embarrassed Citroën offered a free goodwill rust-proofing to all existing customers).

ENVIRONMENTALLY FRIENDLY. The popular image of the 2CV chugging through the French countryside, driven by a friendly farmer carrying a bale of hay to his sheep, has contributed to the idea of the 2CV as an environmentally clean car. In fact, a modern Sports Utility Vehicle is cleaner to the environment than a 2CV. While the 600 cc engines of the later models still managed 56 miles to the gallon, their exhausts emit a 300% higher hydrocarbon output than an SUV. The "ugly duckling" was designed before the days of emission regulations.

MYTH GOES UP IN SMOKE

"It is estimated that the 10% of oldest vehicles are responsible for 90% of car pollution, so the idea that it is 'green' to potter around in an ageing Morris Minor or 2CV is a myth whose sell-by date is long overdue." Reg Boorer, director of Greenpeace U.K. and Executive Director of the Ark Environmental Foundation.

FRANCE'S WINE INDUSTRY TELLS DRIVERS: HAVE A DRINK FOR THE ROAD. OR THREE

To counter a government campaign against drinking and driving, French winemakers launched their own €350,000 ($430,000) initiative in November 2003, telling motorists that they can have a drink before driving. Pascal Rousseaux, director of Afivin – an umbrella group for the €18 billion ($22 billion) a year French wine industry – said that since the government's current DUI campaign began, wine sales at restaurants had dropped 15%. He said drivers should be made aware that they can drink "two or three glasses" of wine with their meal and still be capable of driving.

How could even the French fall so deeply in love with such a deeply flawed car? Perhaps, being the most dangerous drivers in Europe, they are not qualified to notice.

France has the highest number of annual automobile deaths in the European Union, around 8,000 every year. A succession of governments has launched campaigns to cut the number in half (which would then just about fall to the current figure of U.K. fatalities). In 1987, a French government minister revealed the official attitude as supine and indifferent: "We mustn't annoy the French with speed limits and seat belts".

But in 2002, the then Prime Minister, Pierre Raffarin, announced yet another initiative to curb his nation's speed-junky drivers. It involved installing automatic cameras on all the autoroutes, satellite monitoring for arrested speeders and the implementation of a new "highway patrol".

"Road safety must become a national priority. It will demand a massive collective effort on the part of the French people, but also a proper sense of personal responsibility", said the Minister of the Interior, Nicholas Sarkozy. 'Speeding and drink-driving are crimes like any others, we cannot say it loudly enough." Sarko's "get-tough-on speeding" campaign lost a little impetus when he himself was pulled over for travelling 60 kmh over the speed limit in his government limousine while on the way to the 2005 Tour de France.

Nearly 60% of traffic fines in France are never paid. In a recent survey, most drivers insisted the country's generally excellent roads were "the most important cause" of traffic accidents in France, rather than speeding or alcohol.

In 2005, after the failure of the "Yes" campaign to win the referendum on the European Constitution, President Chirac dismissed Raffarin and the campaign faded with him. The automatic cameras were challenged in the courts by civil liberties groups, the satellite monitoring was deemed too expensive by the Ministry of Justice and the Interior Ministry quashed the idea of the highway patrols since it did not want another police force it did not control.

INDEX OF ROAD INJURIES AND FATALITIES IN WESTERN EUROPE 2003 (FROM THE O.E.C.D.'S INTERNATIONAL ROAD TRAFFIC AND ACCIDENT DATABASE)

	Killed per 100,000 Population				Injury accidents		Killed per 1 billion Veh. Km		
	Total	Age 0-14	15-24	25-64	65+	per 100K pop.	per 1 million Veh km	All roads	Outside urban areas	Motor-ways
Denmark	8.0	2.2	13.9	7.7	12.4	125	0.15	9.7	10.3	3.0
France	**10.2**	**2.0**	**20.1**	**10.0**	**11.3**	**151**	**0.19**	**13.8**	**-**	**4.0**
Germany	8.0	1.7	18.0	7.3	9.2	430	0.52	9.7	-	3.8
Ireland	8.4	1.9	14.6	8.1	12.0	150	0.18	10.9	10.8	7.4
Netherlands	6.4	2.1	12.1	5.7	10.0	195	0.24	7.7	6.5	2.1
Norway	6.1	2.2	10.8	5.8	7.9	173	0.25	8.3	-	-
Sweden	5.9	1.3	11.1	5.8	7.7	205	0.23	8.3	-	2.5
Switzerland	7.5	1.9	14.4	6.7	11.0	326	0.39	8.8	8.9	2.8
United Kingdom	6.1	1.3	12.8	5.9	6.9	385	0.52	7.6	7.5	2.0

Dix-Huit

Who Needs Enemas?

Why The French Are The World's Largest "Consumers" of Suppositories.

According to European medical lore, the English and the
Dutch prefer to take their medication in pill form, the
Germans go for an injection and the French, it seems,
like to shove it up their butts.

ARSE NO QUESTIONS

*"The next thing was I woke up in the next bed to O'Toole in the local hospital at
Moisson. As I lay in a half-trance I heard two medical men arguing about our case.
One voice said, 'I disagree with you, Armand. The Cordon Rouge is powerful
enough in a case like this'. The other voice shook its head and said: 'In my opinion,
only the Imperial will answer'. A frail tremor of joy fluttered in my breast. I blessed
a medical profession enlightened enough to prescribe vintage champagne in such
cases; it is good for shock, good for bruises, good for everything. Moreover Imperial
Tokay, Mumm's Cordon Rouge, I didn't care which. I leaned over to O'Toole. 'Did
you hear that?', I said. 'We are going to get the champers treatment. Isn't it bully?'.
But he was bright green. 'You fool', he hissed. 'Don't you know, the Imperial and the
Cordon Rouge are the largest suppositories known to medical science?'"*
Lawrence Durrell, The Little Affair In Paris, 1966.

Medical treatment varies from country to country, not just by disease but by culture. In 2003 the Vanderbilt Institute for Medicine, Health and Society noted "that the preference for different dosage forms – more pills in America, more parenterals (injections) in Germany, more suppositories in France – is fraught with cultural significance".

Basically, the French take their medicine by the path less travelled by, either as a solid capsule (a rectal suppository or vaginal pessary) or in liquid form as an enema.

These are not only prescribed when the patient is unable to receive oral medication, they are administered for almost any ailment "and that means everything", as novelist Lawrence Durrell learnt to his consternation, "from coated tongue to tertiary gangrene".

According to their Health Ministry, four out of five French people shoved something

FOREIGNERS BEWARE
" 'A suppository for a sore throat?', I quavered. I have lived in France long enough to know that the French believe passionately that medications that are in suppository form are more effective than a simple, easy-to-swallow pill or capsule. I never thought to encounter a suppository for a sore throat. Why not a lozenge, maybe even an effervescent lozenge? But a suppository? 'Mais oui, Madame', the pharmacist replied. 'C'est beaucoup plus efficace.' (It's much more efficacious – code word meaning that the medication will be absorbed more quickly from the mucosa of the nether regions). 'But don't you have a different, stronger throat spray?' The canny pharmacist could tell my resistance was faltering before the force of her Pure Reason. 'Les suppositoires, alors?', she asked with finality, setting a box of the dread 'cones' firmly on the counter. Unwilling to belabour the point any longer, especially with an eye to the people waiting behind me, who were probably amused by the spectacle of la petite américaine resisting what every French citizen knows is the best way to take a medication, I gave a small, defeated nod." The experience of one American visitor to Paris, www.frenchgardening.com.

pharmaceutical up one or other of their orifices in 2003. Doliprane is the French version of paracetemol and it out-sells its pill form by a factor of 60 to 1. Aventis, France's largest manufacturer of suppositories, sold 300 million of them in 2004, and they all have to end up somewhere.

There is no real reason for administering a drug rectally unless there is a specific need to avoid liver metabolisation (which occurs with pills taken orally). The French just seem to like it and they are encouraged to get used to it at an early age. The website of the French Health Ministry provides pages of advice to young mothers on the best way of stuffing baby like a turkey "so you can get on with your busy, happy life".

The suppository has always been deeply embedded in French history. As a child, Louis XIII was regularly given clysters (a kind of rectal wash-out administered with a syringe the size of a bazooka) in the presence of numerous lookers-on by his mother. This may or may not explain how he matured into a flamboyant homosexual but he certainly passed on his tastes to his son, Louis XIV, who, according to memoirist the Marquis de Saint-Simon, became a "clystéromane", an enema maniac.

Louis XIV himself had many thousands of clysters and had his hunting dogs regularly douched. According to Saint-Simon, clysters were so popular at Versailles "that the Duchess of Burgundy had her servant give her a clyster in front of the King (her modesty being preserved by an adequate posture) before going to the theatre". Possibly she was on her way to see Molière's *Le Malade Imaginaire (The Hypochondriac)*, whose hero, Argan, is always on the verge of impalement by some syringe-wielding quack. Louis XIV was eventually to die of an anal fistula the size of a boot which historians suspect was brought about by an over-enthusiastic clystering.

THE ENEMA OF MY ENEMY

The French appetite for enemas and their like has often been cause for ridicule by their neighbours and, at times, for overt propaganda. "One particularly explicit political cartoon by Dutch artist Romeyn de Hooghe shows Louis XIV, identified by a sun-burst on his head, sitting atop a terrestrial globe, impaled upon a large clyster syringe. Lacking the necessary commode, the contents of the royal bowel, successfully loosened by the procedure, spill over the world. Holland seems to get the worst of it, with various German cities (Heidelberg, Offenburg, etc) also receiving the exalted anal effluvia In the eyes of a Dutch satirist, the military, religious, and territorial policies of Louis XIV, embodied in the enema syringe and the incontinence resulting from its use, have befouled the earth." Laurinda S. Dixon, Art Journal, 1993.

WAS NAPOLEON HIS OWN WORST ENEMA?

According to a new study conducted by the San Francisco Medical Examiner's Department, Napoleon Bonaparte was killed by too many uncomfortably large enemas. An autopsy performed straight after Napoleon's death, by his personal physician, revealed that he had died from stomach cancer. But over the decades historians have disputed this explanation, suggesting either that the exiled leader might have died from toxic ingredients in his hair ointment or was poisoned by his confidant Charles de Montholon. But after a detailed study of the medical records, forensic pathologists in California have focused on the daily enema he had to relieve the pain caused by the cancer. "They used really big, nasty syringe-shaped things," Steven Karch, head of the researchers, told New Scientist *magazine. In the final crisis of Napoleon's illness, the doctors' decision to administer a purgative of 600mg of mercuric chloride (five times the usual amount) on 3 May 1821 would have further reduced his potassium levels – and may have been fatal. He died two days later, aged 51.*

It was not only the French royals who enjoyed this back alley work. Voltaire the father of French philosophy, had a strong preference for soap enemas. He wrote eloquent passages about a small English enema device that he used. The painter Monet believed that coffee enemas would cure his increasing blindness but being, well, rather short-sighted, once had to be prevented by his wife from douching himself with bleach. In the early 1920s the elderly and house-bound writer Anatole France found the best way to meet women was to invite warm-fingered nurses over to his house to administer smoke enemas.

Today, France's strange predilection for blocking the main exit has, if anything, intensified. Maybe even over-intensified. In 2004, A.N.A.E.S. (*Agence Nationale d'Accréditation et d'Evaluation en Santé*, the National French Agency for Accreditation and Health) issued a stern warning to modern day French clystéromanes, citing the case of the two Orly women who died following excessive enema use. Their deaths were attributed to fluid and electrolyte abnormalities. One took ten to twelve coffee enemas in a single night and then continued at a rate of one per hour. The other took four daily. As A.N.A.E.S. points out, "in both cases, the enemas were taken much more frequently than was necessary for healthy and sociable use".

Wheels on Fire

Why The Tour de France Is Fuelled By More Than Testosterone

An epic twenty-stage endurance cycle race pitting riders and their teams against the landscapes of France, Le Tour de France is a bad dream. What turned it into a nightmare for U.S. rider Lance Armstrong during the 2004 Tour was the French themselves.

A s any traveller will tell you, touring France can be physically, emotionally and mentally hellish. Only the French could turn it into a sport. A typically French sport too, with all its opportunities to wear flashy outfits, drive like a maniac and do down foreigners through your own native, not to say patriotic, fervour.

> *"Suffering on a bicycle is noble since it equates to the full evolution of the will."* Henri Desgrange, editor of L'Auto-Vélo *(ancestor of the present* l'Equipe*) magazine and founder of the* Tour de France, 1903.

The *Tour de France* covers around 2,400 miles and consists of 17 road stages, four time trials and two rest days. It ranges through ocean coastlines, mountain peaks, poplar-lined flats and ends on the Champs Elysées.

ORIGINS OF THE TOUR

Obliged to resign as a legal clerk after being observed by a client cycling with bare calves, dour bike fanatic Henri Desgrange was approached during the Dreyfus Affair by wealthy anti-Dreyfusard, the Comte de Dion, to start a magazine covering bicycling from a more nationalistic, anti-semitic angle than pro-Dreyfusard rival, le Vélo. In January 1903 his new l'Auto-Vélo was sued by le Vélo for stealing half its name and became l'Auto. Calculating that readers would assume the magazine was about cars, he conceived of "the greatest cycling trial in the entire world. A race more than a month long: Paris to Lyon to Marseille to Toulouse to Bordeaux to Nantes to Paris." The first Tour de France, held in July 1903, finished before a crowd of 20,000 paying spectators. L'Auto's sales quintupled to 130,000, le Vélo folded and Desgrange went on to run the race for the next thirty years in a dictatorial and semi-sadistic manner only reluctantly allowing riders such luxuries as eating en route and using bicycles with gears as he softened with old age.

Le Tour has the same iconic status in France as the Superbowl in the United States. The press gives the event blanket coverage, intellectuals analyse the race endlessly and fan clubs set up camps along the route, paint the road in their team's colours and spit at riders of opposing teams as they pass. It is estimated that 10% of the French population is drawn to the roadside during each Tour.

The fiercely partisan crowd has always been a problem. In 1904, only a year after the race's inception, a crowd blocked the route on the Col du Grand Bois,

BREAKING DOWN LE TOUR

1. *The Tour is a "stage race" of around 20 stages, one race being held every day over a three week period.*
2. *Stages include mountain stages, individual time trials and a team time trial. The overall winner is usually a master of mountain stages and time trials.*
3. *After each stage, every rider's accumulated time from all stages to that point is calculated and the one with the lowest overall time becomes race leader, entitled to wear the* maillot jaune *(yellow jersey).*
4. *Most stages take place in France although some occur in nearby countries such as Italy, Spain, Switzerland, Belgium, Luxembourg and Germany.*
5. *In recent years, the first stage has been preceded by a short individual time trial (1 to 15 km), called the prologue.*
6. *The traditional finish is in Paris on the Champs Elysées.*
7. *The race itinerary changes each year but certain famous mountain stages recur annually including the* Col du Tourmalet, Mont Ventoux, Col du Galibier, *the* Hautacam *and* Alpe d'Huez.
8. *Tour racers can hit 70 mph on straight sections of mountain descents. The record average speed for a road stage longer than 100 miles is 23 mph.*
9. *The legal minimum weight for a Tour bike is 14.9 lb.*
10. *Only one man has won the Tour seven times: Lance Armstrong of the United States.*

near St. Etienne. It let through a French favourite, Antoine Fauré, but stopped the Italian Giovanni Gerbi and broke his fingers. The crowd had to be dispersed by race organisers with revolvers.

This was the start of a long tradition of hostility towards foreign riders wearing the coloured jerseys that mark out the leading riders. "I was riding full out 300 meters from the finish line when I got punched in the kidneys by one spectator", says Eddie Merckx, a five-times Tour winner describing the incident that lost him his chance of a sixth title in 1968. "To take a punch like that in full effort was hard to take."

And Merckx is Belgian – so imagine how a French crowd treats an American like Lance Armstrong. "He's not well-liked", shrugs Jean Marie Leblanc, the race director since 1990. "That's not my judgement. It's a fact. *Voilà!*"

Armstrong is a phenomenon. Until 1996, the 35-year old Texan's career was solid rather stellar. He won the 1993 World Road Championship in Norway and some major U.S. races, showing good form on the hill stages of the Tour DuPont. However, riding for the French team, Cofidis, he had participated in the Tour de France only four times and finished just once, taking thirty-sixth place in 1995. A year later, he was diagnosed with stage three testicular cancer that was in danger of riddling his entire body.

Doctors told him he had a 50% chance of survival (they told his family, 3%), cut off a diseased testicle and went to work on the lesions in his brain and his lungs. He came out of the heavy chemotherapy a changed man. "He had no hair and had scars on his head", recalls Merckx, a good friend to Armstrong since they met at the Barcelona Olympics. "He became thinner, he was different morphologically, and above all, he lost a lot of weight. He was completely transformed as a cyclist."

The transformation showed in 1999 when the Texan won the Tour for the first time. Now he rode for the young "Blue Train", the team of the U.S. Postal Service, which gave him his chance when his old sponsors, a French telephone credit company, cancelled his two-year contract during his illness.

Armstrong won again in 2000, in 2001, in 2002 and 2003, equalling records held by Merckx and only three others. It didn't make him popular with the home crowd. When

THE WORLD'S FASTEST FASHION PARADE
The yellow jersey (maillot jaune) is worn by the overall time leader at the end of each stage. Yellow because L'Auto-Vélo, the race's original sponsor, had yellow pages.
The green jersey (maillot vert) is awarded for sprint points.
The "King of the Mountains" wears a white jersey with red dots (maillot à pois rouge) referred to as the polka dot jersey. The colours were decided by the then sponsor, Poulain Chocolat, to match a popular product.
The white jersey is for young time leaders (under 25).
The red jersey is awarded to the most combative rider, as decided by the judges after each stage .

Armstrong and his team were introduced to the crowd at the start of the 2001 Tour in Dunkirk, they were stunned to be booed even before the race had started. This was the beginning of ritual barrackings of the American through all subsequent appearances in France.

Two years later, while cornering on the mountain road to Luz-Ardiden in the Pyrenees, Armstrong was thrown from his bike when his brake levers were snagged by the strap of a fan's plastic shoulder bag. In 2004, during his 15.5 km time trial up the gruelling Alpe d'Huez, much of the stage uncordoned, Armstrong had to be flanked by security outriders on motorcycles. "He had received death threats", explained race director Leblanc. "Whether they were founded or not I don't know."

This was nothing new. Ten years previously Andy Hampsten, the first American to win this legendary stage, had been forced to fend off jostlers with his fists.

During the 2004 Tour T.V. news crews filmed spectators sprinting beside Armstrong's bike, shouting insults in his ear and letting off air-horns, waving flags in front of his face and spattering him with saliva. None of it mattered.

TOUR OF RECORDS.
Lance Armstrong *(U.S.) holds the record as the only rider to have won the Tour seven times (consecutively 1999-2005). Four other riders have managed to win the Tour five times:*
Jacques Anquetil *(France) in 1957, 1961, 1962, 1963 and 1964*
Eddie Merckx *(Belgium) in 1969, 1970, 1971, 1972 and 1974*
Bernard Hinault *(France) in 1978, 1979, 1981, 1982 and 1985*
Miguel Indurain *(Spain) in 1991, 1992, 1993, 1994 and 1995).*
Riders from France have won most Tours (36), followed by Belgium (18), Italy and the United States (9 each), Spain (8), Luxembourg (4), Switzerland and the Netherlands (2 each) and Ireland, Denmark and Germany (1 each).

He won five stages, including the team time trial, and the Tour championship outright. He even let his friend Ivan Basso win Stage 12 by choosing not to contend at the finish line, his way of offering support for Basso's mother's own struggle with cancer.

He is the only man in history to have won the Tour de France so many times. Except that much of the French crowd and its cheerleaders in the French press do not accept Armstrong's victory as clear at all.

Their objection was expressed in a piece of graffiti chalked on the Alpe road that Armstrong must have passed as he raced to victory: "EPO Lance". EPO is short for erythropoietin, a blood-booster banned in sport.

So it is dope, rather than talent, stamina, strength, year-long training programmes, superbly engineered bikes or the famous "rage", that many French hope is responsible for Armstrong's performance.

And they are eager to prove it one way or another. During Stage 5 the sport daily *l'Equipe* revealed from an un-named source that one of four urine samples had tested positive for another banned drug, a corticoid. It was well-known that

THE PEDAL PUSHERS. DOPING IN THE MODERN TOUR DE FRANCE

On 8 July 1998 French police arrested Willy Voet of the Festina cycling team for possessing illegal quantities of performance-enhancing drugs. Two weeks later, they raided other teams in their hotels, finding significant quantities of doping products amongst the T.V.M. team. In response, Tour riders started a "sit-down strike" and refused to ride, jeopardising millions of dollars of endorsements and advertising revenue. The Spanish teams quit the Tour in a show of solidarity led by the ONCE team. In the end, the "Tour of Shame" continued after the U.C.I. backed down and promised to limit heavy-handed actions. Richard Virenque, French star of the Festina team, denied doping himself, arguing that he might have been doped "without his knowledge", a stance which led him to be widely ridiculed. During the 2000 trial Virenque confessed to doping himself. Whilst he was not sentenced (but had penalties imposed on him by the sports authority), the Festina management was found guilty and received fines and suspended jail sentences. Virenque was awarded the title "Race King of the Mountains" in the 2004 Tour de France.

Armstrong had been one of those tested. His team were besieged by the media until the International Cycling Union finally coughed up an emergency press statement stating that Danish racer Bo Hamburger, another of the tested riders, had a certificate to use the drug for his asthma.

The truth is that Armstrong is the most tested cyclist on the Tour circuit. In 2004 he was tested twenty-two times in random spot-checks during competition and out of it by four different official agencies, all of whom found him clean. During the two hundred other checks he has taken since 1999 Armstrong has only tested positive once, the result of a legitimate prescription for a cream containing steroids used for a saddle sore. "The U.C.I. [International Cycling Union] declares with the utmost firmness that this was an authorized usage", reads the official statement, "and does not constitute a case of doping".

Armstrong's unblemished record is a disappointment to the forces who really run the Tour show, the French press with its vast advertising presence along the route, its travelling circus of press vans, special correspondents and access-all-areas passes.

It especially rankles with the sports writers of the influential French newspaper, *Le Monde*. Their crusade against Armstrong unsettles even the riders of opposing teams. During the 2004 Tour, Euskaltel-Euskadi rider Iban Mayo expressed his concerns to the Spanish newspaper, *Sporza*: "We know that *Le Monde* has pursued him for five years with all sorts of untrue stories. It was also the newspaper that wrote in 1999 that he used forbidden products. But they forgot to say that he had a medical certificate for them."

The magazine *L'Express* is equally hostile. The sensation of the Tour was its serialisation of *L A Confidentiel: Les Secrets de Lance Armstrong*. Timed by its author, former *l'Equipe* journalist, Pierre Ballester so it was on the shelves during the height of the race, the book makes no direct charges but features testimony

THEY LISTEN BUT THEY CANNOT HEAR
" *Immediately after the finish, I was asked by a genuinely baffled French radio reporter to explain to his listeners how, after coming back from cancer, a 'non-climber' like Armstrong could win a mountain stage I told him and his listeners: 'Armstrong was already a good climber on shorter hills when he was young, and has lost ten kilos in body weight since then because of cancer treatment. That's given him the build of a climber, tall and lean, and increased his power-to-weight ratio by a good ten percent This year, he has focused his whole season on this Tour, worked on his power, and trained tirelessly in the mountains near his home in Nice. His victory today doesn't surprise me at all.' I could feel that the radio guy didn't believe my explanation at all.*" From 23 Days In July (2004) by John Wilcockson, *sports journalist for* The Times, *editorial director of* VeloNews *and recipient of the* Médaille de la Reconnaissance *and the* Plaque de la Reconnaissance.

from an old team-mate and a former masseuse of Armstrong's, neither of whom actually accused the rider of taking drugs.

Faced with immediate legal action by Armstrong and U.S. Postal, the author has been back-pedalling fast: "It's all circumstantial evidence", he told the *International Herald Tribune*. "We don't actually prove anything." In 2005 a London judge ruled in a libel case brought by Armstrong that the defendants had wrongly repeated and sensationalised a whole stream of false allegations.

Would the French press pursue what has never been proved to be more than rumour against a Frenchman? Armstrong has worn the *maillot jaune* seventy times in the past five years while the French have had it for precisely seven days. One of the French riders who wore it was Richard Virenque, "King of the Mountains". Virenque was at the heart of the Festina doping scandal only a few years earlier. For the home crowd, he can do no wrong – and the French press agrees.

THE FRENCH-SPEAKING MEDIA CELEBRATE ARMSTRONG'S 2004 WIN
" *Armstrong's behaviour is haughty, and contrasts European cycling's camaraderie with a typically American business that scorns humanity. Mankind is not fond of those who gorge themselves on success without suffering.*" Editorial, La Tribune De Genève.

"*The French like winners but when the win is so crushing people get bored. The Tour de France seems over before it starts. French people would like more suspense.*" Jean-Pierre Bidet, *cycling correspondent of* L'Equipe.

"*It's not that we don't like him, it's more that people respect him but don't find him very warm or very human And the French find it hard to believe Armstrong went from being a good rider who couldn't climb well in the mountain stages to being the best rider in 1999.*" Eric Collier, *deputy sports editor of* Le Monde.

"When he [Virenque] won the stage on Bastille Day", recalls Rupert Guinness, sports correspondent for *The Australian*, "all the French journalists in the pressroom stood up and clapped, while the rest of us just groaned. How can the biggest drug cheat in the sport be so popular? He wouldn't be if it weren't for the *Tour de France*."

Lance Armstrong may never be given an easy ride by the French crowd, press or authorities. But perhaps he might have seen the only reply he will ever need to make to them all, written on the road alongside the insults on the road of the 2004 l'Alpe stage. It was obviously written by an American fan, probably very lonely in that crowd, to his hero.

It read: "Rip their balls off, Lance".

THE CYCLE CONTINUES

To no one's suprise Lance Armstrong won the 2005 Tour de France. And, to an equal lack of surprise, the French newspapers again accused him of doping. This time the sports daily L'Equipe *published copies of result sheets that appeared to indicate six urine samples collected from Armstrong way back in 1999 showed "indisputable" traces of EPO. However, the 1999 samples were tested by the state dope-testing laboratories in Châtenay-Malabry. The lab has now issued its own statement saying that the samples, which were labelled with anonymous codes, may not have been Armstrong's and warning that tests on six-year old urine are not reliable. Nonetheless,* Le Monde *newspaper hailed the evidence as "proof" that Armstrong "is no longer the extraordinary champion that some wanted to believe in". Tour de France authorities viewed the evidence for themselves and decided not to press for any further investigation. Armstrong announced his retirement but, to one newspaper, hinted he might return if only "to piss the French off".* (The Statesman, 5 September 2005).

WHO ARE THE DOPES NOW?

May 2006: After a seven year investigation, reports Agence Presse, the International Cycling Union cleared Lance Armstrong of doping in the 1999 Tour de France. The report went on to accuse French anti-doping authorities of "serious misconduct" in dealing with the American cyclist. The ICU appointed Dutch lawyer Emile Vrijman to investigate the handling of urine tests from the 1999 Tour by the French national anti-doping laboratory, known by its French acronym L.N.D.D. Vrijman said his report "exonerates Lance Armstrong completely with respect to alleged use of doping in the 1999 Tour de France" but accused the French authorities of "behaving in ways that are completely inconsistent with the rules and regulations of international anti-doping control testing".

Patently Wrong

Are the great inventions of the world... French?

At the unveiling of the new Airbus A380 in 2004, President Chirac startled the press by claiming that an obscure Frenchman, Clément Ader, invented powered flight. When it comes to the great inventions of the world, French schools, universities and information websites like to rewrite history.

Who invented powered flight?

THE FRENCH CLAIM

Clément Ader was a French engineer born in Muret, Haute-Garonne. His first craze was for telephones (he invented the first – and probably only – stereo phone for listening to the opera). Using the studies of Louis Mouillard on the flight of birds, he constructed his first flying machine in 1886, the *Eole,* powered by a steam engine. On 9 October 1890 Ader attempted a flight and claimed a distance of approximately 50 metres before crashing. The French War Office became interested in his work and, with army money, Ader developed and constructed the *Avion III*, an enormous bat made of linen and wood with a 16-yard wingspan. Ader took the machine out on 14 October 1897 and, before the military commission reviewing his work, wrecked it on take-off. The army withdrew funding but kept the results secret. After the Wright brothers made their flight, the commission released reports on Ader's flights, stating that they were successful. Ader is still considered "the father of flight" in France. In 1938 a postage stamp was issued to honour him and in 1990 Airbus gave his name to one of its aircraft assembly sites in Toulouse.

THE WORLD KNOWS
Bicycle mechanics, Orville and Wilbur Wright, brothers, grew up in Dayton, Ohio. They began their mechanical aeronautical experimentation in 1899, extending the technology of flight by concentrating on navigational control rather than lifting power. They developed the three-axis control still used today. The Wrights had a wind tunnel built by their employee, Charlie Taylor, and tested over two hundred different wing shapes. In 1900 they went to Kitty Hawk, North Carolina to continue their aeronautical work, In 1903 they built the *Wright Flyer* – later the *Flyer I* – with carved propellers and an engine built by Taylor in their bicycle shop. The propellers had an 80% efficiency rate. The engine was superior to manufactured ones, having a low weight-to-power ratio. On 17 December 1903 the Wrights took to the air. The first flight, by Orville, of 39 metres (120 feet) in 12 seconds, was recorded in a famous photograph. In the fourth flight of the same day Wilbur Wright flew 279 metres (852 feet) in 59 seconds. The flights were witnessed by four lifeguards and a boy from the village. The *Cincinnati Enquirer* newspaper printed the story the next day.

Who invented the bicycle?

THE FRENCH CLAIM
According to the French, the earliest bicycle was an unsteerable. wooden scooter-like contraption called a *célérifère*; it was invented about 1790 by Comte Mede de Sivrac of France. It was also known as the Dandy Horse. Most bicycle historians now believe that these unsteerable hobby-horses probably never existed, but were made up by Louis Baudry de Saunier, a nineteenth century French bicycle historian.

THE WORLD KNOWS
The bicycle has many fathers. The most likely originator is German Baron Karl von Drais, who rode his 1816 machine, the *Draisienne*, while collecting taxes from his tenants. It was essentially a pushbike, powered by the rider's feet against the ground. Scottish blacksmith Kirkpatrick Macmillan shares creator credit for adding a treadle drive mechanism in 1840 which enabled the rider to lift his feet off the ground.

Who invented the calculator?

THE FRENCH CLAIM
In the same way that most parents, knowing it will drive them crazy, try to keep their adolescent sons away from porn, the father of Blaise Pascal (1623-62) refused to allow his precocious son anywhere near a maths book. However, the little know-it-all would secretly study geometry under the bedclothes at night and, at the age of twelve, came up with Euclidian geometry by himself. He grew up to become France's greatest mathematician, physicist, and religious bore. In 1642, the helpful child devised the *Pascaline*, a mechanical calculator to assist his father with his work (daddy was a tax-collector). By 1652 fifty prototypes had been produced before manufacture ceased due to lack of demand.

THE WORLD KNOWS
German maths geek Wilhelm Schickard (1592-1635) of Tubingen, Germany, built his own – and the world's first – automatic calculator in 1623, the year that Pascal was born. Contemporaries called it the Calculating Clock. Schickard's letters to astronomer Johannes Kepler show how it was used to calculate astronomical tables, add and subtract six-digit numbers and indicate any overflow of capacity by dinging a little bell. The designs were lost until the twentieth century when a working replica was constructed in 1960.

Who invented film?

THE FRENCH CLAIM
The Lumière Brothers, Louis Jean and Auguste Marie Louis Nicholas, have always been presented by the French as the inventors of "cinema", a claim that rests on their creation of the "cinematographic projector" which allowed the display of moving pictures. They patented a number of significant processes – most notably, the creation of sprocket holes in the filmstrip as a means of getting the film through the camera and projector. They produced a single device that acted as both camera and projector, the *cinématographe*, which they patented on 13 February 1894. The first footage ever to be shot on the device was made on 19 March 1895; the film was *La sortie des usines Lumière* (*Workers leaving the Lumière factory*). If anything, what they invented was that great French tradition, the dull social documentary.

THE WORLD KNOWS
In 1889, William Friese Greene developed the first "moving pictures" on celluloid film, exposing 20 feet of film at Hyde Park, London. George Eastman

then improved on Friese Greene's paper roll film, substituting the paper with plastic. In 1891, Thomas Alva Edison patented the Kinetoscopic camera that took moving pictures on a strip of film. He also devised a method of displaying it when, also in 1891, he successfully demonstrated the Kinetoscope, which enabled one person at a time to view moving pictures. (The Lumière brothers reverse-engineered their own multi-person projection system after experimenting with Kinetoscope filmstrips retrieved from one of Edison's French concessionaires). Later, in 1896, Edison showed his improved Vitascope projector and it was the first commercially, successful projector in the U.S.

Who invented photography?

THE FRENCH CLAIM

In 1825 Nicéphore Niépce created a rudimentary photographic image on a polished pewter plate covered with a petroleum derivative. This process turned out to be a dead end and Niépce began experimenting with silver compounds based on earlier German discoveries. In 1833 he died of a stroke, leaving his notes to artist Jacques Daguerre, whom the French consider to be the "inventor of photography". With no scientific background, Daguerre discovered that by exposing the silver to iodine vapour first, before exposure to light, and then to mercury fumes after the photograph was taken, a latent image could be formed and made visible. By then bathing the plate in a salt bath the image could be fixed. In 1839 Daguerre announced his new process, calling it the *Daguerreotype*.

THE WORLD KNOWS

Across the English Channel, William Fox Talbot had also discovered his own means of fixing a silver process image. He made the earliest known surviving photographic negative on paper in the late summer of 1835, a small photogenic drawing of his home, Lacock Abbey (now in the photographic collection of the Science Museum at the National Museum of Photography, Film and Television at Bradford, U.K.). This was four years before Daguerre's process was announced. In January 1839 Talbot presented a paper on his discovery, which he called the "calotype process", to the Royal Society in London. Unlike a *Daguerreotype*, a calotype negative can be used to reproduce positive prints. Later this process was refined by George Eastman and is today the basic technology used by chemical film cameras.

Who invented recorded sound?

THE FRENCH CLAIM
Edouard-Léon Scott de Martinville certainly produced the *Phonautographe*, a device that made a visual image of sound waves on a resin cylinder, in 1857. French scientists and historians certainly agree that it was the first instrument to record sound. But it had no playback, so how did they know? I have found a stick. I hold it in front of me while I sing my cover of Britney Spear's "Toxic". I claim the stick is recording my voice. I shall call it the *Phonautostick*. Kindly put my head on a €1 stamp. *Exactly!*

THE WORLD KNOWS
In 1877 Thomas Edison, tireless inventor and "The Wizard of Menlo Park", unveiled the phonograph built by expanding on the principles of the phonautograph. This machine incorporated a cylinder covered with a soft material like tin foil, lead or wax on which a stylus drew grooves. The depth of the grooves corresponded to changes in air pressure created by the sound. But he went one further. By tracing a needle through the groove and using mechanical amplification, the recording could be played back.

Who invented the smart card?

THE FRENCH CLAIM
The French are very proud that one of their own, Roland Moreno, a journalist turned inventor, has been loudly proclaimed as the inventor of the "smart card" (the integrated circuit card). He patented his version of the card in 1974 and there are now three billion of the cards distributed worldwide.

THE WORLD KNOWS
The industry generally recognises that the smart card was originated by two German engineers, Jürgen Dethloff and Helmut Grottrupp in 1967. They filed for a patent in February 1969 but were only granted the patent in 1982, titled "Identifikanden / Identifikationsschalter". Independently, Kunitaka Arimura of the Arimura Technology Institute in Japan filed for a smart card patent in Japan in 1970. The following year, Paul Castrucci of I.B.M. filed an American patent, titled "Information Card".

Who identified the AIDS virus?

THE FRENCH CLAIM
Luc Montagnier is a French virologist. His research was done at the Pasteur Institute in Paris. In 1984 he identified a virus he called L.A.V. (later renamed H.I.V.). Importantly, he was not able to prove that H.I.V. caused the Acquired Immune Deficiency Syndrome (A.I.D.S.). Later Montagnier was to encounter international disdain (except in France) after declaring in 1990 that H.I.V. cannot cause A.I.D.S. on its own but needed a co-factor which he believed is a mycoplasma. This has since been proved to be wrong.

THE WORLD KNOWS
Robert C. Gallo is a U.S. biomedical researcher. In 1984 he and his collaborators published a paper in the research journal *Science* arguing that H.I.V., a retrovirus that had recently been identified in AIDS patients by Montagnier at the Institut Pasteur in Paris, France, was the sole cause of A.I.D.S. Controversy followed as to which one discovered the virus. Today it is generally agreed that Montagnier's group was the first to isolate H.I.V. but that Gallo's group identified its nature and function and demonstrated that it causes A.I.D.S. Furthermore, the work of Montagnier had relied on a technique previously developed by Gallo for growing T cells in the laboratory. This technique became the basis for H.I.V. testing of blood samples.

The Little Corporal

The Man Who Invented The Napoleon Complex

The greatest Frenchman ever, proclaim French opinion polls. We take a look at Napoelon Bonaparte, the man and his shortcomings.

Politics rest on principles, and principles are founded on personality. The towering personality of modern French history is Napoleon. He towers literally over Paris. In 1806, as the new Emperor of France, he decreed the construction of the column which still dominates the capital's central square, the Place Vendôme. Standing 44 metres high and encased in 180 tons of bronze melted from 1,200 cannon captured from the Russians and the Austrians, the column is engraved with the words *Monument élevé à la gloire de la Grande Armée* (*Monument erected to the glory of the Grand Army*).

Napoleon had no problems choosing the most perfect crown for this tribute to the men who fought and died at the battle of Austerlitz (1805): a statue of himself, three and a half metres tall, dressed as a Roman emperor.

"*Ce qui est grand est toujours beau*" ("Big is always good"), said Napoleon of architecture in general and probably of monuments to him specifically.

NAPOLEON: A SHORT LIFE

Napoleone Buonaparte, born 1769 second son of eight children into poor Corsican nobility. Military school at Brienne-le-Château 1779, joined royal French artillery in 1785. Thanks to his rabid Jacobinism and his defence of Toulon, made General in 1793. Defended the revolutionary National Convention by turning artillery on demonstrating Parisian crowds in 1795. Married Josephine de Beauharnais in 1796 then led a demoralised Army of Italy to victory over the Austrians. In 1798 invaded Egypt, destroying a Turkish army at the battle of the Pyramids. Returned to Paris, overthrew the ruling Directory and sidelined rivals to become First – and only – Consul. Crowned himself Emperor of France in 1804 and King of Italy in 1805. Victories against Austria at Marengo (1800), Russia and Austria at Austerlitz (1805) and Prussia at Jena (1806) consolidated French dominance of Europe. At home, streamlined his dictatorship with centralising reforms including new civil laws, the Code Napoléon. *Abroad, created the Continental System, a Europe-wide commercial boycott of Britain. Its enforcement prompted disastrous invasions of Spain (1807) and Russia (1812). Weakened, was defeated by a European coalition at Leipzig (1813) and abdicated in 1814. Banished to Elba in 1815, he returned to France and seized power only to be crushed by British and Prussians at Waterloo. Permanently exiled to the mid-Atlantic island of St. Helena, died 1821.*

The French are still impressed. In Paris alone there are over two hundred streets, squares, monuments and institutions commemorating the Napoleonic era in France, a period that lasted only fifteen years. Such symbols are important to any country as the outward expression of internal values.

There are 600,000 volumes relating to Napoleon in France's National Library, *La Bibliothèque nationale*, equivalent to ten miles of shelf space. In 2001, despite heavy duties as President Chirac's then Foreign Minister, Dominique de Villepin added to them with his own six-hundred-page book on Napoleon, called *Les Cent-Jours ou l'esprit de sacrifice* (*The Hundred Days or the spirit of sacrifice*), one chapter called "Waterloo, or the Crucifixion".

Napoleon was hardly Jesus. Personally, he was a sadistic fruitcake, so bizarre that he had his own mental disease named after him. Politically, he was the military dictator of a totalitarian state, both the first of their kind but neither the last.

THE NAPOLEON COMPLEX MADE SIMPLE

In the fields of psychology and psychoanalysis, the Napoleon Complex is a colloquial term used to describe a type of inferiority complex more formally known as Small Man Complex and suffered by people who are physically small. Alfred Adler pioneered the psychological work on inferiority complexes and used Napoleon Bonaparte as an example of someone who he thought was driven to extremes by a psychological need to compensate for what he saw as a physical handicap.

If anyone suffered from a Napoleon Complex, it would seem to be Napoleon. His temper was uncontrollable. No-one was safe, high or low. "At Posen, already, I saw him mount his horse in such a fury as to land on the other side," remembered his Foreign Minister Talleyrand, "and then give his groom a cut of the whip". He kicked Senator Volney, a trusted friend from his Corsican childhood, in the stomach, knocking him to the ground, for making an approving remark about the previous royal family. On parade, he struck a Captain Fournois with his cane and when the officer's company set up "a general murmur", Napoleon in a rage had them all disarmed and ordered every tenth man to be shot ("...but Bonaparte pardoned them on condition of penal servitude for life in the colonies").

STORMY TEMPERAMENT
In 1804 Admiral Bruix refused Napoleon's instructions to send flat-bottomed ships out into the Channel for a landing exercise because of a threatening storm. Napoleon flew into a rage, went for Bruix with his riding crop and demanded the Admiral embark with the vessels within twenty-four hours. More than twenty guard boats filled with his troops ran aground. Two hundred dead bodies washed ashore the next day. Agents had to be sent into the town with gifts of gold to stop the news spreading.

There are many such stories recorded by impartial witnesses. He cheated at cards with children, he smashed furniture, he shot the swans in the lake of his house at Malmaison to spite Josephine. After such fits, he would sob for a quarter of an hour and suffer from stomach cramps or attacks of vomiting. Madame de Rémusat, who once loved him, eventually had to write: "Bonaparte has an innate evil nature, an innate taste for evil not only in small things but in great".

After the first success of his career, at the siege of Toulon, Captain Buonaparte (he did not lose the "u" until 1798) had a large number of surrendered Royalists and liberated convicts herded into the town's square and used artillery to mow them down. He then announced that the vengeance of the French Republic was satisfied and they should now rise and go to their homes. As the bleeding and cowed survivors stood up, he fired again.

Napoleon invented the idea of military and police terror as a political weapon and turned it into a system. Having taken Hamburg after a hard siege, he ordered the city's population evicted on pain of flogging (though "French gallantry substituted with respect to females the birch for the cane," noted one observer) and then pilfered 4,000,000 francs from their banks for his personal use.

His armies' atrocities against Portuguese and Spanish civilians between 1807 and 1814 earned him the nickname "the Ogre". One of his own officers later wrote that "if we had carried out to the letter our orders concerning the Spanish insurgents, we would have had to put almost the entire population of the country to death".

He cared as little about his own men. At the battle of Eylau (1807), Napoleon

THE LIVING PLAGUE

Victor Hugo, author of Les Miserables, *called Napoleon a "living plague", vividly accurate given his behaviour in 1799 when his forces stormed Jaffa. His men were given leave to run amok, raping and killing thousands of civilians. He himself ordered the slaughter of 3,000 surrendered Turkish soldiers. Napoleon then retreated, leaving behind fifty of his own men sick with plague. Before doing so, he ordered them poisoned. His motives were not merciful. The Ottoman Turks had a good record in their treatment of foreign prisoners while Sir Sydney Smith's Royal Navy squadron off the coast would have given his wounded safe passage under the then rules of war. Napoleon simply did not want any evidence of his defeat to reach Europe. Hospital doctors bravely refused Napoleon's order.*

entered the field with an army of 50,000. Though he forced the Russians from the battle, 22,000 of his own army were dead or wounded. He rode amongst the bodies muttering: "Small change, small change. A night in Paris will set this right".

This was no shell-shocked reaction. "A man like me doesn't give a shit about the lives of a million men", he screamed at an Austrian diplomat in 1813, before attacking him with his hat.

As usual, this was a half-truth: of the 675,000 men he used to invade Russia in 1812, only half a million died. This figure was published in Paris in the notorious *Twenty-Ninth Bulletin*, which ended reassuringly "but the Emperor's health has never been better". And so it should, since he had long dumped his retreating army and returned home by fast sleighs and heated carriages.

Towards the end, as the allies closed in on Paris, he boasted: "I shall bury the world beneath my ruin".

Military terror abroad, police control at home. Napoleon's legal, financial and administrative reforms have provided the foundation of all France's political regimes since, including another empire and four republics.

NAPOLEON'S BILL.
"No accurate estimate exists of the casualties which resulted from the Emperor's career Between 1804 and 1815, at least 1,700,000 French soldiers died on active service; the true figure is probably nearer two million. Certainly well over two million of Napoleon's allies and opponents were killed. Such figures are enormous when one remembers that there was no mechanised transport."
Desmond Seward, Napoleon and Hitler, *1988.*

Their purpose was to create a centralised command structure with himself at the top in total control and administered by a set of prefects, tax-collectors and police officials totally loyal to him, "an intermediate caste interposed between myself and France's vast democracy".

It included personalities like Joseph Fouché, his Minister of Police who had political opponents executed in batches with cannon-fire; René Savary, head of *Gendarmerie d'Elite*, who forged banknotes for the state and invented the clockwork time bomb; and Charles de Talleyrand, his Foreign Minister, who was so corrupt that his demand that the fledgling U.S. democracy pay him $250,000 before he would begin treaty negotiations almost led to a war.

Together, Napoleon and his administrators sent opponents to concentration camps on the Ile d'Oléron or exiled them to the jungles of Guiana. The press was suppressed. Slavery was restored. Those who managed to survive the midnight arrests and military trials were "disappeared" or "suicided".

AMONG THE DISAPPEARED

1801 *Comte de Frotté, leader of Chouan dissidents. Surrendered on promise of free pardon, shot: "I didn't order it but I can't say I'm sorry", Napoleon.*

1804 *General Pichegru, political opponent, found "self-strangled" in his cell. "We must all ask what peculiar circumstances caused this noble man to end his life", Napoleon.*

1804 *Duc d'Enghien, royalist, kidnapped from neutral territory, shot. "I caused the Duc d'Enghien to be arrested and tried, because that step was essential to the safety, interest, and honour of the French people", Napoleon.*

1815 *Marshal Berthier, one-time chief of staff to Napoleon, refused to join him before Waterloo, found "fallen from a window". "I have ordered an immediate investigation into the circumstances of this mysterious incident", Napoleon.*

Eventually, Napoleon's control was so total that he was able to crown himself Emperor in Notre Dame cathedral over a country that had only recently been a revolutionary and atheistic republic. Surveying the pomp, one republican officer, General Delmas, grumbled: "All that was missing was those hundred thousand Frenchman who died to be rid of all this". Delmas was placed immediately on the retirement list.

Was it all about his height? George Washington (6' 3") or the Duke of Wellington (6' 1"), tough soldiers and political leaders, never made themselves dictators. Once, in his library at Malmaison, his private residence, the Emperor was observed standing on tip-toe to reach a book on an upper shelf. Marshal Moncey offered to retrieve it for him. "I am taller than Your Majesty," he remarked. "No, Marshal," Napoleon screamed, "you're just longer!".

HOW HE MEASURED UP

After his death, Napoleon's body was autopsied by French anatomist Dr François Antommarchi and his height noted as 5 foot 2 inches. However a French foot (pied de roi) was equivalent to 1.067877 English feet or roughly 13 inches. In the universally accepted British system, Napoleon was just over 5' 6" (around 168 centimetres). Mulhall's Dictionary of Statistics (1891) gives the average height of French males in the nineteenth century as 5' 5" so Napoleon was slightly over the median height for Frenchmen for the time, though English males averaged 5' 7½".

In fact, though Louis Marchand, the Emperor's valet, would shove lifts into his master's boots every morning and remove them every night, in case the Emperor died in his sleep and history discovered he was shortish, Napoleon stood 5' 6" in his stockinged feet, more than average for the time.

But perhaps some of the rage has a physical basis. French writer Madame de Staël once managed to force her way into Napoleon's

THE HEIGHT OF MASS-MURDER	
Attila the Hun	4ft 6in
Stalin	5ft 4in
General Franco	5ft 4in
Pol Pot	5ft 5in
Hitler	5ft 6in
Napoleon	5ft 6½in
Tamerlane	5ft 8in
Mao Zedong	5ft 11in

quarters when he was in the bath. She retired with a stifled laugh murmuring, "Genius has no sex". Hortense, his stepdaughter, once told him: "Women are not for you because you do not have the resources to please them". The Emperor had many mistresses but, as he himself admitted: "Love is not for me; I am not as other men". His autopsy noted "strikingly small, infantile and undersized genitals". The organ in question was measured at 1½".

Whatever the cause of his personal defects they were projected in giant scale in his political and military heritage, which today still dominate France. In 2004, France's Defence Minister, Michèle Alliot-Marie, told *Le Figaro* magazine that "if Napoleon remains a reference for the French, it's surely because he appears in our collective memory as the creator of the modern state".

NAPOLEON'S SHORTCOMING EXPOSED

In a memoir published in 1852 in the Revue des mondes, *Napoleon's manservant, Ali, claimed that he and the attending priest, Vignali, had removed parts of Napoleon's body while preparing the body for burial. In 1916 Vignali's descendants sold his collection of Napoleonic artefacts to a British rare book firm which in 1924 sold them on to A. S. W. Rosenbach, a Philadelphia bibliophile, for $2,000. Among the relics was "a mummified tendon taken from Napoleon's body during the post mortem". The putative penis, couched in blue morocco and velvet, was displayed at the Museum of French Art in New York. According to a contemporary news report, "In a glass case [spectators] saw something looking like a maltreated strip of buckskin shoelace or shrivelled eel!". The organ was described as "one inch long and resembling a grape". In 1977 it was put up for sale and purchased by John K. Lattimer, professor emeritus and former chairman of urology at the Columbia University College of Physicians and Surgeons for $3,000. He acknowledged having it in 1987 and presumably still does.*

The Devil's Own Cowpat

The Curse of the Beret

As a hat, the beret is functionally useless. Why did it become such a fashion statement at home and abroad – and why has it proved more destructive than W.M.D.s to the United States?

BERET-BERET DISEASE
"Oh, the connotations; and the connotations! France, Picasso, Che, Revolution, Romance, Art, Existentialism, Special Military Forces, Spain, The Basque, Impressionism, Surrealism, Bohemians, Beatniks, Monica Lewinsky, The Pyrenees, Camus, Sartre, The Underground, Bob Marley, and on and on. Is there an article of clothing that drips with resonance and symbolism more than 'The Beret'? I think not."
www.berets.com, website dedicated to all things beret, 200

In many ways, the beret is France's most enduring motif. For years, even centuries, it was as much a part of the national uniform as the smouldering butt-end dangling from the lower lip or the condescending sneer. Stone carvings from the Middle Ages show French beret-wearers. Maurice Chevalier sported a Basque beret while cycling through Montparnasse burbling,

"The Song of Paree". Jean-Paul Sartre topped off his "dirty thinker" look of Mac, N.H.S. specs and squint with a larger, droopier Hoquy beret. Infamous mime, Marcel Marceau, never pretends he is trapped inside a glass box without his sprigged All-Seasons beret and boat-necked stripy jumper.

In 1939, there were over three hundred factories churning out thirty million berets every year in France, the birthplace of this devil's own cowpat of a hat. Most of them were based around Pau in the Béarn region, which recently fixed beret emblems on to its lamp posts and bus stops to rub in the message. The beret originated amongst Basque farmers and fishermen either side of the nearby Pyrenees. The name itself is derived from a Latin word, "birretum", which means "cap".

Deconstructed, the beret is not a cap. It is hardly a hat. It has no brim to keep the sun out of your eyes, and no space between your head and the crown to allow the collection of warm air. Ear protection? Forget it. In the rain, the little shape it has collapses and it seeps down your head, as if someone had cracked an ostrich egg on your skull.

GREAT BERET WEARERS OF HISTORY (FRANCE)

François Mitterrand, French president
Brigitte Bardot, movie star and sex-bomb
Olivier Messiaen, atonal composer
Jean-Paul Sartre, Frank Spencer-lookalike philosopher
Jean Moulin, genuine Resistance hero
Claude Monet, blind artist
Maurice Chevalier, cheeky cabaret singer
Gérard Depardieu, stock Frenchman
Jean Cocteau, artist, film-maker and compulsive cottager
Eric Cantona, lugubrious soccer star and kung fu artist
Jacques Tati, horse-faced comic actor
Marcel Marceau, mime "artist"
Françoise Sagan, novelist and speed freak

GREAT BERET WEARERS OF HISTORY (FOREIGN)

Pablo Picasso, billionaire artist and communist
Che Guevara, revolutionary and patented T-shirt motif
Benny Hill, sex pest
Madonna, gristly pop singer and Euro wannabe
John Malkovich, intense movie actor
Frank Spencer, Jean-Paul Sartre-lookalike T.V. cretin
Johnny Rotten, deranged punk musician
Bette Davis, pop-eyed film star
Field Marshal Montgomery, oddball British soldier
Patty Hearst, crazed kidnap victim
Monica Lewinsky, wide-mouthed White House intern
Huey Newton, Black Panther activist
Saddam Hussein, dictator currently on trial for beret-related crimes

---

The classic beret, the *béret basque*, is just a flat, one-piece circle of wool (now more usually wool felt), created by knitting outward from a central three inch "tail" and then draped over the head. The soft material could be shaped in a variety of ways but is pushed to one side to the head, giving the wearer a monolobal brachycephalic – or Elephant Man – touch.

It never mattered that the beret is functionally useless *qua* hat. The Basques wore it because they were too poor to afford anything else but it really only took off in the late 1800s onwards, when it was taken up by artists, most famously by long-time French resident Picasso, to make a *statement,* the statement being: "Look at me. I don't care what I look like. I don't care what you think I look like. Look at me more."

During the twentieth century, the beret became and remains standard issue for anyone with artistic or radical "tendencies", not just in France but around the world. Revolutionaries like Che Guevara and the Black Panthers, jazzmen like Dizzy Gillespie and Sidney Bechet, intellectuals from Camus to Linus Pauling, general-purpose attention cravers from Madonna to Paris Hilton, all of them have been congenital beret wearers. Simply, anyone you would imagine wears a beret, does. Visit www.johnmalkovich.com to view a selection designed by this deeply intense actor.

TOUGH BERETS
The "artists" who now sport berets will be dismayed to learn that the most numerous wearers of berets are soldiers (in 2005, the US Army, the world's largest beret consuming organisation, ordered 600,000 of them, from China).

The military use of the beret originated in the French Army, in the shape of the wide and floppy headdress worn by the Chasseurs Alpin (mountain light infantry) from the early 1880s. A tight fitting version was subsequently adopted by French armoured troops towards the end of World War I. Between the wars special fortress units raised to garrison the Maginot Line wore khaki berets to stop them scraping their helmets on the low ceilings. The French service currently provide the following colour-coded berets to the following units:

Khaki – *Standard issue;*
Wide, black – *Chasseurs alpins;*
Green – *Naval commandos and Foreign Legion paratroops (on operations);*
Dark blue – *Air commandos and* Troupes de Marine;
Red – *Paratroops;*
Electric blue – *Army Light Aviation.*

Here's where the joke comes in. The French don't wear them anymore. "Though berets may be more common in France than bowler hats are in Britain," says journalist and France-watcher, Jonathan Fenby, "you could drive from Calais to Cannes without seeing one". The beret is just too, well, *ringard* (naff). In 2000, there were only three beret factories left in France, employing one hundred and eighty people and making only a million berets annually with a third of them being bought by the French army. In 2006, there is only one factory remaining and that has to make wool caps and "event headgear" (American-style baseball caps) to stay ahead.

THE FINAL WORD?
"Honey, I thought we talked about the beret. Even Patty Hearst couldn't pull one off, and she had money and a gun." Megan Mullally, Will & Grace, U.S. sitcom, 2004.

While the French have quietly cured themselves of their beret problem, the nation that has become the world's largest consumer of France's tonsorial joke is now the United States. What must make the joke all the more delicious to the French is that the addiction is already kicking in, with the last two presidencies of its great geopolitical rival shaken to their foundations by the simple beret.

Monica Lewinsky and Saddam Hussein, anyone?

Blown Away

Chirac, Muroroa and Nuclear Tests

President Chirac's decision to resume nuclear testing in French Polynesia disregarded the interests of its people, its neighbours and the international community.

Mururoa Atoll, a tiny French possession, is located in the southeast corner of the Taumotu archipelago in French Polynesia. It could have been an island paradise except that in 1966 France began using the site for atmospheric nuclear testing.

In 1992 President Mitterrand announced a complete end to all testing under the Nuclear Non-Proliferation Treaty. The cold war was over, international tensions had eased and the world had other W.M.D.s to worry about. In 1995, to international disbelief, a new president, Jacques Chirac announced France's intention to resume underground nuclear testing.

OCCUPIED POLYNESIA
When asked by ABC, "Most people call this place French Polynesia. What do you call it?", Mr Temaru replied: "This is French-occupied Polynesia. That is the truth. This country has been occupied."
Australian Broadcasting Corporation interview with Oscar Temaru, new President of French Polynesia.

THE GODFATHER OF FRENCH POLYNESIA

Polynesia was ruled for twenty years by French-backed President Gaston Flosse, whose main basis of support was the annual €1 billion ($1.2 billion) in aid that Paris pumps into the islands' economy each year. He also built himself a monumental presidential palace that houses "623 employees and courtiers" (Pacific Islands Report). In May 2004, Oscar Temaru's pro-independence party, the Union for Democracy, won a narrow victory at the polls. Flosse, who enjoys a warm relationship with Chirac (he is godfather to Flosse's youngest son), did not want to go. His supporters cut the telephone lines to the presidential offices and started running the country from nearby government buildings. In France, the French Socialist party alleged that Paris was "methodically destabilising" Temaru's government. Chirac refused to intervene. "The people of French Polynesia", he said, "must be free to settle their own affairs". They did; fresh elections enlarged Temaru's majority.

THE PEOPLE

Whilst the British, Dutch and Germans gave their colonies in the Pacific independence decades ago, France has held on to French Polynesia. During a visit to its capital, Papeete, in August 2002 the Overseas Territories Minister Brigitte Girardin said, "Without French Polynesia, France would not be a great power".

BLOWN AWAY

Mururoa is the home of the Centre d'Expérimentation du Pacifique (Pacific Experimenation Centre), France's nuclear testing agency. Between 1966 – when the French were forced to leave their former test site in Algeria – and 1995, France conducted 41 atmospheric and 138 underground tests at the atoll. All that remains is a thin crescent-shaped strip of lightly forested beach, fifteen miles long.

The main point and purpose of France's continuing Pacific presence is to provide somewhere to develop France's nuclear weaponry. French aid – €1 billion ($1.2 billion) in 2003 – and especially funding for the giant *Centre d'Expérimentation du Pacifique* (C.E.P.) dominates the economy which has little else to offer except tourism and pearl fishing.

When Chirac announced that France was going to resume nuclear testing in their islands, it was the usually tranquil Polynesians who exploded in rage. Polynesians burned French flags at a rally in Sydney and protesters held a

THE NUCLEAR ECONOMY

"French military spending [has] distorted the communal Polynesian society and created a middle class that feeds on French-subsidized government jobs and patronage and enriched itself through corrupt business monopolies and real estate investments at the expense of the laboring majority," says David Chappell in The Contemporary Pacific *magazine (Spring 2005). As a result the 245,405 inhabitants of French Polynesia are either nicely paid civil servants or, the larger part, their cabana staff.*

candlelight vigil in Fiji. When the testing began, in September 1995, protests rocked Tahiti with rioters wearing pro-independence T-shirts. Chirac had Foreign Legion units choppered in to restore order.

Demands for independence have not gone away. In May 2004 a pro-independence party, the Union for Democracy, won a narrow victory at the polls.

THE BOMB

There was only one reason President Chirac ordered a resumption of nuclear testing at Muroroa: he wanted to snub someone he loathed; his predecessor, François Mitterrand.

Mitterrand ceased testing in 1992 in accordance with a number of international non-proliferation obligations. When he came into office, Chirac unilaterally overturned Mitterrand's directive and ordered eight new tests. "You only have to look back at 1935", reasoned Chirac rather weakly. "There were people then who were against France arming itself, and look what happened."

France's Pacific neighbours – unconsulted – were furious. France was condemned at the UN, Australia and other Pacific states withdrew their ambassadors while Japan convened the Tokyo Forum, a meeting of eighteen prominent diplomatic and strategic experts from sixteen countries to discuss "the impact of nuclear testing". France's actions "remind us of the threats and horrors that haunted the collective imagination during the Cold War years", was one typical comment, this time from Brazil's Foreign Minister Luiz Felipe Lampreia.

Meanwhile, the people of the region voted with their wallets, boycotting French wine (one order for 44,000 cases of Beaujolais was terminated) while Club Med's resort in Tahiti received 15,000 cancelled orders. The French aircraft manufacturer Dassault lost business worth $370 million when banned from bidding in Australia.

In the wave of governmental and public hostility, Chirac lost his nerve. France stopped nuclear testing on 22 February 1996, three months short of the expected testing intervals with only six of the eight tests completed.

In May 1996 France finally signed the Comprehensive Test Ban Treaty.

LAW-BREAKER
In terms of international legality, the tests broke Article VI of the Nuclear Non-Proliferation Treaty to which France had just signed an extension which committed France to "pursuing negotiations in good faith on effective measures relating to cessation of the nuclear arms race at an early date and to nuclear disarmament". France also contravened the 1957 Euratom Treaty since it also roundly refused to provide information on the effects of its tests. Cases brought against France at the European Court of Justice in the Hague were dropped when Chirac stopped the tests before completion.

THE ENVIRONMENT

The overall effects of the French nuclear tests at Mururoa will not be known for years. The French government is secretive when it comes to releasing information about environmental hazards associated with nuclear testing.

It is known that the blasts inflicted long-term environmental damage to the structure of the atoll and the surrounding coral reefs. Comparing official French maps from 1980 and 2000 show that years of nuclear testing have cracked the atoll and altered land plates.

In May 1999 the director of France's Atomic Energy Commission, René Pellat, had already admitted that the nuclear tests had caused cracks in the coral atolls. Resulting radioactive leaks have drastically increased the risk to aquatic life in the surrounding sea and, more ominously, to the food chain which obviously ends with the human inhabitants of Polynesia. The *Sydney Morning Herald* has reported that fish near Mururoa have died after their eyes popped out and their internal organs were forced out of their mouths and anuses.

UNWISE CRACKS
International scientists are concerned about the real danger that radiation is seeping through fissures in the Mururoa atoll. Dr Murray Matthews from New Zealand's National Radiation Lab has warned of the spread of radioactive material from wind storms and rain while the vulcanologist Pierre Vincent has stated "these tests seem to have ruptured the rock and released radionuclides from underground cavities".

The impact on human health is also uncalculated. Since August 2002 former French Pacific test site workers have been demanding a complete medical investigation into their abnormally high rates of cancer.

In a 2003 flying visit to Papeete, Chirac proudly announced to the Polynesians that France would pay them "compensation" for the years of nuclear testing and would take responsibility for any test-related health problems, "if proof could be provided that such a link existed". Two years later, the €200 million ($250 million) compensation, as well as other amounts pledged for infrastructure improvement, have still not been paid.

THE LAST LAUGH
Chirac's resumption of nuclear testing at Mururoa was designed to tick off his old rival, former President Mitterrand. He, in turn, gleefully relished the international outrage and humiliation suffered by Chirac. Even though dying of cancer, Mitterrand gave a well-publicised interview to reporters, saying he had received so much cancer treatment he was "as radioactive as Mururoa Atoll".

Vingt-Quatre

The Cohabitee

Edith Cresson: "She's Not Really Corrupt"

The career of ex-Prime Minister and ex-European Commissioner Cresson says a lot about the state of French politics and its influence in Europe.

I terviewed recently by *Le Monde*, Edith Cresson was asked what she got from being Prime Minister of France for just ten months in 1991 to 1992. "Nothing. It wasn't worth it," she said. Her subsequent career as a European Commissioner showed that wasn't a mistake she was going to make twice.

The man who got her both jobs was François Mitterrand. French prime ministers are not elected directly but appointed by the president to manage the National Assembly. This balance is called "*cohabitation*", although the relationship can be rocky when president and prime minister come from different parties. The relationship between Mitterrand and Cresson brought a whole new meaning to the word.

POLITICALLY UNSTABLE. *With the title* Président du Conseil de Ministres, *France has had over 150 prime ministers since 1815 (compared with 52 in the U.K.). Politically, France has never been particularly stable but then, like Cresson, neither were many of its prime ministers.*

Charles Floquet. *1888-89. Along with 510 other politicians, received share of 23 million francs in bribes during Panama Canal scandal. Exposed, forced to resign from parliament after public outcry. Re-elected a year later.*

Joseph-Marie-Auguste Caillaux. *1911-12. Pacifist, resigned when his wife shot and killed the editor of* Le Figaro *newspaper. Arrested for treason during First World War, banished for ten years, yet managed to serve in governments during the 1920s.*

Pierre Laval. *1931-32, 1932, 1935-36, 1942-44. Prominent in 1930s governments, high level Nazi collaborator during Second World War, supervised persecution of French Jews, fled with retreating Germans, returned by U.S. army and shot.*

Georges Bidault. *1946, 1949-50, 1950, 1958. Convinced French colonialist. Quote: "Ho Chi Minh is about to capitulate. We are going to beat him." Beaten by Ho Chi Minh, supported de Gaulle's return to power. Fell out with de Gaulle and, as head of terrorist* l'Organisation de l'armée secrète *(O.A.S.: Secret Army Organization), spent the early '60s trying to kill him. Amnestied 1968.*

Pierre Bérégovoy. *1992-93. Replaced Cresson as Prime Minister. Deeply implicated in President Mitterrand's widescale bugging of opponents, apparently shot himself beside a canal towpath. He left no note and his personal diary, known to have existed, was not found.*

More than most, Mitterrand and Cresson were well suited to cohabit. Though not conventionally beautiful (if anything, conventionally ugly), she had enjoyed a sexual relationship with Mitterrand since 1965 when she had assisted with his first presidential campaign. Thanks to France's stringent privacy laws, the relationship was never publicised at home.

After securing the presidency in 1981, Mitterrand named her successively Minister of Agriculture, Foreign Trade, Industry, and European Affairs. While maintaining her cabinet position, he "parachuted" Cresson into the provincial city of Châtellerault to became its mayor in 1983. Eight years later, Mitterrand set her up in the sumptuous Hotel Matignat, the prime minister's official residence.

THE THOUGHTS OF EDITH CRESSON (1)
"The truth is no ugly woman can succeed in politics", Edith Cresson, red-headed and squinting former Prime Minister of France (1991, two months before she was dismissed).

It didn't work out. She couldn't stem France's rising unemployment, which

*"In the U.S.A. there are already
25 percent of them [homosexuals]
and in England and Germany it
is much the same," she said in
1987. "You cannot imagine it
[homosexuality] in the history of
France.", Edith Cresson, reported
in the Observer newspaper, 16
June 1991.*

reached over a million, and a series of aggressive public statements about *"les Anglos"*, the Japanese and gays suggested she was little more than an aggressive but over-promoted local hack who'd been sleeping with the boss.

Her popularity ratings crashed (she became known as "Madame 19%") and, with his own political position in jeopardy, Mitterrand dumped her. She wasn't a woman to go quietly. Her widely publicised letter of resignation complained that she had not been allowed to "fully complete" her mission and she blamed her dismissal on "a macho plot".

Mitterrand, the old smoothie, adroitly shut her up and got her out of town by naming Cresson as one of France's two (now reduced to one) delegates to the European Commission in Brussels. She demanded a Commission Vice-Presidency as the only position befitting her rank. Commission President Jacques Santer declined, palming her off with Research, Education and Training, the Siberia of Commission portfolios.

She soon turned on the heat. Arrogant and abrasive, she needled colleagues by showing up unprepared and using Commission meetings to catch up with personal correspondence. More serious was the criticism she received for the hands-off way she administered her budget and worked with contractors.

THE THOUGHTS OF
EDITH CRESSON (3)
*"The Japanese are like ants.
They stay up all night working
out how to screw you in the
morning." Edith Cresson,
reported in* Business Week
magazine, 1 June 1991.

European Union investigators looking into "serious irregularities and / or fraud" during Cresson's period as Commissioner focused on the case of Forma in Quarto, a Brussels-based printing firm. Not only were tender specs altered to suit Forma in Quarto but, according to the official report, "the company was always invited to quote last and always managed to tender prices slightly lower than the last estimate". No surprise then that the firm won bulk printing contracts worth

CRESSON AND AGENOR
Cresson was also responsible for the Leonardo da Vinci *programme for vocational training. Despite its €620 million ($765 million) budget, her department apparently did not have the staff to administer the programme itself which was contracted out to a private company, Agenor. Numerous internal audits raised concerns about Agenor fixing bids for lucrative contracts, paying on fraudulent invoices and hiring family members at lavish salaries. Cresson failed to inform the European Parliament about any of this. After her resignation, the contract was immediately cancelled.*

€3 million ($3.7 million). Forma in Quarto has only three employees.

Laurens Jan Brinkhorst, a member of the European Parliament's Budget Control Committee summed up Cresson with withering accuracy: "She showed herself to be, truly and honestly, a French-bred local politician".

Just how local became clear when she appointed a highly paid "scientific visitor" to "co-ordinate research on A.I.D.S.". Amongst the nominated candidates presented to her were the 1992 Nobel Prize Winner for Physics, George Charpak. Instead, Cresson chose René Berthelot, her personal dentist.

IN THE TEETH OF THE EVIDENCE

A long-time friend of Cresson's, dentist René Berthelot had no background in the H.I.V. sciences. During his two year employment, which cost European taxpayers €150,000 ($185,000), he submitted only twenty-four pages of notes. His work was officially described by Brussels investigators as "infantile". His travel expenses for "field trips", on examination, turned out to be mostly to his home town, Châtellerault. Cresson initially denied any knowledge of Berthelot's appointment. Improbable, since she was not only Mayor of Châtellerault but, on his arrival in Brussels, Berthelot had promptly moved into her flat.

When the appointment became public knowledge, there was uproar in the European Parliament. E.U. investigators then established that M. Berthelot's notes, supplied to them by Cresson to justify his work between October 1995 and March 1997, had been forged a year later after the scandal had broken. They advised the E.U. commission that Cresson "should have been aware of the reality of these documents which were intended as a cover up". Since she refused to resign, in March 1999 all the other European Commissioners resigned instead, taking her with them.

Charged with fraud by Belgian magistrates, she fought back. She claimed she was the victim of a right wing conspiracy "by the Germans", that her Paris apartment had been burgled, that she was suffering from cancer. More tellingly, she announced that the charges against her were "designed to tarnish the image of France" and wrote to President Chirac demanding "the full protection of the Republic". Belgium, very much the "Mini-Me" of France, dropped the charges a year later for "lack of evidence".

A parallel investigation by the European Commission is still under way. A case against Cresson has been submitted to the European Court of Justice with a view to stripping her of her €40,000 ($49,000) annual pension.

Yet in France, it's as if nothing had happened. In 2004 Cresson was selected to sit on a prestigious high-level government panel tasked with shaping "the future of Europe" and examining Europe's nascent constitution. More recently, she chaired a session of the Paris-based Global Forum on Sustainable Development. The event's patrons included President Jacques Chirac.

The French are forgiving. "She is incredibly maladroit. She attracts hostility and enemies everywhere she goes," says French political commentator Alain Duhamel, "but she's not really corrupt".

Le Roi du Crazy

Jerry Lewis and French Humour

National humour doesn't travel – and French humour, in particular, is for domestic consumption only. Yet when it comes to imports, the French are far from choosy, as their legendary appetite for Jerry Lewis shows.

By the 1970s, Jerry Lewis' career as a film actor had ebbed away. At its high water mark, just a few years before, he had been a global entertainment phenomenon.

Partnered with crooner Dean Martin, he parlayed their cabaret act into a wildfire film career, playing variations on a character variously described as "an over-grown juvenile" (Leonard Maltin), a "nebbish man-child" (*Variety*) or, to put it bluntly, "a spaz" (Dennis Leary). Even when the partnership

THE FOREMOST COMIC ARTIST OF THE TIME
"I consider Jerry Lewis, since the death of Buster Keaton, to be the foremost comic artist of the time. He corresponds to his era both reflecting and criticising our civilization." Robert Benayoun, French critic, intellectual and (obviously) surrealist.

imploded, Lewis's brand of "jazz screwball", veering wildly from klutzy slapstick to tear-brimming slush, kept his solo career alive and well. The box office gross receipts of his films total about $800 million (and this was when tickets cost between 25 and 50 cents each).

Tastes changed. Comedy evolved. Beside more nuanced comics like Woody Allen and Mel Brooks, Lewis seemed cornball, even crass. The man who had giant hits with *The Bellboy* (1960) and *The Nutty Professor* (1963) bombed big-time with *Which Way To The Front* (1970). His self-directed, -produced and -scripted story about a masochistic buffoon entertaining Jewish children in Auschwitz, *The Day The Clown Cried* (1972), was so excruciating it never got a release. Cinematically, the world regarded him as a one-off, time-expired.

Finally, in 1982, he had a heart attack and was pronounced clinically dead. Rushed to hospital for triple-bypass surgery, he was then pronounced alive again. And this is exactly what the French seem to be doing with his career. Over there, Lewis is an immortal, *le Roi du Crazy* – the King of Craz-eeee!

This twisted love-affair started with Lewis' visit to France in 1965. Mobbed at Orly airport by fans, he was the toast of Paris. French critics voted *The Nutty Professor* the best film of the year (this was the same year that *Dr Zhivago*, *Thunderball* and *The Sound of Music* came out). An art cinema put on a three-week festival of his films, and the *Cinémathèque Française* (the French film library) held a retrospective on his "art".

His wild popularity among the French public has its roots in what the French actually think is funny. In 2003 the *Economist* magazine summed it up: "The French Have Jokes, But Do They Have A Sense Of

FRANCE'S TOTAL FILM-MAKER

"Watching Lewis' films again, one more than ever notices how contrived and, at times, counterproductive their formal sophistication can be . [But] once all the necessary reservations have been duly entered and once it has been recognised that Lewis's work, as a result of its inner contradictions, imposed some serious limitations upon itself, the inescapable fact remains that Lewis was the only Hollywood comedian to rise from mere performer to 'total film maker' of the sound era." Jean-Pierre Coursodon, American Directors, Vol II, *1983*.

BONJOUR MONSIEUR LEWIS *(1982) is the title of a documentary about Jerry Lewis by French critic and film maker, Robert Benayoun. It runs for six hours: "The pic loses a little steam in the third and fourth hours, when focusing on his relationship with children and his smarmier edge. You also have to wade through several renditions of 'You'll Never Walk Alone', while his ancient 'musical typewriter' routine is so grating that you'll want to drive your shoe up his shrivelled ass. Even if you can't understand one word of the un-subtitled French narration, almost everything else is in English and, as we all know, Jerry's (alleged) talent spans language barriers. Though far from the last word on this repellent comic genius, this fabulous love letter will leave any Jerry Lewis fan drooling and limp with joy".* Review, Shock Cinema.

Humour?". While French society, like all societies, breaks down into the routine political, economic and other groups, France has always divided itself into two categories, "*Parisien*" (from Paris) and "*de la province*" (essentially, from anywhere *except* Paris). And each category has its own sense of humour.

This is more than a geographical divide; it's two different styles of living developed in almost deliberate opposition to each other. The first is hyper-chic, intellectual and verbal; the second is earthy, passionate and emotional. It's Charlotte Rampling vs. Gérard Depardieu, it's Citroën vs. Renault, it's Louis Vuitton vs. Carrefour. Lewis' talent is to tickle the funny bone of both sides.

IT'S OFFICIAL: THE FRENCH ARE HUMOUR-LESS (UNTIL 1932)
Are the French humourless? Until recently, the official answer was "yes". Before the French revolution, the French spoke of l'esprit *(wit) or* la farce *(joke) or* la bouffonnerie *(banter), but the word "humour" had no French equivalent. Only in 1878 did* l'Académie française *(the French Academy), a collection of intellectuals that decides what goes into the French language and what doesn't, accept "humoristique" as a French word – but only if it appeared between apostrophes. A year later, author Edmond de Goncourt used "humour" without italics in his novel* Les Frères Zemganno. *Not until 1932 did* les academiciens *finally allow "humour" in their dictionary.*

For those "*de la province*", Lewis ties in with a long French tradition of physical comedy heroes from film star Jacques Tati (who was making interminable silent films long into the '70s) to the "crying clown" mime Marcel Marceau. They see his mugging as a jet-age version of Chaplin (*Charlot* in France), the little man expressing his emotions through painfully mawkish slapstick. To French film critic Jean-Pierre Coursodon, Lewis "represents the lowest degree of physical, moral and intellectual debasement that a comic actor can reach". He means it as a compliment.

INSIDE THE FRENCH MIND
"Self-deprecation, another essential ingredient of a 'detached' sense of humour, is not the forte of the French. If the Latin emotions of the French sit uneasily with humour, so does the French logical mind. French children are instilled with Cartesian esprit (here meaning mind) at school. When your correspondent was at university in France, she was told her poor performance was due to an Anglo-Saxon mind that made her unable to think properly. A French Cartesian mind does not know what to make of a nonsensical story, such as this one: The Governor of the Bank of England began an address to an assembly of bankers with these words: 'There are three kinds of economists, those who can count and those who can't.' A joke of this kind would be met with incomprehension by French listeners. It is not logical." Economist *magazine, 2003.*

Lewis appeals to "*les Parisiens*" on another level. To put it simply, highbrow French critics (is there any other type?) believe Lewis is so bad that he *must* be good. Or, to translate it into their language, his sloppy, uneven film-making is actually "Godardian anti-formalism". Jean-Luc Godard, the bottomlessly pretentious director now worshiped as the father of New Cinema and *auteur* of numberless botched-up films, is a major fan. "Jerry Lewis", he concludes, "is the only American director who has made progressive films; he is much better than Chaplin and Keaton".

For critic and film-maker Robert Benayoun, another of the leaders of the strange, intellectual cult surrounding the toothy clown, Lewis actually has supernatural powers. He describes his idol's 1965 release *The Family Jewels* as "audacious" because it "deliberately severs space-time".

Since 1960, Jerry Lewis has won three Best Director Awards in France. In the 1970s the French gave him his own two-hour, prime-time chat show which featured guests like famed director Louis Malle, sitting literally at his feet.

While his film career is pretty much at a full stop in the U.S., in France they're begging him to make movies. In 1984, with the opening of one of his French movies *Retenez-moi ou je fais un malheur!* (*Stop me, Or I'll have an accident!*), he was made a commander of the Order of Arts and Letters, France's highest cultural honour (perhaps not so high since even Sylvester Stallone has one of those). Incredibly, just two months later he was awarded the Legion of Honour, France's highest any kind of honour, traditionally awarded to French generals who storm enemy bunkers so you can understand how rare that is.

On 15 September 1999 Jerry made his first live appearance on France's new COMEDIE! channel. It got the same kind of audiences as the moon shot. The publicity material was headlined simply *Jerry*. No further explanation was necessary for Jerry's French fans.

THE OUTRAGE OF JERRY!

What other comedian could dial up Paris and immediately be put through to Jacques Chirac? Only Le Jerry. In 2003, Ralph Garman, an entertainment reporter with Los Angeles-based radio station, K.R.O.Q. 106.7, made a prank call to the French president and duped him into a bizarre eight-minute conversation that covered Saddam Hussein and the war in Iraq. During the call, Chirac assured Garman: "I recognize your voice, no doubt about that," and invited the imposter to visit him next time he was in Paris. When the joke was revealed, Lewis issued the statement: "Jerry is outraged that this impersonation occurred, especially at this critical time in the conduct of foreign policy".

The Duck Stops Here

Arnold Schwarzenegger tells the French to Get Stuffed

Foie gras has been called the "emblem of French national cuisine". Produced by methods close to torture and fiercely protected by the government, *foie gras* production is ruffling the feathers of France's neighbours.

GOVERNATOR TO FRANCE: "CRAM IT, FRENCHIE!"
"Cramming food down a duck's throat to make a gourmet item known as foie gras *is not only unnecessary, it's inhumane." California Senate President Pro Tem John Burton on the passage of S.B. 1520 banning the eventual sale of* foie gras *in his state.*

Arnold Schwarzenegger has done some pretty disgusting things in his life, "Jingle All The Way" for one and Maria Kennedy Shriver for another, but there are some things even he won't stomach. Like *foie gras*.

On 29 September 2004, the Governor signed into law a bill immediately banning the force feeding of ducks and geese in California and, from 2012, prohibiting the sale of any foodstuff produced by force feeding. Not only is this

FOIE GRAS
"(fwÃ-grÃ) [Fr., fat liver], livers of artificially fattened geese. Ducks and chickens
are also sometimes used in the making of foie gras. The birds, kept in close coops to
prevent exercise, are systematically fed to the limit of their capacity. Under this
treatment the livers are brought to weigh 4 or 5 lb (2.5-3kg) or more. Foie gras was
prized by epicures in Egypt, Greece, and Rome, but the fattening of geese for their
livers became a lost art during the Middle Ages except in Strasbourg. The industry
was revived in the 18th cent. following the creation of pâté de foie gras by Jean
Joseph Close (or Clause), a chef brought to Alsace by a French governor of the
province. The making of foie gras has become a famous industry of Strasbourg and
of Toulouse, France." Columbia University Encyclopaedia, 2003.

good news for geese and ducks everywhere but it also stuffs a large number of
rich, powerful French farmers whose business has rested for centuries on the
torture of poultry.

Foie gras is one of those French delicacies, like oysters or calves' brains in
black butter, that you would not naturally eat unless told they were a French
delicacy. The grossly enlarged liver of a duck or goose, it is in effect a balloon of
semi-solid fat in a gelatinous sac. If you like offal that bursts in your mouth, *foie
gras* is for you.

To French food writer Charles Gerard, and to many of his countrymen, it is
"the supreme fruit of gastronomy". Seared and doused with a port-wine
reduction, or baked with truffles into a terrine, it is the holy grail of the French
restaurant industry: the €20 ($25) *hors d'oeuvre*.

What leaves a nasty taste in the mouth is
how these birds are treated on the way to the
slaughterhouse. To make their livers larger,
ducks are force-fed enormous quantities of mash
three times a day using air pumps attached to
long metal pipes forced into their gullets. This
process of deliberate and painful over-feeding,
up to three kilos a day, is called "*gavage*"
(stuffing). The human equivalent would be to
eat thirteen kilos of pasta. It continues for up to
a month, by which time the birds' livers swell
up to ten times their healthy size.

**WHAT FOIE GRAS MEANS
TO THE FRENCH (1)**
"*It has an unctuous texture
and it fills your palate. Foie
gras makes a meal special and
it's a symbol of celebration – of
Christmases and New Years,
marriages and baptisms. In
Gascony, where we celebrate
around the dinner table, foie
gras is always invited.*"
Claude St. Blancard, owner of
a foie gras *farm that
slaughters 3,000 ducks a year.*

One German newspaper reporter visited a *foie gras* farm in Gascony and saw
how large the livers become: "After removing the intestines and the gizzard, [the
farm worker] lifts out an enormous, tan coloured *foie gras*, the size of a small
melon, that fills the entire belly of the small bird". French farmers defend the
distortion of the bird's internal organs by saying the migratory ducks over-eat

prior to long flights, swelling their livers naturally. Naturalists at P.E.T.A. (People for the Ethical Treatment of Animals) respond that such natural swelling is no more than 50% rather than 1,000%.

In another investigation, by GourmetCruelty.com, into French *foie gras* farming, reporters discovered corpses of ducks that had burst open through over-feeding, many choked to death on their own vomit. Necropsies performed by vets determined others had died from aspiration pneumonia caused when, during the process of forced-feeding, food is pushed into the lungs of the birds.

The process is so traumatic, and the confinement and conditions on *foie gras* farms so debilitating, that the pre-slaughter mortality rate for *foie gras* production is twenty times the average rate of other duck factory farms.

These figures apply solely to drakes since only male ducks are used for *foie gras*. They produce larger livers and are considered better able to withstand the four-week force-feeding. Female hatchlings are simply killed. GourmetCruelty.com found this was usually done by stuffing female chicks in a sack and drowning them.

Although some free range producers are promoted as tourist attractions in France, 80% of all ducks are now kept in individual cages, known as *épinettes*, in factory farms strictly closed to visitors. This change has enabled costs to fall and production levels to increase by more than 100% over the past ten years.

Much of the world, not just Schwarzenegger's California, rejects this industrialised process. Animal protection laws in Denmark, Germany, Norway, Poland and Austria specifically prohibit force-feeding. In 1998 the Council of Europe issued a directive stating that no animal should be "provided with food or liquid in a manner which may cause unnecessary suffering or injury". The Council and many other European bodies, up to and including the European Commission, have since made many more rulings and

WHAT FOIE GRAS MEANS TO THE FRENCH (2)

"They are kept in individual cages for about 10 days. They are force-fed with a tube, twice a day into their throats, about five pounds of corn per day. And that makes their liver swell many, many times its normal size so they can't breathe, they don't sleep any more and some of them die before the end. That's what foie gras *is."* Dominique Hoffpower, French Animal Rights League.

GETTING FAT OFF FOIE GRAS

Making the stuff is big business in France, which accounts for 70% of the 20,000-odd tonnes produced in the world each year and for 85% of global consumption. The industry, centred in the south-west, employs 30,000 people directly and indirectly, and the average French person eats foie gras *at least ten times a year . In 1998, over 25 million ducks and geese were raised for the production of* foie gras *in France.*

AND FATTER

*"*Foie gras *gets 85 percent of its calories from fat – more than twice as much as a hamburger! This fat is mostly palmitic acid, a saturated fat known to increase cholesterol."* David T. Nash, cardiologist quoted by P.E.T.A.

recommendations, all of which – if they were ever observed – would end the force-feeding of ducks and geese for *foie gras*.

France either refuses to implement these directives or else delays them. Not only does it decline absolutely to consider the end of force-feeding but it blocks even the smallest changes to the conditions in which the birds are farmed.

THE DUCK BILL?
Foie gras *is supplied either in its natural state or as a paté and sells for as much as €260 ($320) per kilo. A jar of the best pate de foie gras serves four people and costs €65 ($80).*

In September 2004, the French Agriculture Ministry infuriated animal welfare organisations by giving the country's 6,000 industrial producers an extra five years – until 2010 – to scrap the cramped individual cages, arguing that a European ruling on the subject was just a recommendation, not a directive.

"We will implement the recommendation on individual cages, but we need more time and we're glad the government has recognised that," said Marie-Pierre Pé of the powerful industry association C.I.F.O.G. "Bigger cages will make it harder to grab the birds." (This is also the reason most French *foie gras* production now uses ducks rather than geese, since a goose – a larger, bad-tempered bird – is more likely to beak the hand off any Frenchmen unwise enough to shove a pipe down its throat). "Feeding them will take 20-30% longer", he complains. "That will cost us money".

The French *foie gras* lobby is fighting back fiercely to protect its money. Recently, a committee of eminent scientists from France's National Veterinary School and the State Agricultural Research Institute produced an 80-page report claiming, to the incredulity of non-French scientists, naturalists and activists, that the birds are not being cruelly treated.

GET STUFFED (1)
"Gavage is a veritable form of torture for ducks and geese, which have to absorb huge quantities of food in a matter of seconds." Brigitte Bardot, 1984.

The French *foie gras* lobby is not winning sceptical hearts and minds outside Europe. When it asked Nobel Prize winner and goose expert Konrad Lorenz to read its report promoting the *foie gras* industry to the European Parliament, he refused, saying he felt "hot with anger" as he read the report.

"My viewpoint towards the 'expert opinion' which further permits forcible fattening of geese can be expressed briefly", he replied in anger. "The 'expert opinion' is a disgrace for the whole of Europe."

GET STUFFED (2)
"They say they are not against foie gras but against gavage and that we should look for alternative methods of production. What methods? There are none. Why don't they also ban butterfly collecting?" Marcel Saint-Cricq, foie gras *producer from Landes, south of Bordeaux.*

The Smell of Victory

Did you mean "French military defeats"?

On Bastille Day, every 14 July, tanks thunder down the Champs Elysées while jet fighters roar in formation overhead. But as the French commemorate their spectacular military history, have they forgotten some equally spectacular fiascos?

THOUGHTS OF THE GREAT GENERALS (1)
"It is not big armies that win battles, it is the good ones." Maurice de Saxe, Maréchal de France, 1696-1750. This statement of the obvious comes from Saxe's memoirs, Mes Rêveries, described by historian Thomas Carlyle, as "a strange military farrago, dictated, as I should think, under opium". Saxe took opium for his chronic piles, of which he eventually died. His last battles were won because of his insistence on leading cavalry charges, slowly, from a wicker bath chair so that the enemy ran out of ammunition long before his horsemen got within range.

Military Disasters (Land)

Everyone knows of France's less glorious military moments, from Waterloo and to, well, really the entire Second World War. Here are a few neglected classics.

Crécy (1346): Philip VI hurls 24,000 knights at an invading 10,000-strong English army who open up with armour-piercing arrows. The French lose eleven princes, 1,200 knights and 8,000 troops. The English lose 300 men. Ninety years later, the English leave France.

Pavia (1525): Francis I, invading Naples, doesn't detect a 20,000 Habsburg army less than one mile from his camp. Boldly, he leads a cavalry charge, giving his infantry time to face the enemy. The infantry prefers to withdraw. The King is captured by the laughing Imperials who lose 1,000 men to 8,000 French. Naples stays Italian.

THOUGHTS OF THE GREAT GENERALS (2):
"Nous sommes dans un pot de chambre, et nous y serons emmerdés." (*"We're in the crapper, getting crapped on"*). *General Auguste Ducrot, Battle of Sedan, 1871. Unusually frank despatch summing up his position as the French are, as usual, surrounded by a German army.*

Blenheim (1704): As Louis XIV advances on Vienna, his 56,000 troops are surprised by the British and Austrians who march unnoticed halfway across Europe. 30 French squadrons of horse drown in the Danube, 200 standards, 50 guns and all the French baggage are lost along with 21,000 dead. The Sun King stays out of Germany.

THE LOSING STREAK: COMPLETE MILITARY HISTORY OF FRANCE – AN AMERICAN VIEW

GALLIC WAR (58-52 B.C.)
Lost. In a war whose ending foreshadows the next 2,000 years of French history, France is conquered by, of all things, an Italian.

NORSE INVASIONS (841-911)
After having their way with the French for 70 years, the Normans are bribed by a French King named Charles the Simple (really!) who gives them Normandy.

THE HUNDRED YEARS WAR (1337-1452)
Mostly lost, saved at last by female schizophrenic who inadvertently creates the First Rule of French Warfare: "France's armies are victorious only when not led by a Frenchman".

ITALIAN WAR (1494–1559)
Lost. France becomes the first and only country to ever lose two wars when fighting Italians.

WARS OF RELIGION (1562-98)
France goes 0-5-4 against the Huguenots.

THE THIRTY YEARS WAR (1618-48)
France is technically not a participant, but manages to get invaded anyway. Claims a tie on the basis that the other participants started ignoring her.

WAR OF THE AUGSBURG LEAGUE / KING WILLIAM'S WAR / FRENCH AND INDIAN WAR (1688-97)
Lost, but claimed as a tie. Three ties in a row induces deluded Frogophiles the world over to label the period as the height of French military power.

WAR OF THE SPANISH SUCCESSION (1701-14)
Lost. The War also gave the French their first taste of a Marlborough, which they have loved ever since.

Leipzig (1813): Despite the Retreat from Moscow, Napoleon's army is intact and threatening. His tactics have been learned by his enemies who mass 300,000 Austrians and Prussians to trap him outside Leipzig, inflicting 50% casualties on his 155,000-strong army. Desperate for a way out, he orders Poniatowksi's Polish corps to cover the withdrawal. Every last Pole is slaughtered. Napoleon goes back to France and his abdication.

THOUGHTS OF THE GREAT GENERALS (3): *"If they had given me 10,000 S.S. troopers, I could have held Dien Bien Phu."* General Marcel Bigeard, expressing his "wish list" after commanding the French paratroop forces at Dien Bien Phu during France's greatest post-war defeat of the twentieth century. Uniquely enough, his wish was answered since when the Viet Minh processed the Foreign Legion prisoners that they had taken at the battle, it emerged that most of the German-origin legionnaires were actually Wehrmacht and SS veterans.

The Aisne (April 1917): Robert Nivelle, new French commander, convinces Paris he'll win the war in three weeks. His new plan, like all the old plans, involves an artillery barrage to announce the fact his soldiers are walking slowly towards the machine-gun-bristling German trenches. After two weeks of slaughter, his surviving troops refuse to fight on. 23,000 mutineers are later convicted. Nivelle is fired and the French army is unable to take the offensive again for the rest of the war.

WAR OF THE AMERICAN REVOLUTION (1775-83)
In a move that will become quite familiar to future Americans, France claims a win even though the English colonists saw far more action. This is later known as "de Gaulle Syndrome", and leads to the Second Rule of French Warfare: "France only wins when America does most of the fighting".

THE FRENCH REVOLUTION (1787-1879) *Won, primarily due to the fact that the opponent was also French.*

THE NAPOLEONIC WARS (1793-1815) *Lost. Temporary victories (remember the First Rule!) due to leadership of a Corsican, who ended up being no match for a British footwear designer at Waterloo.*

THE FRANCO-PRUSSIAN WAR (1870-1) *Lost.*

WORLD WAR I (1914-18)
Tied and on the way to losing, France is saved by the United States. Thousands of French women find out what it's like to not only sleep with a winner, but one who doesn't call her "Fräulein".

WORLD WAR II (1939-45)
Lost. Conquered French liberated by the United States and Britain just as they finish learning the Horst Wessel *song.*

WAR IN INDOCHINA (1948-54)
Lost. French forces plead sickness; take to bed with the Dien Bien Flu.

ALGERIAN REBELLION (1954-62)
Lost. Loss marks the first defeat of a western army by a non-Turkic Muslim force since the Crusades.

WAR ON TERRORISM (2002-?)
French attempts to surrender to German ambassador fail after he takes refuge in a McDonald's.
From satirical U.S. website
www.albinoblacksheep.com

"The official figure of 96,000 [casualties] is one of the most suspect in military history, especially as the Germans, who won, admitted a loss of 163,000." – John Laffin, *Brassey's Battles*, 1986.

THOUGHTS OF THE GREAT GENERALS (4):
"We come to give you liberty and equality, but don't lose your heads about it – the first person who stirs without permission gets shot." Marshal François Lefebvre, quoted as he stormed parliament on behalf of Napoleon Bonaparte. Politically, France's senior officers are notoriously fickle. Lefebvre went on to sell out Napoleon to Louis XVIII, then, before Waterloo, Louis XVIII to Napoleon and, after Waterloo, Napoleon to Louis XVIII. He died rich, a duke and a member of the parliament he had originally overthrown.

Military Disasters (Sea)

France's military record on land is equalled only by its record at sea, enough to submerge any other nation. The battle of Trafalgar is well-known but the French navy boasts many more watery disasters on its score card.

Moribhan Gulf (56 B.C.): The first ever naval battle in the Atlantic. The Veneti tribe of Brittany bases its strength on its large fleet of 200 vessels. Julius Caesar builds his own ships in the Loire and sails into battle. Using sickles attached to long poles to disable the Veneti's rigging, the Romans systematically burn every ship and throw the crews overboard.

Sluys (1340): Off the coast of Holland, the fleet of English King Edward III attacks 200 French ships at anchor. A leading ship-to-ship action is between a barge containing the ladies-in-waiting of Edward's queen and a French warship which the English overwhelm with the loss of one lady-in-waiting. Ultimately, the entire French fleet is destroyed and 25,000 men drowned.

FRANCE GOOGLEBOMBED
After 13 March 2003, a Google search for "French military victories" would bring up a page registering "0 hits" and then ask: "Did you mean 'French military defeats'?" The page was actually a mock-up created by a Canadian student, miffed at France's diplomatic campaign against the war in Iraq. Steve Lerner, a 22-year-old Toronto student, said he created the page as "a humorous way of showing political opposition against France's weaselling". Whether an accurate comment or not on French martial prowess, in two days the page became the #1 search result on google.com. Based on a report by Richard J. Dalton Jr, Newsday, March 2003. (Visit the page at: http://www.albinoblacksheep. com/text/victories.html).

La Hogue (1692): Admiral de Tourville's 44 ships of the line carrying an army to invade Ireland meet a combined English-Dutch squadron. In a stunning reversal of form, the French attack and actually sink one English and one Dutch ship. Next day, while celebrating in the Bay of La Hogue, sixteen of their warships and the invasion vessels are sent to the bottom by the allied squadron, which had come back for more.

Battle of the Saints (1782): A French fleet of 183 ships commanded by the Comte de Grasse proceeds towards British-held Jamaica to invade it. Sighting a British force of 37 warships under Admiral Rodney, three French warships immediately collide. The British break the French line, those ships not sunk, flee and de Grasse surrenders his flag ship *Ville de Paris*. "All considered, rather a quotidian little victory, and one hardly worth the noting, being once more against the French." Rear-Admiral Sir Samuel Hood, 1793.

Mers-el-Kebir (1940): Unique in that the French lost their fleet while not actually at war. After France's surrender, the British fear its powerful sea force at Mers-el-Kebir will fall into Nazi hands. On 3 July Admiral Sommerville's Force H begins battleship and aircraft operations against the French. The battleship *Bretagne* is sunk, the *Dunkerque* and the *Mogador* badly damaged, and the *Provence* runs

WAITING FOR HEROES
Les Invalides *in Paris' seventh arrondissement (district) consists of a complex of museums and monuments all relating to France's military glory, as well as a large church often referred to as the* Dôme des Invalides. *This is reserved as the resting ground for the greatest of its war heroes (not unlike Washington's Arlington Cemetery, which contains service people from Ulysses S. Grant to Omar Bradley, and London's St. Paul's Cathedral, which contains the remains of the Duke of Wellington and Admiral Nelson among hundreds of other military tough guys).*

Directly under the dome itself lies Napoleon in a gigantic red marble catafalque. Arranged in a circle around this tomb are a series of smaller "lady chapels", one for each of the other great French military heroes at rest. These include Marshal Foch, responsible for some of the most futile assaults in World War I, and Marshal Lyautey who pacified a section of desert in North Africa. The rest of the chapels are empty, waiting for more French heroes, as and when – and if – they should arrive.

THOUGHTS OF THE GREAT GENERALS (5): *"I am not afraid of the word torture, but I think in the majority of cases the French military men obliged to use it to vanquish terrorism were, fortunately, choir boys compared to the use to which it was put by the rebels. The latter's extreme savagery led us to some ferocity, it is certain, but we remained within the law of eye for eye, tooth for tooth." General Jacques Massu, commander of French forces during the war in Algeria and responsible for placing two million Algerians in prison camps during the emergency.*

aground. Only the *Strasbourg* escapes to Toulon. Winston Churchill notes wryly that the French finally fought "with all their vigour for the first time since the war broke out". The commanders of eleven other ships, including two battleships, in Alexandria prefer to allow themselves to be immobilised peacefully by the British.

Vingt-Huit

Stinking from the Top

Corruption in the Botswana of Europe

In the past decade over five hundred French politicians and businessmen have been investigated or convicted for corruption. In France, officially the most corrupt country in Western Europe, many of them still walk free while the magistrates investigating them face death threats, press hostility and political interference.

In January 1998 Roland Dumas – Resistance hero, connoisseur of the arts and of beautiful women, lawyer to artists like Picasso and Giacometti, former Foreign Minister of France, friend to presidents and currently President of its highest court, the *Conseil Constitutionnel* – found himself trapped in his own apartment. With mounting fury, he watched as the place was thoroughly ransacked by a shortish, fiftyish woman.

He told the woman he had urgent business and would have to leave. The reply, reported in a French paper, was humiliating: "You stay," snapped Eva Joly,

THE REASON
"France fell because there was corruption without indignation."
Romain Rolland, writer, 1940.

"or I'll have you arrested". Mme. Joly was a *juge d'instruction* (investigating magistrate) with wide powers to root out the corruption endemic at the highest levels of French society.

Dumas, as it turned out, was implicated up to his eyeballs in a set of interlocking corruption cases.

These cases, known as *Les affaires*, touch every aspect of French life. Scandals erupt in every western liberal democracy, from Enron and Worldcom in the U.S. to Jeffrey Archer's trial for perjury in the U.K. In those countries, public sentiment is outraged, judicial investigations are conducted swiftly and the guilty end up in jail. In France, in the words of French philosopher Montesquieu, writing in the sixteenth century, "The law is like a web, big insects fly right through it, only the little ones get caught".

Today France is officially rated by Transparency International, the Berlin-based think-tank, as the most corrupt country in western Europe while analysts Fredrik Galtung and Charles Sampford, working for the 2003 U.N. Anti-Corruption Convention, give France a corruption rating of "3", on a par with Botswana.

"THE FIREBOMBER"

In 1993, Eva Joly became one of France's six hundred juges d'instruction. She was a Norwegian former au pair, who married a Frenchman and then attended nightclasses to get her law degree. Her first office in Paris' Palais de Justice was a dark cubbyhole with a desk and a pile of dossiers gathering dust in a metal locker. She borrowed her daughter's old PC and bought her own fax machine. In the spring of 1994, Joly targeted one of France's most flamboyant public figures, Bernard Tapie, a bouffant-haired pop singer who had bought Marseilles football club. In 1992 President Mitterrand had named him Minister of Urban affairs. Joly found that Tapie was guilty of outrageous scams, from registering his yacht as a commercial vessel to embezzling €15 million ($18 million) from his football club and paying another team to throw a match. He got a prison sentence for fraud. She became a public figure, given nicknames like "The Firebomber" and "The Bulldozer from the North" by the media. In 1995, Joly investigated the bizarre financial dealings within Elf, France's leading oil company, and in 2001 brought charges against a string of senior business people and politicians . In June 2002, after facing death threats, a co-ordinated press campaign and constant political interference, she resigned her post, left France and became special adviser to the Ministries of Justice and Foreign Affairs in Norway .

ELF: PAYMASTER TO THE "WHORE OF THE REPUBLIC"

Roland Dumas was mixed up in the case of Elf-Aquitaine, the gigantic state-owned oil firm. Under President Mitterrand (now safely dead) the company had been used as a general piggybank by successive governments. A €305 million ($375 million) slush fund was created from the loot that was then passed on as bribes, sweeteners and kickbacks. Allegedly, "royalties" went to African leaders for drilling rights; commissions were paid to acquire desirable industrial properties and sweetheart loans were granted to undeserving companies.

The most infamous instance concerned the 1991 sale to Taiwan of six modern frigates built by the French defence firm Thomson-CSF. The contract was worth more than €1 billion ($1.25 billion), but the deal conflicted with French government policy towards mainland China which aggressively opposed the deal. The sale was cancelled, then reversed. The Taiwanese, who were near to completing a similar deal with Hyundai of Korea, pulled out of that sale and opted for the French offer. By the time the six frigates were finally paid for, their price had rocketed to €2.44 billion ($3 billion), of which nearly a third was estimated to have been the cost of the bribes and commissions.

The warships were delivered to Taiwan. At just about the same time, Mitterrand's Prime Minister Edith Cresson was passing on full details of the commercial and technical specifications of the deal to the People's Republic of China in order to soften the transaction – and allegedly getting herself a €1.5 million ($1.85 million) kickback from Elf.

The deeper Eva Joly, dug, the deeper she got in. In 1996, she began receiving death threats and was assigned a police bodyguard. A year later, a case of documents disappeared from a locked police storage room. Then her office was broken into and two computers tampered with.

ELF PAYS OFF ITS FRIENDS...
President Mitterrand used the Elf slush fund to contribute millions of francs to the 1991 re-election of his friend Helmut Kohl, the German Christian Democrat leader. Elf also helped Kohl smooth over the awkward economics of German reunification by buying 2,000 unprofitable petrol stations in East Germany. It was alleged that Chancellor Kohl returned the favour by approving a favourable deal for Elf to buy the former East German Leuna oil refinery.

AND ITS ENEMIES?
"Who today can remember details of the two suicides that threatened to bring down President Mitterrand's government? Exactly. In 1993, Pierre Bérégovoy, the former French Prime Minster, was found with a bullet hole through his head by a canal in Nevers. The following year, François de Grossouvre, Mitterrand's head of personal intelligence, was found shot dead at his desk in the Elysée . Both incidents were dismissed as suicide. Yet no suicide note was found on either man. And both men just happened to be implicated in the enquiry [about Mitterrand's relationship with Elf]. The reason we cannot recall such details is that, this being France, no independent inquiry was set up to investigate". Nigel Farndale, Daily Telegraph newspaper, 2003.

Only when Joly zeroed in on Roland Dumas did the press start taking notice, reporting the 1.4 million ($1.75 million) luxury Paris apartment and a €6,000 ($7,300) monthly expense budget allotted to Dumas's mistress, Christine Deviers-Joncour, who had been put on the Elf payroll for unspecified duties. Joly banged up Deviers-Joncour in jail, called Dumas in for questioning and, with relish, presided over a search of that expensive Parisian apartment.

She found links to Loïk Le Floch-Prigent, boss of Elf in 1989-1993, and Alfred Sirven, his deputy, as well as to their ex-"Mr Africa", André Tarallo.

These three insisted that they were operating an inherited *système Elf* designed to further French oil policy and benefit certain African leaders. So, the palatial Paris apartment that he acquired, insisted Tarallo, was for the use of Gabon's president, Omar Bongo. A villa in Corsica was intended to house a "Franco-African foundation".

This defence evaporated under Joly's fiery scrutiny. Sirven, who fled to the Philippines (and swallowed the chip in his mobile phone) before his arrest, turned on his former boss. He had spent over €100 million ($120 million) on Le Floch-Prigent's behalf, he said. This included purchases like yet another multi-million euro house in Paris that Le Floch-Prigent had reported (for tax purposes, naturally) as a "business flat". This extraordinary world of bribery and personal profit, of jewellery and furs, villas and mistresses was all revealed in a carnival of trials lasting well into the 2000s. To court uproar, it was revealed that Le Floch-Prigent had used €4.5 million ($5.5 million) of company money to fund his divorce.

As a result of Joly's investigations, Le Floch-Prigent, Sirvent and Tarallo, as well as twenty-seven others, all got prison sentences and combined fines of nearly €20 million ($24 million).

"THE WHORE OF THE REPUBLIC"
Roland Dumas was Foreign Minister in 1990 when Thomson-CSF, a then state-owned defence company, wanted to sell ships to Taiwan. The Socialist government blocked the sale, anxious not to damage relations with China. Elf, expert in "facilitating" sensitive international deals, was brought in to lobby on Thomson's behalf. In turn, Elf hired the 42-year old Christine Deviers-Joncour. In August 1991, the veto was lifted; no explanation was ever given. In fact, Deviers-Joncour had become Dumas' lover. During her time on Elf's payroll, she was set up in a designer apartment on the Left Bank, just a stroll from the Foreign Ministry. She lavished gifts on Dumas, twenty-six years her senior, including €1,500 ($1,850)-pairs of hand-made Italian shoes. At her subsequent trial on charges of corruption, it was found that she received around €10 million ($12 million) in salary, expenses and bribes for her trouble. A magistrate called her the "whore of the Republic" and Deviers-Joncour used it as the title of her best-selling memoirs. Now released from jail, she maintains that she has enough dirt to "sink the Fifth Republic". "If I die tomorrow," she once said, "it won't be an accident or suicide".

But not Dumas. In 2001, he was convicted of complicity in taking bribes. At his sentencing, he warned the judges: "You will hear from me after this trial". On appeal, in 2003, he was cleared of all charges. "I am happy that I have been given justice," he told the French news agency A.F.P. His former mistress, Christine Deviers-Joncour, was not so happy. She got three and a half years.

THE CONTINUING TRIALS OF ROLAND DUMAS
Just as Dumas was finally cleared, after many appeals, for his alleged role in the Elf scandals, he was arrested again for (no surprises here) corruption. He is now accused of accepting a bribe in connection with the sale of artworks by sculptor Alberto Giacometti. Dumas was an executor of the will of Giacometti's widow . He is charged with receiving a pay-off to keep silent about proceeds allegedly retained illegally by the auctioneer in return for a €370,000 ($455,000) pay-off. Dumas says the money he received was for legal services. The case continues.

CRÉDIT LYONNAIS: THE BANK THAT DRIPPED RED INK
In 1988 Crédit Lyonnais, France's biggest state-owned bank, began a dynamic programme of explosion and acquisition under its peppy new C.E.O., Jean-Yves Haberer.

Haberer had a mighty dream. He wanted this staid, solid bank to be a French rival to Germany's Deutsche Bank or the vast U.S. investment banks. So he began creating a giant portfolio of stakes in French companies, splurging large sums buying other banks and giving loans to rackety businessmen, many of whom were tainted by their association with other French business and financial scandals.

This explosive growth was overseen by the governor of the Banque de France, Jean-Luc Trichet, acting as Treasury Director, and the French government, which saw Crédit Lyonnais as a channel for its industrial policy.

But in the early 1990s France's economy slumped and Crédit Lyonnais began bleeding red ink. In the words of Rob Jameson of financial analysts, *eRisk*, "It seemed that no one with authority over the bank was able to draw a clear line between the bank's risk capital and the deep pockets of the French taxpayer".

By 1992, though the bank's management had deliberately inflated its results, it was obvious that Crédit Lyonnais was bankrupt. The savings of eight million people were in jeopardy. The French Finance Ministry stepped in with a vast injection of taxpayer's cash, saving it from collapse at a total cost of €190 billion ($234 billion).

New management, led by Jean Peyrelevade, was installed in 1993 and the bank was privatised in July 1999, lending it some respectability. In late 2002 Crédit Lyonnais was bought by Crédit Agricole.

Investigations into criminal wrong-doing were hampered by the destruction of crucial archives in a fire that began in the main trading room of the bank in May 1996. Another fire at a Le Havre depot later destroyed documents that were critical to unravelling the story behind some of Credit Lyonnais' worst property-linked investments.

Nonetheless, Jean-Yves Haberer was found guilty of fraud in 2003, and given an 18-month suspended sentence and a €50,000 ($62,000) fine. Two other former officials, François Gille and Bernard Thiolon, were also convicted and given

177

suspended sentences and fines of €10,000 ($12,000). All are appealing.

Jean-Luc Trichet, the link between the government and the bank, was also tried. He claimed that he "was given little information by the bank's management while, as Treasury Director, I was not given access to internal Ministry reports". He was acquitted. In the same year, President Chirac appointed him to head the European Central Bank.

CLEAN HANDS OR BUTTERFINGERS?

Jean Peyrelevade was the executive brought in to Crédit Lyonnais to clean up the mess left by his predecessor, Jean-Yves Haberer. He seems to have fumbled the pass. In America, Crédit Lyonnais is now subject to a criminal lawsuit over its 1991 purchase of Executive Life, a Californian insurance company. Contrary to U.S. rules, the bank used a series of front companies to get round laws barring banks and foreign governments from owning more than 25% of any U.S. insurance firm. To stave off further charges, Crédit Lyonnais has already agreed to pay $100m to the U.S. government. The payment is believed to be part of the biggest criminal settlement in U.S. history. Criminal charges are now pending against Jean Peyrelevade, who masterminded the deal. On 2 October 2003 Peyrelevade resigned with immediate effect from Credit Lyonnais and, if found guilty by U.S. authorities, he could face a personal fine of $500,000 and a lifetime ban on working in the U.S. banking industry.

PARIS: THE GARDENS OF CORRUPTION

Between 1977 and 1995 Jacques Chirac was Mayor of Paris – the city called, not without affection, "the Gardens of Corruption" by poet Charles Beaudelaire.

Chirac has been named in numerous cases of corruption and abuse relating to his time as Mayor. However, as President, Chirac has near total legal immunity for acts not only as President but for acts preceding his time in office. This is thanks to decision 98-408 D.C. of the *Conseil Constitutionnel* (Constitutional Council). The Council committee that made the decision was handpicked by Chirac and headed, inevitably, by Roland Dumas.

Maybe he should not be blamed. Paris seems to bring out the worst in everybody involved in its governance.

Vote Rigging. This is endemic across the different districts of Paris. In the third arrondissement alone, 859 (being 5% of the registered voters) were fraudulently registered on the electoral rolls during Chirac's time as Mayor. During the tenure of his successor, Jean Tiberi, 7,228 dead, missing or simply made-up names were registered in the fifth arrondissement (allowing Tiberi to win his election with a 2,725 vote majority).

Kickbacks. One easy way to raise funds is by manipulating the bidding of public contracts. Charles Pasqua, one of Chirac's former interior ministers, was allegedly involved in a kickback scheme for works on the public housing projects of the Hauts-de-Seine *département*. Forty other officials are under investigation for corruption in the Ile-de-France regional council. Police investigations show that at least 2% of the payments from companies involved in building or repairs on the region's high schools were channelled back to political parties.

Payroll Padding. On 31 January 2004, Alain Juppé, former Prime Minister of France and also former Deputy Mayor in charge of finances of the City of Paris (1983-95) was sentenced to an 18-month suspended sentence for paying party workers from the city employee payroll.

Jobs for the Boys (and Girls). Xavière Tiberi, the wife of Mayor of Paris Jean Tiberi, received €30,000 ($37,000) for a report on *la francophonie* (the coalition of French speaking nations) for the Essonne *département*. This 36-page report was poorly written and littered with child-like spelling and grammatical mistakes. Police now suggest it was written after payment when investigators actually asked what was being paid for.

Uphill Gardening. In 2004, current mayor Bertrand Delanoë complained that for the last decade City of Paris gardeners have been diverted from their jobs to tend the gardens of senior figures in President Chirac's R.P.R. party (*Rassemblement pour la République*, Rally for the Republic). He estimates the loss to the public purse to be upward of €700,000 ($860,000).

THE HORRORS OF TOULOUSE

Something macabre is unravelling in Toulouse, known as *la ville rose* because of the pinkish terracotta frontage of its Spanish-style villas.

In 2002, Patrice Alègre, a pimp and cocaine pusher, was convicted of five murders and six rapes in the region during a decade-long murder spree. He was only caught when a special homicide squad began to investigate the unexplained disappearance of 115 women and girls in the Toulouse region dating back to 1992.

At his trial, policeman's son Alègre claimed that the reason his crimes had gone undetected so long was the official protection that he received from the local police and government officials who attended the regular sado-masochistic orgies he hosted in a council-owned chateau and, bizarrely, a courthouse.

At first, his claims were dismissed as fantasy until two prostitutes, given the witness-protection pseudonyms "Patricia" and "Fanny", corroborated his story. The women testified repeatedly that they informed gendarmes about Alègre and the parties years ago but had always been ignored. This was during a time when, the investigations revealed, the region's police were reclassifying some of Alègre's murders as "suicides".

Their testimony included the description of Alègre's strangling a transvestite, Claude Martinez, who had boasted of secretly filming the orgies and was threatening to name names. Those names soon came out, including the former Mayor of Toulouse, three judges and, incredibly, one of the prosecutors conducting the case against the killer.

The appointment of Michel Barrau, to replace the dropped local prosecutor, concerned some observers because he had been blamed for blocking an investigation into corruption among senior right-wing politicians in Paris before the 2002 general election.

As it stands, Alègre is still to be tried for five other suspected murders. In 2005 charges of rape against two of the leading names implicated, Dominique Baudis, the former Mayor of Toulouse, and Marc Bouraque, the substituting prosecutor of Toulouse, were dropped. Investigations continue into many other suspected "party-goers" and into the conduct of Toulouse's police and judiciary during Alègre's career of rape and murder.

THE CULTURE OF CORRUPTION

Why the French people seem to care so little about the corruption that riddles the upper echelons of its business, political and judicial institutions is a mystery to its English, Scandinavian and German neighbours. Eva Joly, former investigating magistrate, sums up the current situation: "The law applies to all, *except* for those who wield political or economic power".

THE OCEAN OF FRAUD

"I had no idea of the extent of the corruption. I'd assumed that people respected the laws. But reality outstripped fiction. Corruption was endemic. There was an ocean of fraud at the highest level. Every day I found something new."
Eva Joly, 2003.

The problem is that corruption seems not simply endemic, it is systemic, built into the structure of public institutions in France. During his time as Mayor, President Chirac was able to pay for twenty, first-class trips abroad for himself and his family – at a cost of €440,000 ($540,000) – using an official but "secret" fund available to him by virtue of his office. The source of this cash is officially unaccountable and, as Eric Halphen, the investigating magistrate looking into "travelgate" found out when he tried to explore how it was spent, so is its disbursement.

Slowly but surely, the investigating magistrates, the only people in France with the power to clean it up, are being sidelined, pressurised and forced from their jobs. Halphen resigned in disgust at Chirac's refusal to testify in the myriad cases of bribery regarding his time as Mayor of Paris. Eva Joly took early retirement and went back to her native Norway, intimidated by political and police pressures. She had received police protection after receiving death threats but found the 24-hour armed guard "more like police arrest than police protection". When she asked that the guard be removed, her request was denied and the guard was doubled. Joly's colleague Laurence Vichnievsky has also resigned.

Perhaps the problem is that corruption at the top reflects the attitude of French society generally. A government report in 1996 estimated that the cost of tax evasion in France could be as high as €30 billion ($37 billion) per year – equal to two-thirds of the revenue from income tax. French authorities are so bad at collecting income taxes (or the people so good at evading them) that between a third and a half of the adult population pay no income tax at all.

THERE IS NO LAW BUT OURS
"Why does no one seem to care? One explanation suggests that the idea of a state based on the rule of law is just an Anglo-Saxon obsession. In France the revolution of 1789 gave power to the people. Quite naturally, the elite who rule in the people's name feel above the law." The Economist magazine, 2003.

In 2002, while covering the French presidential election, a B.B.C. reporter asked a selection of French voters why they were not more worried about the crooked tendencies of their politicians. One answer provided by a chuckling waiter sums up the attitude of the entire country:

"Don't talk about corruption in France or in Paris – everybody is corrupt, myself too."

YESTERDAY – AND TODAY?
"Among a people generally corrupt, liberty cannot long exist." Edmund Burke, Reflections on the Revolution in France, *1790*.

BREAKING: CLEARSTREAM, MUDDY WATERS

In 2006, a new corruption scandal broke in France. The so-called Clearstream Affair involves spies, defence contracts, money-laundering and an alleged attempt by Chirac and his Prime Minister Dominique de Villepin to smear their arch-rival, Interior Minister Nicolas Sarkozy.

In 2004 anonymous documents were sent to a French judge looking into Clearstream. The letters named Sarkozy as one of the politicians who had received a pay-off. This information was leaked to the press and was extremely damaging to Sarkozy while boosting his political

[THE SECOND AFFAIR
To be precise, this is Clearstream Affair No. 2 and should not be confused with Clearstream Affair No. 1. The first Affair centres on Clearstream Banking S.A., a clearing bank based in Luxembourg, the secretive, French-speaking enclave sitting off France's right shoulder. In 2001, both French and E.U. police began investigating Clearstream as a major platform for money laundering. Investigators are now looking into the hundreds of undeclared accounts it operates on behalf of French politicians including the major players in the Elf-Taiwanese frigate scandal].

rival, Villepin. But an investigation then showed the letters were extremely sophisticated forgeries. Attention then focused on three questions: who fabricated the evidence? Why did they act? And above all, at what point did Villepin and Chirac know what was going on?

The two magistrates now looking into the affair have suggested Villepin and his boss, Chirac, not only knew from the start of 2004 that Sarkozy was innocent but that they might have ordered the French secret service, the D.G.S.E. to frame their cabinet colleague.

Sworn testimony from the spy chief General Philippe Rondot suggests that Villepin told him in January 2004 that he had Chirac's authority to conduct an investigation into Sarkozy. In notes seized by the judges, Rondot showed his masters' concern that his work remain secret. The words "protect the president" appear and Rondot quotes Villepin as saying: "If we appear, the President and me, we're done for."

Villepin and Chirac have reacted with outrage. The President went on television to denounce the "dictatorship of rumour" and the Prime Minister has told the National Assembly there was no secret inquiry. But the atmosphere inside the government is now poisonous, with Sarkozy – who has made himself a civil plaintiff in the case – demanding that the full truth be told. In the latest move, the magistrates sent in the police to raid the headquarters of the D.G.S.E. for further evidence.

Vingt-Neuf

France's Internet

Minitel – the 2CV of Information Technology

In the 1980s, France thought it had stolen a lead on world telecommunications – with Minitel. Today, this clunky pre-Internet communications system has been blamed for the national phone company's gigantic debt and the growth of a bizarre porn industry.

THE ALLURE OF DURAN DURAN:
"Minitel machines are a pure product of the early 1980s. They look like a cross between a mobile phone, a T.V., and a computer, and in many ways they are. Our version was a four-pound, beige plastic box, equipped with a built-in handle, featuring a 5 x 7-inch greyish-glass screen protected by a collapsible brown keyboard and old-fashioned springboard keys. Its earth-tone colouring and Duran Duran allure evoked the years when disco was going belly-up, but neon colours still hand't hit." Jean-Benoît Nadeau and Julie Barlow, Sixty Million Frenchmen

B y the end of the 1960s, only 60% of French households had a telephone (even tiny, concretised East Germany had 78% phone penetration). For a nation making its own atom bombs, it was unacceptable that France could be a third-world country when it came to communications. The government ordered the Direction Générale des Télécommunications (D.G.T.) to modernize the phone system and so Minitel was born.

Minitel is technically a "dumb computer", one of the dumbest. These are not anything recognisable as a P.C. Instead, they provide minimal brain power and the graphic capacity of a typewriter. All you can really send and receive is text, mostly in black and white, and usually against a dark background. In 1983, the D.G.T., which had turned into France Télécom, distributed millions of these boxes free across France – and suddenly it was *bienvenue au Jet-Age*!

Now the French could use the blender-sized box plugged into their phones to look up numbers, shop, make hotel reservations and get news, weather and stock reports. It was like France Télécom had combined the phone with a newspaper that didn't run photography – but more expensive. (It still is. The first three minutes of Minitel connection are free, but then consumers pay a per-minute fee of 2 cents to €1).

Naturally, the French were cock-a-hoop at their new toy (bear in mind, the rest of the world was still marvelling at that other new breakthrough in communications, the fax). By the start of the '90s there were 6.5 million Minitel terminals in France, 80% of them in private households. By 1996, there were an estimated 17 million Minitel users in France, almost 30% of the population.

Its growth was all down to the popularity of Minitel's chat services. At first, consumers began using the bottom line of a naval battle game to type simple messages to one another. The Minitel team recognized the potential and so constructed the *Messageries Conviviales* service – the first chat rooms. They soon accounted for about 20% of Minitel traffic.

What the French were chatting about was, naturally, sex. This led to

MINITEL ADDICTION

" *Like the Internet, Minitel creates its own bizarre addictions – they just cost a lot more.*

" *'In 30 days, there are 720 hours. How many hours would you say our first addict spent online in 30 days?' Landaret asked me. I figured that a truly obsessive user could devote about half that time to chatting online, given time for meals and normal sleep.*

" *'520 hours' he finally declared grimly.*

" *'What is the maximum number of hours that a single person can spend in front of a terminal without leaving it to drink, eat, or sleep?' was Landaret's next question. I guessed a few hours, five or six maximum.*

" *The maximum we recorded was seventy-four. What do you think the maximum bill for a period of two months might be?'*

" *'I guessed $1,000 or more. Landaret came back with another stunning figure – more than $25,000."* Howard Rheingold in conversation with Michel Landeret, Minitel content provider, from The Virtual Community, *second edition, 2000.*

the creation of *messageries roses* or sex chat lines. These proliferated wildly with chat services springing up to service the entire spectrum of French sexuality which, according to *Le Guide du Minitel* (the Minitel directory), apparently includes never-ending multi-user, painstakingly typed orgies (contributing to the to explosive growth in Mavis Beacon and YESolo touch-typing courses across France in the 1990s) to chat rooms specifically for "*les types qui adorent les fromages*" (men who love cheese – presumably not in the platonic sense).

In 1985, heavy traffic generated by these sex lines caused what remains the system's only large-scale crash, drawing the attention of the national news media. At its peak, the *messageries roses* represented about 4 million hours traffic a month though this has now dropped to about 1.5 million hours per month. "And in my opinion, about a million of those hours every month are through the chat services that create 'false persons'", comments Henri de Maublanc, a former France Télécom executive. These are the *animateurs* that the sex-chat services hired to keep conversations going, almost all of them being young men whose job is to pretend they are young women.

THE ANIMATEUR EXPOSED
"My friend Annick knew a young fellow named Denis, an actor whose day job was to pretend to be several women at a time, via Minitel, from 8:00 p.m. to 2:00 a.m., three days a week, plus all weekend from 8:00 p.m. to 4:00 a.m. for thirty francs an hour. I met Denis at Annick's house, and he used her Minitel terminal to show me what he did during his work online. He gleefully explained that it was a fun job for an actor, to try to create four or five different women at once, and keep up four or five conversations with credulous men, preventing them from guessing the duplicity as long as possible. Denis was cynically gleeful about his performance: 'This fool still believes I'm a woman!'."
Howard Rheingold, The Virtual Community, *second edition, 2000.*

The French don't seem to care. In October 1991, as politicians raged against the "moral pollution" of Minitel, a Harris France opinion poll showed that 89% of the French people polled were against banning the *messageries roses*.

Minitel use peaked in 1997, with about 6.3 million free terminals in use. Today, around 4 million terminals are still used although traffic has been falling by 20% a year since 1998. The slow, clunky network faces almost inevitable death by Internet, its faster, freer and even more sex-stuffed rival.

That said, there is nothing that the French enjoy more than a losing battle (as if they had any choice). To the exorbitant cost of launching Minitel is now added the cost of successive relaunches – and an attempt to integrate Minitel's black-and-white, text-only services onto the Internet. All this has contributed to France Télécom's current debt levels of €57 billion ($70 billion).

NOT FOR EXPORT
"Minitel's place in this story is not merely a nostalgic one; the boondoggles of the 1980s begat the hubris of the 1990s. Ultimately, the Internet overtook Minitel, despite France Télécom's global aspirations. The Minitel was too proprietary, too limited and too French to be successful internationally." Brian Carney, International Policy Unit.

The English language flavour of the Internet is unlikely to be overwhelmed by the Trojan donkey from France. The French are very aware that only 2% of all Internet data is in their home tongue. In 1997, Prime Minister Lionel Jospin recognised the truth when he complained bitterly that the huge investment of national pride in Minitel, "this defiantly French invention", was retarding his country's commercial presence on the Web.

The brown box still holds a place of choice in more than 20 million French households. And for as long as it still provides a revenue stream for cash-strapped France Télécom, Minitel is likely to rattle on for many years, derided and outdated, but beloved and very French, like that other redoubtable zombie, the 2CV.

The Dirty Dogs

The French and their Dogs

The French are generally believed to hate everything, even themselves. So why do they love their dogs so much? Though not enough, admittedly, to clean up after them.

MERDE MOST FOUL
"All persons accompanied by a dog are henceforth obliged to remove immediately, by whatever means is appropriate, all deposits that said animal abandons on the public highway, including pavements and gutters, as well as in squares, parks, gardens and green spaces." One of the 200,000 new signs that appeared in Paris during 2002 as the city once again tried to persuade its dog owners to clean up after their pets.

I once saw a woman fly in Fréjus, a little town in the south of France. I walked out of the darkness of the lobby of the Auberge des Adrets and saw her in the blazing sunlight flying above the pavement on the other side of the road. Not exactly flying, more floating. She was absolutely horizontal, looking up at the sky, and hanging about two and a half feet off the ground. She was middle-aged, she wore a headscarf and a beige kind of housecoat. Her shopping bags, one held in each hand, hung down either side of her. I saw all this in a split second. It was noon.

Then she came down with a muffled thud, a whole body impact that knocked the breath out of her. People ran over while she lay on the stones waggling her arms and legs like an upturned beetle. There was also a horrible smell. She wasn't hurt, she was younger up close. She got up, very embarrassed and then very angry. She brushed off her helpers and walked away.

Looking after her, I saw a bright orange streak running down the back of her coat. It matched an orange skid mark on the ground where she had fallen. Thirty yards away, she stopped, emptied her pockets of small things into one of the bags, took off the coat and threw it in a bundle onto the road, then walked on.

Just another simple dog turd-related incident in France.

Figures aren't available for the whole of France but in Paris there are 650 *glissades* – "slip-ups" – on dog mess every year that require hospitalisation. Not surprising, since France's pet dogs drop 16 tonnes of rich, steaming shit on the street each day. That's an annual 5,840 tonnes, a load equivalent to two-thirds of the Eiffel Tower or 3,000 Citroën Xsara Picassos.

It is a strange fact that the French have more pets per head than any other nation, including 7.6 million dogs; strange, because when it comes to animals, the French have a tendency to shoot, poison, trap, crush, stuff and then eat almost any living thing smaller than themselves. After all, this is the country in which box-nets are laid down across the Aquitaine countryside to trap skylarks and in which, every May, Languedoc hunters celebrate spring by blasting turtledoves out of the sky.

But dogs are different. More than half of all French households have a pet with about a quarter owning a dog. The most popular breed is naturally the poodle (9.3%, according to French pet food manufacturers, FACCO) but all the smaller, yappier types are favoured (with rat-like Yorkshire Terriers coming in at 5.6% and Spaniels at 4.6%). A bizarre sight to be experienced in almost every French city is the local, crop-haired gangster sinking brandy in some seedy back street bar at ten in the morning, cradling a coiffeured

NOT FOR EATING
France has more household pets per head than any other country.

21.4 million fish
8.1 million cats
7.6 million dogs
5.7 million birds
1.5 million rodents

DOG IN A BAG
If you travel by bus or train in a French city, you will often see cute little dogs poking their heads out of their owner's handbag or shoulder bag. This is not a fashion statement. It's because the owner doesn't have to buy a dog ticket – if the dog is stuffed into a container it classifies as hand luggage. This is not good news for blind travellers like Briton Verity Smith, who is currently suing French railway operator S.N.C.F. for insisting she buy a ticket for her guide dog. "The French only count you as disabled if you are in a wheelchair, and since my dog is sighted, she has to buy a ticket."

toy poodle, sometimes in doll's clothes, under his armpit.

The French love their doggies deeply, perhaps even more than they do other humans. Certainly it seems easier for a dog to get a seat in a five star restaurant. No one turns a hair at the sight of a dog, sometimes with a napkin tweely tucked into its collar, sitting at table, on its own chair, at even the most exclusive eateries. Some even offer special canine menus. They get in everywhere including parks, shops, cinemas and even, as one British visitor complained when his wife went into premature labour, hospital emergency units.

They're everywhere you go and, if they're not, then their crap is. Paris spends €9-14 million ($11-17 million) a year clearing up its dog dirt. In 1998 the city hygiene department calculated that the cost to the taxpayer worked out at some €5.20 ($6.40) a kilo, or roughly 50 cents (62 U.S. cents) a turd. This is nothing compared to the €3 billion ($3.7 billion) spent every year on French dog food – and its end products carpet the pavements.

The trouble is, French dog owners just won't clean up after little Toutou. A variety of expensive initiatives have been tried to solve the poo problem, none of which has worked. One included a series of "doggy loos", each one costing €7,000 ($8,600), but these proved unsuccessful since the dogs refused to go "on order" and preferred to find their own tree or footpath, much like their owners (the French penchant for public urination, as noted most recently in Sarah Turnbull's *Almost French* (2004), is a psychosis deserving of its own textbook). Another scheme involved recruiting fifteen "canine counsellors" to reason with often argumentative Parisian dog owners and guide them politely in the direction of the gutter. The counsellors found that the owners preferred to set their dogs on them. That's an occupational hazard. French dogs bite 500,000 people annually, most of them children between one and fourteen but also including 1,900 postmen.

DOG'S BREAKFAST

The Trianon Palace is a four-star hotel in Versailles. In 2003 it launched a VIP service for dogs . This includes a room service menu for dogs and a gourmet bill of fare offering pure beef hamburger, fillet of fish or chicken breast – all served with fresh vegetables. "We also propose dog biscuits for those who have a specific dietary or religious requirement," said Trianon Palace spokeswoman, Vanina Minassian-Sommer. Dogs may sleep in a designer basket with a luxury blanket and pamper themselves with a range of pet toiletries such as a fragrance called "Oh My Dog!" Other services, including "psychological support", are available for a supplement.

EXECRABLE ART

France, the home of surrealism, has inevitably found an artist who makes "works of art" out of dog mess. Whenever the artist, known only as Cho, finds likely material on the pavement where he lives in the capital's eleventh arrondissement, he draws around the mess, sticks a specially-made flag in it and signs and dates the spot. "I am raising public awareness about the problems of street pollution and making a statement about the war in Iraq", he says. The point is that the turds have turned Paris streets into minefields for anyone who walks down them, apparently.

The next most gloriously stupid solution was a fleet of seventy *motocrottes*, bright green mopeds with an attachment for turd capture even while mobile, introduced when Jacques Chirac was Mayor at an annual cost of €4.2 million ($5.2 million). The mosquito whine of these scooper-scooters was a regular and annoying feature of Paris' soundscape until scientific analysis showed that picking up dog mess at high speed usually resulted in catching only 20% of the object while the rest emerged as a fine brown mist over anyone and anything within a ten metre radius.

NO SHIT

"The problem of la merde *remains. Why? No 'SENS CIVIQUE'. The idea is: when I'm out on the street, I do what I want and my dog does what it wants where it wants which most of the time is RIGHT IN THE MIDDLE OF THE SIDEWALK. As a result, the City of Light has become laced with filth." Harriet Welty Rochefort, American expatriate and ardent Francophile puts her finger on why the French don't clean up after their dogs,* Letter From Paris, 2002.

Nothing seems to work. Only very recently have fines been introduced for dog owners who refuse to clean up after their pets. These are set only at €400 ($494) for repeat offences, unlike the €8,000 ($9,870) first offence tariff imposed over the border in spotless Switzerland. Anyway, as one defiantly lazy dog-owner interviewed by the *Guardian* newspaper made clear: "We won't pay them anyway. People will get up at 2 am to avoid the cops if we have to," which would rather seem to obviate his laziness in the first place. The authorities are in a losing battle; there are only two "dog police" per arrondissement but one dog for every three Parisians.

It was the French philosopher Voltaire who said that a dog is a creature who will love you more than you love yourself. But, even for a dog, the French must be a stretch.

The Indochina Syndrome

Imperial Meltdown at Dien Bien Phu

How French bungling of a forgotten battle in a far-away war shaped international politics for half a century and destabilised south-east Asia.

"I fight the war like a game. I like combat, the risk, like others enjoy bowls or fishing. I fight for myself, for my legionnaires, for the Legion – France??? Yes, I believed when I was younger, but the mentality of most of the French is so rotten that I cannot pretend to fight for them." Lieutenant Basset, 2ᵉ étranger, Indochina, 1952.

A cluttered village, peopled by Hmong and Black Thai families, it lies in the Muong Thanh valley of north-west Vietnam. Shaped like a heart, the valley, 20 km long and 6 km wide, is cupped by steep, jungly mountains. In the centre, on the banks of the Nam Yum River, is Dien Bien Phu. Fifty years ago, it was the scene of a military fiasco catastrophic even by French standards.

France's empire has long ebbed away, leaving not much trace. Always smaller than the British, its administrators invested only haphazardly in its infrastructures, institutions or peoples. While English remains the official language of 1.2 billion Indians, less than 1% of the population of Vietnam, the jewel of France's Asian empire, now retain any French at all. Perhaps this was because France rarely considered its overseas possessions as more than a playground for its freebooting army, historically too unreliable to keep at home.

It is now largely forgotten that there were two Vietnam Wars (except by the Vietnamese who suffered in both). In the 1950s, the first was being lost by the French. At talks being held in Geneva, French negotiators had already acknowledged the inevitable with– drawal. All that remained was haggling over the small print of independence.

In Indochina itself, General Henri Navarre's strategy of launching search and destroy raids from a network of armoured bases had managed to stalemate the Viet Minh which itself had suffered 280,000 dead in the eight years of war.

Except, for the French army and its hardcore paratroop and Foreign Legion (*Légion Etrangère*) officers, this was not enough.

TIME RUNS OUT FOR THE FRENCH

Indochina was a federation of French colonies in south-east Asia: Cochin China, Tonkin, Annam (which now form Vietnam), Laos and the Khmer Republic (now Cambodia).

1884-85   *France seizes Annam and Tonkin after the Franco-Chinese War, ruling through puppet Emperors.*

1940   *Vichy France accepts Japanese occupation of Indochina, keeping the French in place to run the territories.*

1945   *After the war, French attempts to regain control are opposed by the Viet Minh, an organisation of Communist Vietnamese nationalists under French-educated Ho Chi Minh. A force of British and Indians restore French authority.*

1950   *Ho declares an independent Democratic Republic of Vietnam, recognised by the fellow Communist governments of China and the Soviet Union. The war against French occupation intensifies.*

May 1954   *The Viet Minh win military victory over French forces, leading to the partition of Vietnam into North, under Viet Minh control, and South, called the Republic of Vietnam, which has the support of the U.S.A.*

Navarre's staff wanted a victory. Operation Castor was created to provide it. The plan, so top secret that even the government in Paris was kept out of the loop, was to create a massive *base aéroterrestre* in the north behind enemy lines, fill it with tough, leathery paras and legionnaires and, when General Vo Nguyen Giap's Viet Minh were drawn to the bait, smash them once and for all in a set-piece battle. The base was 500 kilometres from the French-held capital of northern Vietnam, Hanoi, but this was irrelevant since the troops could be supplied by air. The place chosen was Dien Bien Phu.

ALWAYS TIP THE WAITER
During the Versailles Peace Conference after the First World War, the French delegation complained of being "annoyed" by an informal group of Vietnamese waiters then working in Paris. Their petition for Vietnamese self-government within the French Union of Nations was dismissed out of hand. The leader of the delegation, Nguyn Sinh Cung, was a pastry chef who had trained under the famous Escoffier. Humiliated, he threw himself into Communist organisation and changed his name to Ho Chi Minh. The American actress Mae West recounted that she met "Ho Ho Ho something" while she was staying in the hotel where he worked. "There was this waiter, cook, I don't know what he was. I know he had the slinkiest eyes though. We met in the corridor. We – well..."

The French government did not want a battle. Peace with "Uncle" Ho had nearly been agreed at Geneva and a unified state was on the cards. When it finally heard of the operation, it rushed its representative, Admiral Cabanies, to Saigon to stop it. But when he arrived on 20 November 1953, 5,000 paratroopers had already seized the village, led by three generals who insisted on jumping first.

The completed camp consisted of a central position, with airstrip and dispersals for Bearcat fighters, guarded by an uneven circle of ten outlying firebases. The garrison was made of up twelve paratroop and legion battalions supplemented by Algerian and Moroccan *tirailleurs* and Thai troops. In total, around 14,000 men, backed by twelve Chaffee tanks and twenty-eight heavy guns.

Castor was a dazzling success right up until the moment the French made first contact with the enemy on the afternoon of 13 March 1954. What the high command had not realised was that Giap had infiltrated four divisions, around 45,000 regular troops, right under its *képi*. Along with two hundred artillery pieces carried by hand through the jungle by 75,000 porters, this army was now sitting in well-camouflaged positions in the ring of mountains directly overlooking the camp. They were delighted to see that in the interests of smartness, the French had cut down almost every tree in the valley, removing the only available cover.

THE COLONEL'S LADIES
Base commander Colonel de Castries organised the defences in a "clock" of independent firebases around the central airstrip, called "Gabrielle", "Beatrice", "Dominique", "Eliane", "Isabelle", "Claudine", "Françoise", "Huguette" and "Anne-Marie". Asked by his Intelligence Officer for the rationale behind the codenames, de Castries informed him that they were the names of his mistresses.

The first real inkling the French had that the Vietnamese were attacking in strength came when two regiments popped screaming out of trenches just two hundred yards from the *Beatrice* firebase and stormed it. Meanwhile, Viet Minh guns knocked out the airfields, blowing up planes, munitions and fuel. "The shells rained down on us without stopping like a hailstorm on a fall evening", recorded Legionnaire Sergeant Stefan Kubiak. "Bunker after bunker, trench after trench, collapsed, burying men and weapons."

OVERCONFIDENT. . .

December 1953: French Artillery Colonel Charles Piroth, deputy commander of the forces at Dien Bien Phu, stated: "Firstly, the Viet Minh won't succeed in getting their artillery through to here. Secondly, if they do get here, we'll smash them. Thirdly, even if they manage to keep on shooting, they will be unable to supply their pieces with enough ammunition to do us any real harm."

As the Vietnamese attacked in "human waves", it became clear that the French had failed to take basic precautions. The officers thought the construction of deep defences would be an admission of fear. Most positions were vulnerable not only to Viet Minh artillery but also to the monsoon, about which the French seemed to have forgotten. The valley of Dien Bien Phu always received more rain, almost five feet, than any other valley in northern Indochina. Giap had counted on the heavy rains and low cloud cover to hamper French air support and aerial resupply. The French found themselves pinned down in a drowning swamp.

Fifty-seven days of losing battle followed. The historian Bernard Fall described it as "hell in a very small place". Base commander, lanky, aristocratic Colonel Christian Marie Ferdinand de la Croix de Castries, was not the man to turn back the tide. He isolated himself in his central bunker to dine off the family silver laid out on a spotless white tablecloth.

Infuriated at his passivity, his paratroop colonels took effective command. This made things worse since their dashing frontal assaults to retake the firebases lost one by one were repulsed by entrenched Viet Minh machine gun fire.

All sense of competence seemed to lose the besieged. On 22 April De Castries (bizarrely promoted to Brigadier-General over the radio by an insensible Paris) was pushed by the colonels to order a night attack on the captured Huguette base. The Second B.E.P. (*Bataillon Etranger Parachutiste*) marched into a wall of fire thrown up by the Vietnamese guns. They could not call for support since their battalion commander, deep in his bunker, had his radio tuned to the wrong frequency. They suffered 150 casualties.

Despite the spiralling situation, the French were still pouring men and supplies into this long-lost battle, including untrained reserves who, with oblivious courage, were volunteering to jump into the hell-

. . . AND OVERBLOWN

In the first 48 hours of the attack, Colonel Piroth's crews in open, undefended gun emplacements took terrible losses. He had fired over 25% of his total 105-mm ammunition without effect. He toured the command posts under heavy fire to apologise for his failure. With tears in his eyes, he said: "I am completely dishonoured. I have guaranteed that the enemy artillery couldn't touch us – but now we are going to lose the battle. I'm leaving." He went into his dugout and laid down on his cot. Since he had lost an arm in an earlier battle, he could not load his pistol so he pulled the pin from a hand grenade with his teeth and held the explosive charge to his chest.

hole. As the base perimeter shrank, many dropped straight down the gun barrels of the Viet Minh.

With the landing strip wrecked, Dien Bien Phu could only be supplied by air drop, and only when the driving monsoon rains allowed. Even then, incoming C-47s had to risk the fire of Giap's A.A. batteries which the French intelligence services helpfully informed the base "could not be operated, being too advanced for the Vietnamese". Of the 420 aircraft available in all of Indochina then, 62 were lost in connection with Dien Bien Phu and 167 sustained hits.

Just to survive, the garrison required 200 tonnes of supplies a day to maintain combat effectiveness. The tired and hungry French were never able to drop more than 120 tonnes. Because of the murderously accurate flak, parachute drops could only be made over 8,500 feet, so most of the supplies landed on the Viet Minh, including de Catries's new general stars and a celebratory bottle of champagne. In the last phases of the battle, Vietnamese artillery used 105 mm shells captured from French parachute drops and dressed their shock troops in French para camouflage and steel helmets.

On 4 May the Legion paras in Huguette were submerged by the 308th "Iron Division" and three days later the rest of the French positions were over-run. De Castries, in faultless dress uniform with white gloves, was captured in his command bunker, proving that in today's wars victory goes to the general with the least impressive costume.

The starving and exhausted garrison was rounded up. Nearly two thousand had been killed during the siege. Another seven thousand were to die on the fifty-six day, six-hundred kilometre

"I TOLD YOU SO"

Not all French generals were convinced that Dien Bien Phu would be a great victory. On 19 November 1953, as the first French paratroopers were dropping into the valley, the overall French commander for northern Vietnam, General René Cogny was interviewed by a Newsweek *reporter. "This is headed for disaster," said Cogny. Pressed to explain what he meant, Cogny explained, "Navarre [the supreme commander] won't give me enough troops to hold the high ground around the valley," he said. Told that the nearest enemy units were two hundred kilometres away, he replied: "You don't know Giap". When the battle was good and lost in April 1954, six months later, Cogny had to be escorted from a staff meeting having informed General Navarre: "If you weren't a four-star general, I'd slap you across the face".*

THE BILL

Between 19 November 1953 and 8 May 1954, Giap engaged the equivalent of 17 French battalions or 15,709 men. Killed in action were 1,726; missing were 1,694 (most of the captured were to die of malnutrition, disease and exhaustion); wounded, 5,234; deserters 1,161 . The Viet Minh counted 11,721 prisoners, including 4,436 wounded. Under the Geneva Accords, the Viet Minh returned only 3,290. Some 7,570 – about 70% of the survivors – died on their way to and in POW camps, where they stayed for years. Viet Minh gunners shot down 48 French aircraft. Approximately 12,000 Viet Minh troops died, and 30,000 were wounded.

march to the prison camps in the north and in captivity that was to last until 1958. Eight thousand miles away in Geneva, the Vietnamese and Red Chinese delegations attending the nine-power conference intended to settle the Indochinese conflict, toasted the event with pink Chinese champagne.

Bungling Dien Bien Phu meant the final and immediate end for the French in Asia. Now there would be no gradual, consensual transition. After its smashing victory, Ho Chi Minh's Viet Minh dug its heels in, refusing to dissipate its political control over the territory held in the north by joining the nominally democratic south. Vietnam was formally divided into two warring camps.

AND WHO PAID

The Eisenhower administration in the United States was determined to "contain" Communist influence in south-east Asia. By 1953, the U.S. was paying 80% of the war's costs. As Dien Bin Phu descended into chaos, plans were made to support the garrison using U.S. B52s from the Philippines. Vice-President Nixon even suggested dropping two tactical nukes in the forests around the camp. Luckily, the French, convinced of victory, refused the offer. Later, President Johnson committed over 540,000 U.S. troops to Vietnam to plug the gap left by the French in the "containment" zone. Ironically, the first Americans to die in the Vietnamese war were two civilian pilots, James McGovern and Wallace Buford, shot down as they tried to resupply Dien Bien Phu.

Defeat had not been a foregone conclusion in Asia. The United Nations had stopped – just – Mao's million-strong armies in Korea while, in Malaysia, the British won a jungle war against 500,000 Chinese communists and then gave the country its independence.

The loss of Dien Bien Phu destabilised all of south-east Asia, creating an horrific future of chaos for all its peoples. Into the gap left wide open in Vietnam by the French stepped the only power believed capable of checking the refreshed, motivated forces of the North Vietnamese and their Soviet and Chinese sponsors – the United States.

ROUND 2?

In 1963, Soviet Premier Nikita Khrushchev remarked to a U.S. official: "If you want to, go ahead and fight in the jungles of Vietnam. The French fought there for seven years and still had to quit in the end. Perhaps the Americans will be able to stick it out for a little longer, but eventually they will have to quit, too."

Too Many Cooks

A Guided Tour to French Cuisine

In France, cuisine has been elevated almost to religious status
– and its bible is the Michelin Red Guide. But is that religion
now dying? And is its bible the gospel truth?

D ying from cancer, barely able to breathe or speak, the last meal
ordered by President Mitterrand was a dish of ortolans. These tiny
birds are fabulously expensive. Then, as now, they are not only an
endangered species, they are illegal to hunt. They are consumed
according to a showy ritual which involves swallowing the bird whole while the
eater wears a napkin over their head. The corruption, cruelty and lunacy of
President Mitterrand's final supper sums up not only his career but also much of
France's attitude to food.

For a hundred years that attitude has been expressed, recorded and guided by
a single book, described as "the industry standard" (Harold Jackson, food critic,
The Guardian), "the word of God" (Paul Bocuse, French master chef) and "the
Frenchman's food bible in heft, volume and reverence" (Joe Ray, journalist and
commentator on all things Parisian).

HOW TO EAT AN ORTOLAN

"The ortolan (or bunting in England). The gourmets of France consider the ortolan, an endangered species, to be one of the world's greatest dishes. L'ortolan is a little lemon coloured songbird that weighs only a few ounces or 100 grams. First you force feed them. When they've reached four times their normal size, they're drowned in a snifter of Armagnac. Then you pop them in a hot oven for six to eight minutes and serve. Now the eating part is really far more remarkable than the cooking. First you cover your head with a traditional embroidered cloth. Then you put the entire bird into your mouth. Only its head should dangle out from between your lips. Bite the head off. The hot bird should cool in your mouth as its delicious fat drips past your tongue. Now, slowly, chew. Most appreciated are the tiny lungs and heart, which have been saturated with Armagnac from its drowning. There are those who say you can taste the bird's life essence as it trickles down your throat." Alasdair Sandford, EuroQuest, 25 April 2005.

This is the world-famous *Michelin Guide*. Every year, foodies riffle through its Bible-thin pages, red ribbon place-marker and incomprehensible symbols, to compare annual ratings of their favourite restaurants, or look to see if a chef has been elevated to the hallowed status of the three-star ranking. Then they check to see if anyone has lost their grip. For a chef, demotion can mean, literally, death.

In Mitterrand's time the small town of Saulieu in the Burgundy region often heard the beat of helicopter blades signalling the arrival of the President, flying several hundred miles from Paris for dinner at Michelin three-star restaurant, *La Côte d'Or*. It was owned and run by chef Bernard Loiseau. His signature dish was frogs' legs in garlic *purée* on a bed of parsley sauce.

In February 2003 Loiseau was informed that another guide, *Gault-Millau*, had just down-graded his restaurant. He feared that a knock-on effect would cause Michelin to drop him from three- to two-stars. He went upstairs to his bedroom and shot himself.

The French take cuisine seriously. Its landscapes have always been varied and fertile. The peasants who worked them were historically paid in kind by the land-owning *aristos*. Without money (and with sex strictly regulated by a repressive church), food became the national distraction and comfort. Many of today's French delicacies, truffles, oysters, *petits pois* and even horse, were considered either vermin or animal fodder until the French Revolution, fit only for the garbage-disposal appetites of the peasantry.

By combining and recombining available, low quality ingredients, surmises Jonathan Fenby, author of *On The Brink* (1999) the art of cuisine was created: "the original versions of modern dishes may have been horribly effective – sausage juice offsetting rotten fish, tart apple sauce sharpening the gelatine of trotters".

Over the centuries, each region developed its own distinctive cuisine based on local produce; butter from the Charente-Maritime, poultry from Burgundy and

THE GROWTH OF THE *GUIDE*

1900   *Tyre manufacturers André and Edouard Michelin distribute 35,000 booklets free to motorists. They rate restaurants primarily on the basis of whether they sell Michelin tyres.*

1908   *The* Guide *widens its scope, rating hotels in categories like comfort, amenities, price, room size and "adequate lunch and dining services".*

1914:   *Copies are issued to French troops, looking for lunch between battles.*

1920:   *For the first time, a price is charged for the* Guide. *By eliminating advertising, Michelin can select and rate restaurants and hotels as it likes.*

1931-33 *Michelin's rating system evolves into a one-, two- and three-star classification.*

1933   *Anonymous inspectors visit restaurants.*

1944   *Michelin representatives greet landing allied troops at D-Day with free* Red Guides.

1970   *Michelin recognises not everyone can afford gourmet meals and introduces a "quality meals at reasonable prices" distinction, represented by a red "R" and later by the "Bib gourmand" symbol.*

2006   *The* Michelin Guide to New York City *announced. This will feature 500 New York restaurants and 50 hotels. Reaction from Ruth Reichl, editor of* Gourmet *magazine and* New York Times *restaurant critic: "The French can say what they like but we know what we like. Who cares what they think?".*

olive oil from Provence. These foodstuffs are highly regulated by the *Appellation d'Origine Contrôlée* system, ostensibly to protect their purity (and not, as foreign exporters complain, to create *de facto* closed markets). Prices for some of the best produce are so high that food pirates are known to buy green lentils from the Cantal *département*, dye them with green ink and pass of them off as the A.O.C.-approved pulses from the neighbouring Haute-Loire.

Crimes against food are a grave business in France, a country that has no qualms in force-feeding geese to produce *foie gras*. In 2002 French superchef Jean Bardet suffered his profession's equivalent of a summary execution when a French court fined him €4,500 ($5,550) for "menu lies".

In his summing-up, the prosecutor, Christian Dreux, described the chef as a "poet of French *haute cuisine*, part of our national heritage", who had

THE TASTE OF FRANCE

" *The French insist on being reminded where their food comes from. Ideally, cheese made from cow's milk should taste like a cow, and cheese made from goat milk should taste like a goat. The nuance seemed beyond us until we tasted andouillette, a speciality made out of pig's intestines It really did taste like a pig. A French politician is famous for having said that andouillette, like politics, is better with a whiff of shit". Jean-Benoît Nadeau and Julie Barlow,* Sixty Million Frenchmen Can't Be Wrong, *2004.*

"behaved like a chop-house proprietor of the very lowest order". His celebrated two-star restaurant in the Loire valley town of Tours was found, amongst other blasphemies, to have been passing off "dairy cheese" as "farmyard cheese".

Needless to say Michelin immediately stripped him of his stars and drummed him out of its *Red Guide*. When it comes to food, what Michelin says goes without question or appeal. Last year it sold 415,000 copies in France and had a total sale of about one million for all its food guides around the world.

MICHELIN'S STAR SYSTEM
One star: "worth a visit".
Two stars: "worth a detour".
Three stars: "worthy of a special trip".

There are five other levels for judging restaurants, represented by crossed spoons and forks.

A symbol, the "Bib Gourmand", is for good value.

Until very recently, Michelin's methods were more secretive than a papal conclave. Former Michelin editor Derek Brown is prepared to say that the Guide employs seventy inspectors for Europe who visit establishments included in the guides at least once every year. They pay their own bills and work anonymously.

The precise criteria for star-dispensing are known only to Michelin. "If we published guidelines," Brown says, "we'd have five hundred restaurants all the same. We want to encourage the differences that exist".

Recently, though, Michelin's infallibility and impartiality have been questioned. In 2004, Michelin sacked Pascal Rémy, who had been working for sixteen years as a Guide inspector. He went on to spill the beans on the workings of the secretive *Guide* in his book *L'Inspecteur se met à table* (*The Inspector Sits Down To Eat*). He claims that Michelin in reality has fewer than a dozen inspectors at work at any one time and each tested only about two hundred restaurants per year, a tiny fraction of the establishments listed.

"There's a myth that 'the inspector comes each year'. In fact, it used to be every two years, and now it's every three and a half years," he writes.

To Michelin, according to Rémy, certain restaurants were "untouchable", which meant they could never be demoted. "More than a third" of the three-star establishments, he concluded, were "not up to scratch". Rémy's main complaint is that the *Guide* has become too complicit with France's chefs. "Marketing has crushed gastronomic good sense," he says.

Slowly but surely even some French are beginning to agree. While a number of famous foreign establishments, like Marco Pierre White's *Oak Room* and Nico

MICHELIN'S GUIDE TO NON-EXISTENT RESTAURANTS
"Michelin has removed one of its renowned gourmet guides from sale and pulped 50,000 copies after it emerged it carried a top review for a restaurant that had not yet opened. The Ostend Queen in Belgium had been awarded a 'Bib Gourmand' even though it opened several weeks after publication of the Benelux Red Guide 2005 *. The owner of the restaurant told a Belgian newspaper he got into the guide via his 'good relations' with Michelin." B.B.C. news, April 2004.*

Ladenis's *Chez Nico at 90*, both in the U.K., have asked not to be considered by the *Guide*, some in France are making the same request. Loire valley restaurant, *La Chancelière*, made news across France when it renounced its own Michelin stars.

Perhaps the guide's greatest challenge is that it is just too French. "One problem with Michelin has been that they tend to reward restaurants with a traditional French style rather than on their own terms," says Colman Andrews, editor-in-chief of *Saveur*, a food and drink magazine based in New York.

This blasphemy is spreading to France itself. In May 2005 Alain Senderens, one of the most flamboyant Paris chefs, announced that he was spurning his three stars and returning to simpler fare.

HOW THE FRENCH RATE OTHER NATIONS' COOKING
The 2005 Michelin Red Guide to Paris lists 399 restaurants including 10 given the top rating of three. The Michelin Guides list over 9,000 restaurants across France, with 26 restaurants receiving three stars. Germany has six three-star restaurants, Italy and Spain have four each, the U.K. and Belgium each have three and the Netherlands and Switzerland two each. The rest of the world has none.

"I want to have fun and do something else", said the man who invented the Nouvelle Cuisine movement in the 1970s. "A three-star is too formal, too stuffy. I have had enough of the obligations that go with the three stars."

Michelin's reaction to this – and other – mutinies is to ignore them. On hearing the news of Senderens' apostasy, Michelin's Marie-Benedicte Chevet icily reminded him that: "As far as the stars are concerned, it is only Michelin who can decide whether to award them or not".

Trente-Trois

O-Chirac

Too Close To Iraq?

What connects a "dear friend" of Jacques Chirac, €1.44 billion ($1.78 billion) in bribes and the Total Elf Fina oil company? Why, France's opposition to the invasion of Iraq.

LOOK WHO'S TALKING
*"We consider that all military action not endorsed by the international community, through, in particular, the Security Council, **was** both illegitimate and illegal and **is** illegitimate and illegal. And we have not changed our view on that." President Jacques Chirac, Address to G8 Summit Conference, June 2003.*

International opposition to the attack on Iraq and the removal of Saddam Hussein in 2003 was widespread and loud. It was led by the French. There were good reasons for opposing the invasion by the Coalition of fifty-one nations that in one way or another did support the action initiated by the United States. Those reasons were moral, political and legal, and all of them were voiced by President Chirac and his government.

Now, as the clouds of war recede, France's real motivations can be seen more clearly. Interesting connections are coming to light between high-up personalities in France's government, systematic bribery conducted by the Iraqi regime, the preponderant influence of the Total Elf Fina oil company and a highly dubious approach to military adventurism abroad by anyone but the French themselves

PERSONAL CONNECTIONS: "MY DEAR FRIEND"

In 1974 Jacques Chirac, then Prime Minister of France, travelled to Baghdad and met the No. 2 man in the Iraqi government, Vice President Saddam Hussein. He was the personal spearhead of a major French trade initiative to the regime based on the sale of nuclear reactors to Iraq.

In September 1975 Hussein returned the favour, flying to Paris where Chirac personally gave him a tour of a French nuclear plant. Two were sold, along with €1.2 billion ($1.5 billion) worth of weapons, including an air defence system and sixty Mirage F1 fighter planes. The Iraqis, for their part, agreed to sell France €57 million ($70 million) worth of oil.

Chirac and Hussein formed what Chirac himself called "a close personal relationship". How close is still speculated. One persistent rumour is that Hussein helped to finance Chirac's run for Mayor of Paris in 1977, after he lost the French premiership. Verified are the annual donations that Saddam made to the R.P.R., (*Rassemblement pour la République*), Chirac's political party. The relationship reached the point that Iranians began referring to Chirac as "Shah-Iraq" and the Israelis spoke of the Osirak reactor in Iraq, built with French technology, as "O-Chirac".

BEFORE AND AFTER (1)
Jacques Chirac discusses the sales of nuclear technology to Iraq in the 80s before and after it became obvious Saddam Hussein was using it in his attempt to create atomic weapons.
Before: *"Iraq is in the process of beginning a coherent nuclear program and France wants to associate herself with that effort in the field of reactors." Jacques Chirac, September 1975*
After: *"It wasn't me who negotiated the construction of Osirak with Baghdad.. I never took part in these negotiations. I never discussed the subject with Saddam Hussein.. The fact is that I did not find out about the affair until very late', Jacques Chirac, 1986*

BEFORE AND AFTER (2)
Jacques Chirac's views of Saddam Hussein before and after the Iraqi dictator was captured by the Americans
Before: *"A personal friend and a great statesman." Jacques Chirac, 1975, hosting a banquet in Saddam Hussein's honour in Paris.*
After: *"I feel exactly the same way about Saddam Hussein as my friends George Bush and Tony Blair!" Jacques Chirac, 2003, C.B.S. 60 Minutes interview.*

In 1979 Saddam seized control of Iraq, murdered his political opponents and then invaded Iran. Two years later, Israeli planes attacked Osirak facilities, claiming it was about to be used to develop weapons grade materials, and reduced it to rubble.

The French satirical and investigative magazine *Le Canard Enchaîné* published a letter from Chirac to Hussein dated 24 June 1987, which seemed to indicate that Chirac was negotiating to rebuild the Iraqi reactor. Obviously, this would have been illegal under United Nations resolutions signed by France. In the letter, Chirac addresses Hussein as "my dear friend".

DIPLOMATIC CONNECTIONS: THE €1.44 BILLION ($1.78 BILLION) BRIBES

Throughout the '90s, as different U.S. administrations prodded the United Nations into enforcing its own resolutions by isolating Iraq, the French ran static interference.

Only grudgingly did the French go along with the allied forces that ejected Saddam's army when it invaded Kuwait in 1990. After the war, the UN imposed sanctions on Iraq, including the imposition of no-fly zones over parts of the country. Almost all the enforcement resources came from the U.S. and the U.K.; France made a symbolic commitment of a dozen planes. When Iraqi forces killed opposition leaders in Kurdistan, the no-fly zone was extended from the 32nd parallel to the 33rd, a distance of about sixty miles. The French then announced that their planes would not observe the new boundary.

As America began contemplating the use of force to prevent Saddam stockpiling Weapons of Mass Destruction, France's opposition transformed from passive resistance to active blocking, both in the U.N. and outside. At one stage, a N.A.T.O. proposal to send Patriot missiles to Iraq had to be submitted through an obscure sub-committee only because it had no French representative to veto it.

There is now growing evidence that significant elements of France's political and diplomatic machinery were fuelled or, at the least, greased by bribery from Baghdad.

THE BANK THAT LIKES TO SAY "OUI".

The sole bank handling fund transfers for the $64 billion oil-for-food programme was the French Banque Nationale de Paris – Paribas, or BNP Paribas. A U.S. Congressional investigation found that Paribas made payments without proof that goods were delivered and sanctioned payments to third parties not identified as authorised recipients. Investigators estimate that the bank received more than €565 million ($700 million) in fees under the UN programme that began in 1996 and ended after the ousting of Saddam in March 2003.

In 2004 the Iraq Survey Group (I.S.G.), a 1,400-member international team, reported on the thousands of documents seized from the Iraqis after the invasion. A campaign of systematic bribery had been conducted, using the "oil-for-food" scheme by which the UN lifted some embargoes on the country to allow Iraq to sell oil for medical supplies. $1.78 billion, according to the Duerffer report, was used by Saddam to finance the campaign from funds meant to go to sick and suffering Iraqis.

Memos from Iraqi intelligence officials show the dictator knew as early as May 2002 that France, having been granted oil contracts, would block American plans for war. Iraqi intelligence officials, according to the testimony of Tariq Aziz, the former Iraqi Deputy Prime Minister, had "targeted a number of French individuals that Iraq thought had a close relationship to French President Chirac", including two of his "counsellors" and the spokesman for his re-election campaign.

A French investigating magistrate, Philippe Courroye, is now exploring how far the corruption went. Diplomats Serge Boidevaix, ex-head of the French Foreign Ministry, and Jean-Bernard Merimée, French ambassador to the UN in the 1990s, have so far admitted receiving hundreds of thousands of dollars from Iraq. A former French Interior Minister senator, Charles Pasqua, is also under formal investigation.

Significantly, Patrick Maugein, the chief executive officer of the S.O.C.O. oil company, is being questioned about his acceptance of a "gift" of 13 million barrels of oil. Maugein, a close supporter and friend of Jacques Chirac, has been accused of being Iraq's "conduit" to the President himself, an accusation still unproven.

COMMERCIAL CONNECTIONS: NO PEACE FOR OIL

Tariq Aziz, the former Iraqi Deputy Prime Minister and one of Saddam's highest-ranking officials, has told both U.S. and U.N. investigators that the "primary motive for French co-operation" was to secure lucrative oil deals when U.N. sanctions were lifted. Considerations of oil do indeed appear to have played a large part in France's opposition to the war.

> WHAT THE FRENCH REALLY WANT
> "What Messrs. Chirac and de Villepin want is significant and, for the people of Iraq, dangerous. They want Iraq's oil, and they have France's oil and industrial lobby cheering them on." Kenneth R. Timmerman, Wall Street Journal, 2003.

Before the war, France was the most favoured trading partner of the middle-Eastern dictatorship. France was its largest supplier of arms – 25% – after the former U.S.S.R. and Le Monde newspaper has calculated that, during the '80s, 40% of the French arms industry was devoted to just one customer, Saddam Hussein.

In turn, France became the largest customer for Iraqi oil. Iraq has proven reserves of 112 billion barrels of crude oil, plus an estimated 150-250 billion barrels of as yet unproven oil, the second largest reserve in the world after Saudi Arabia. These reserves are critically important to Total Fina Elf, the hugely influential French energy giant. The company had multi-billion-dollar oil contracts with Saddam but, because of UN resolutions, these contracts were not signed and could not be executed until sanctions were lifted. In 2002, even as the Coalition closed in on the Iraqi regime, Total successfully negotiated an agreement to develop the Majnoun and Bin Umar oilfields, which contain 35 billion barrels of oil, more than three times Total's current reserves.

Total Elf Fina is the world's fourth-largest publicly-traded oil company. The largest stake in the Total company is owned by Power Corp of Canada (which also has a major stake in the international bank, Paribas). The chairman of P.C.C. is French-Canadian billionaire Paul Desmarais. His brother, André, sits on the Total board. Before the war, Total expressed its "extreme concern" that its oil contracts were with the Saddam regime and that, in the event of a new government in Baghdad, they might be repudiated.

To complete the connection, Jacques Chirac spends summer holidays in the Desmarais' compound near Montreal. Other regular guests include the then French Foreign Minister, Dominique de Villepin, and Nicolas Sarkozy, France's former Finance Minister.

TOTAL COVERAGE

In 2005, after regime change in Iraq, officials from the French Justice Ministry raided Total's headquarters in Paris, investigating claims by Total's former head of operations, Jean-Michel Tournier, that the company had used a Geneva-based firm, Teliac S.A., to funnel bribes to "certain beneficiaries" in return for "political coverage to protect our interests in Iraq". The investigation continues.

Continues overleaf

IRAQ AND THE IVORY COAST: "NO CONNECTION"

In September 2002, as the U.S. was contemplating sending troops into Iraq, the French were sending actual troops into the Ivory Coast, one of its former colonies. They were there to enforce a peace deal between rebel forces and those of France's client president (one in a long line of stooges propped up by Paris), Laurent Gbagbo, that had been brokered by the French Foreign Ministry. But Gbagbo thought the French had given him a raw deal and, in resumed fighting, his forces killed nine French soldiers. The French then destroyed the tiny Ivorian air force on the ground in an air strike.

In the demonstrations that followed, 70 Ivorians were killed and over 1,000 injured by French troops firing on unarmed crowds. In a move which further infuriated the Ivorians, the French chief of the general staff dismissed claims of a "massacre", only admitting that his troops might have "wounded or killed a few people".

Disturbances against "foreign interference" became widespread amongst the indigenous population, directed against the large French expatriate community that runs France's oil interests in the country. In 2004 – two years after their entrance to the country – the French were finally given an official U.N. mandate to be there. Additional UN troops were sent to help the increasingly-beleaguered 4,000 Foreign Legion forces restore order. Accusations of routine atrocities against the French army are now surfacing. Three army captains have already testified to military authorities, that in one May 2005 incident a French colonel, Eric Burgaud, congratulated his men when they told him of the death of an Ivorian, suffocated to death with a plastic bag inside a French armoured vehicle. The officers also swore that when they reported the incident to Burgaud's commanding officer, General Poncet, he tried to buy their silence by promising them medals. The occupation continues – and so does the resistance.

CHIRAC ON THE IVORY COAST OCCUPATION:

"You bring up Cote d'Ivoire (the Ivory Coast). The situation there is altogether different. This is not Iraq. The two cases are quite distinct, and there is no connection between the two." President Chirac, B.B.C. interview, 17 December 2004.

Trente-Quatre

The Cavalry of Sodom
vs
The Pornographic Pig

The Dreyfus Affair

Sentenced for a crime his superiors *knew* he did not commit, the case of Captain Dreyfus tore France apart and left it with a stain still not eradicated a century later.

THE AFFAIR THAT NEVER GOES AWAY
"Even after a century, nothing beats the Dreyfus case for emotional power. It's an incident that never goes away, because it was rich with meaning in itself and even richer in what it exposed about the world around it. It's impossible to read modern French history without encountering, again and again, the name of Alfred Dreyfus, the Jewish army captain who was falsely convicted of trying to sell military secrets to the Germans." Robert Fulford, The National Post *newspaper, 17 October 2000.*

"DEGRADING AN INNOCENT MAN"
Early on Saturday, 13 October 1894, 35 year-old Captain Alfred Dreyfus, a junior army officer, received orders at his home in the Avenue du Trocadero in Paris to report in civilian dress to the Ministry of War.

He was met by Colonel Georges Picquart, chief of the *Section de Statistique* (Statistics Office, France's military counter-spy service), and taken to meet a solemn, uniformed officer, Major du Paty de Clam. Dreyfus was asked to write a letter, du Paty dictating, that contained the phrase: "A note about the hydraulic brake on the 120 cannon".

Halfway through the dictation, du Paty asked: "Is something the matter, Captain? You're trembling!". As Dreyfus explained that it was winter and his fingers were cold, Du Paty grabbed his shoulder and shouted: "In the name of the law, I arrest you for high treason".

Dreyfus was court-martialled in secret, convicted and sentenced to deportation. On 5 January 1895 he was brought into the courtyard of the *Ecole Militaire* (Staff College) before a full parade of his fellow officers. Watched by a mob screaming "Judas" and "Death to the Jews!", the buttons and epaulets of his uniform were ripped off and his sword was broken.

WHY DREYFUS?

Why did the French army go to such lengths to frame Dreyfus? Primarily, it was because he was a Jew, despised by his very Catholic fellow officers. After a staff college examination in 1892 he was deliberately marked down by an adjudicator, General Bonnefond, under the pretext that "Jews were not desired" in the army. Paradoxically, Dreyfus was probably more loyal than any of them. He originally came from Alsace-Lorraine and applied for the army after witnessing Prussian troops enter his home town. He was such a rigid conservative himself that one of his greatest supporters, politician Leon Blum, said: "Had he not been Dreyfus, he would not have been a Dreyfusard".

As he was marched off to spend the rest of his life in solitary confinement on Devil's Island, he only said: "You are degrading an innocent man! Long live France! Long live the army!".

SPY MANIA

Before Dreyfus' arrest, the most valued asset of the *Section de Statistique* was a cleaning lady, Madame Bastion.

Every Tuesday and Thursday, she cleaned the German Embassy. More importantly, she passed over anything she found in the wastepaper basket of the military attaché, Colonel Maximilian von Schwartzkoppen, who also acted as German spy chief in Paris.

In 1894, she found an anonymous, hand-written letter which came to be known as the *bordereau, the 'note'*. Written on thin blue paper, it was from a spy operating at a high level in the French

THE NOT-SO-ANONYMOUS TIP OFF

The most Jew-hating of all France's newspapers was La Libre Parole. *On 28 October its editor received a letter tipping him off about the arrest of Dreyfus – and sparking a storm of controversy that spread across all the entire French press: "My dear friend, As I told you, the man arrested on the fifteenth for spying and who is in custody at the Cherche-Midi Prison is Captain Dreyfus. He is said to be away but – this is a lie, as they wish to hush up the Affair. All of Israel is on the move. Yours, Henry." The letter was sent by Major Henry. When reminded that it was illegal for a military officer to communicate with the press in his own name, Henry replied that this did not apply since, as an intelligence officer, he often used his own name, "Henry" as a codename "to confuse the enemies of France".*

army and included the words: "A note about the hydraulic brake on the 120 canon". Schwartzkoppen, not exactly James Bond, had torn it up and binned it.

Bastion gave the letter to her controller, Major Hubert-Joseph Henry. For reasons only to become clear later, Henry kept the letter for some months before showing it to a superior, who happened to be Colonel Fabre. Like many of the strongly Catholic, highly conservative officer corps who wanted a return to the monarchy rather than the existing republic, Fabre was an anti-semite. He suggested that the handwriting of the *bordereau* was like that of a trainee staff officer whom he disliked, Captain Dreyfus. He mentioned that Dreyfus was Jewish. "I might have known", replied Major Henry. Dreyfus was then arrested.

Almost by accident, Dreyfus got caught up in the army's machinery. Handwriting specialists were called in, including an expert from the *Banque de France*. They agreed the writing was not Dreyfus'. It was no good, the general staff under the Minister for War, General Auguste Mercier, had already begun leaking details to the right-wing press, which was delighted at winkling out a Jewish traitor in the ranks of the French army.

That there was no evidence against Dreyfus was immaterial. At the secret trial, du Paty testified that the expert graphologists were simply wrong while Henry, the chief witness, kissed a crucifix to prove his sincerity and swore that the defendant had been identified by another of his agents "whom I cannot name". He pointed at Dreyfus and said, "And here is that very traitor".

Dreyfus was convicted by unanimous decision. He had to be. The army had spun itself into a corner. As one pro-army editorial in the newspaper *L'Autorité* made plain: "If Dreyfus is acquitted, no punishment would be too severe for Mercier".

"DOUBLE SHACKLES"

At every stop of the sealed train taking Dreyfus to Marseilles, lynch mobs gathered. At the port, though in chains, Dreyfus was punched in the face by an officer in view of a cheering crowd. He was transported to the Iles du Salut off the coast of French Guiana and placed on Devil's Island in the middle of a yellow fever swamp.

The government ordered that Dreyfus be kept in especially harsh conditions. He was kept in a small hut (only four cubic metres) specially built for him and surrounded by a fifteen foot high wall. To ensure that he did not kill himself and cheat French justice, an armed guard was posted at the door night and day. The guard was under strict orders not to talk to him at any time. Letters from his wife were checked by code-breakers and sent on as typed summaries.

In 1896, the most vicious anti-Dreyfusard newspaper, La Libre Parole, published a rumour that a Jewish "syndicate" was planning to invade the island and free him. New security measures included "double shackles" that locked his feet into place on the iron bedstead so that he could not move or turn in the boiling heat.

On 5 May 1896, he wrote in his diary (the only thing he was allowed to keep as his own in the hope he would confess): "I have no longer anything to say; everything is alike in its horrible cruelty".

He stayed there for five years.

COUNTER-UNINTELLIGENCE

Marooned on Devil's Island, Dreyfus did not know that his case was causing a building storm in France, conjured up by an unlikely ally – Colonel Georges Picquart, head of the same counter-intelligence service that arrested Dreyfus.

Picquart was a strong anti-semite and pro-monarchist. He was also a professional and concerned that even though the "traitor" had been dealt with, French secrets were still leaking to Schwartzkoppen.

Capturing one communication, he immediately saw that the handwriting was the same as that of the *bordereau* with similar spelling and grammatical mistakes. Everything matched the style of Major Marie-Charles-Ferdinand Walsin-Esterhazy, an infantry major of Hungarian family.

A gambler, a boozer and constantly in debt, Esterhazy had been attached to the French intelligence service. Unusually for a French officer, Esterhazy was loudly pro-German in his opinions which, equally unusually for an intelligence officer, he compulsively wrote down. (Piquart, following his paper trail, got his hands on one letter to a girlfriend in which Esterhazy had written: "What a sad figure these people would make under a blood-red sun over the battle-field, Paris taken by storm and given up to the pillage of a hundred thousand drunken soldiers! That is the fate that I long for!").

Picquart took his suspicions to the army general staff. Reviewing the new evidence, the generals acted at once: in September 1896, they fired Picquart from his position and posted him to far away Tunisia. Major Henry, promoted to lieutenant-colonel, took his job.

THE RIGHT STUFF

Almost everyone in the Affair behaved greedily, dishonestly and hysterically except Dreyfus himself and one other, Colonel Georges Picquart. When he took his doubts to General Gonse of the General Staff, Picquart found it was determined to keep Dreyfus in jail indefinitely, guilty or innocent.

"What can it matter to you," the general said to me, "whether this Jew remains at Devil's Island or not?"
"But he is innocent."
"That is an affair that cannot be reopened; General Mercier and General Saussier are involved in it."
"Still, what would be our position if the family ever found out the real culprit?"
"If you say nothing, nobody will ever know it."
"What you have just said is abominable, General. I do not know yet what course I shall take, but in any case I will not carry this secret with me to the grave."

Conversation quoted during Le Procès Dreyfus Devant le Conseil de Guerre de Rennes *("Appeal of the Dreyfus Case before the Rennes Court Martial") I. 440, 441, Paris, 1900.*

Picquart might have been out of the picture but, before he left, he handed over his findings to Dreyfus' brother Mathieu. He had never given up hope. He had posters pasted across Paris carrying photographs of the *bordereau* side-by-side with the new spy communication. People could see for themselves that the handwriting was identical.

By now Esterhazy was being mentioned in the press. He demanded a court-martial for himself to clear his name. The army court took less than three minutes to acquit him. The judges were particularly impressed by a new dossier put together by Henry that contained absolutely cast-iron *new* evidence against Dreyfus which could not be released to be the public for reasons of state security.

"I ACCUSE"

By 1898, four years after the original trial, France was in uproar, divided between anti-Dreyfusards, mostly right-wingers and the Catholic church who imagined some vast Jewish conspiracy to destabilise the army, and Dreyfusards, left-wing republicans who wanted to purge the army of political enemies and break the ties between church and state.

As newspapers launched vicious attacks on each other and fistfights broke out in France's National Assembly, the writer Emile Zola published an open letter in the newspaper *L'Aurore* to the President François-Felix Faure accusing the government, the army and the church of conspiring to keep Dreyfus on Devil's Island.

Tying together all the threads, Zola's letter, entitled *J'Accuse* (I Accuse) unleashed chaos. Anti-semitic riots broke out in Nantes, Bordeaux, Montpellier, Tours and Toulouse which saw Dreyfus burned in effigy and Jewish businesses besieged. In French-held Morocco, the authorities turned a blind eye to attacks on synagogues and the stoning to death of worshippers.

To calm the country, a senior government minister read out a letter

FOR AND AGAINST
During the Dreyfus Affair, each side poured hysterical abuse on the other as they fought to control the fate of Dreyfus, who quickly became secondary to the political and religious agendas of the different factions.

DREYFUSARD: *"Who is defaming this innocent man? The army of France itself, the generals of debacle, this cavalry of Sodom who know nothing but flight and surrender and bring no victories except over the French. All because they are in the hands of the Jesuits That is the root of the entire Dreyfus case." Georges Clemenceau, later Prime Minister of France, in* L'Aurore *newspaper.*

ANTI-DREYFUSARD
"...The traitor Dreyfus is now under the protection of that pornographic pig, Zola, the purveyor of filth which he now hopes to heap upon the army of France at the behest of his masters in the Syndicate [the supposed international conspiracy of Jews behind Dreyfus] *and their paymasters in turn, the militarists in Berlin." Edouard Drumont, editor of* La Libre Parole *newspaper.*

from the Dreyfus dossier supplied by Henry. This damning evidence was intended to silence the Dreyfusards once and for all.

Colonel Picquart happened to read the letter in the newspapers. He was baffled. If anyone knew the contents of the dossier, it was Picquart. He realised instantly that it was a forgery and he informed the newspapers.

ARTISTIC DIFFERENCES

During the affair, blazing rows broke out, as always, amongst France's intellectual community, especially its artists. For years, anti-Dreyfusard Edgar Degas, one of the most famous of the Impressionists, had had dinner with Camille Pissarro, an equally influential painter, a Dreyfusard and a Jew, at a friend's house every Thursday night. One night, they argued about the Dreyfus and Degas stormed out, never speaking to Pissarro again. He started abusing Pissarro's paintings as "rotten". Everyone knew that he had once been among the first to buy his friend's work. "Yes", he said, "but that was before the Dreyfus Affair". Around this time, a model in Degas' studio also expressed doubt about Dreyfus' guilt. Passers-by in the street outside heard him shout, "Put your clothes on and get out, Jew!". His mind remained unchanged when he learned she was a Gentile.

"A PATRIOTIC FORGERY"

Now came the most bizarre twist of all. Colonel Henry had led the Dreyfus investigation from the start and, with his former superior sent off to the desert, he now controlled the dossier.

What only became clear after Picquart raised the alarm was that Henry knew the real spy, Major Esterhazy, very well. They had worked together in the *Section de Statistique*. Not only were the two men close friends but Esterhazy was in the habit of lending Henry money. As the Dreyfusards applied pressure, Henry had asked Esterhazy for help to take the heat off him. Esterhazy had promptly forged some "evidence" incriminating Dreyfus and Henry put it in the dossier.

Now the only thing to do was shut Picquart up. Henry challenged him to a duel. In a nice touch, Picquart won, skewering Henry through the arm. Esterhazy also challenged Picquart but was refused with contempt. "That man," said Picquart, "belongs to the justice of his country".

Justice came swiftly but from the wrong direction. It was Picquart who was put on trial for "revealing military secrets". His lawyers,

THE PATRIOTIC FORGER

The confession and suicide of Lieutenant-Colonel Henry, the man who admitted he had forged the evidence framing Dreyfus, should have been an end to the matter. But the anti-Dreyfusards were in too deep to stop digging. In an incredible piece of political spin, Charles Maurras, writing in the Gazette de France, *came up with the idea of a "faux patriotique" ("a patriotic forgery") created by Henry as "a man of honour since the real proofs were too sensitive to reveal". This ludicrous theory was enough to keep the Affair rolling along for another year.*

backed by Dreyfusard journalists, turned the tables, proving beyond doubt that Esterhazy was not only a spy but that Henry, the head of the French counter-intelligence service, had schemed with him to fabricate evidence against Dreyfus. Now it was all in the open.

One step ahead of the gendarmes, Esterhazy took the next steamer to England where he stayed till he died in 1923. Henry was arrested and imprisoned in Mont Valérien military prison. The next day, while shaving, he cut his own throat. The army chief of staff resigned and then finally the whole government. A new cabinet was formed of moderate republicans, some known to be Dreyfusard.

At last, they ordered that Dreyfus himself, still rotting on Devil's Island, be recalled to Paris for a new court-martial. In an atmosphere charged with tension (his defence lawyer was shot in the back outside the courtroom by an unknown anti-Dreyfusard), the now white-haired and broken Dreyfus made his case before the court-martial in Rennes.

On 9 September, true to form, the panel of army judges delivered their verdict. Dreyfus was still guilty. Because of "extenuating circumstances" that they did not explain, the judges reduced his sentence from "life" to only "ten years imprisonment".

AFTER THE AFFAIR

Dreyfus did not stay in jail long. Ten days after his trial, he was granted a presidential pardon. Only in 1906, was the Rennes verdict overturned and Dreyfus declared innocent of all the charges against him.

"L'Affaire" (The Affair), as it is still known in France, did not fade away as its main characters grew old and died. Its echoes still reverberate in France today.

Its immediate effect was to unite, and bring to power, the French left wing. The Dreyfusards gleefully purged the army of monarchist and conservative officers, reducing its size by 75,000 just as the First World War approached. All ties between the French state and the Catholic church were ended (14,000 church schools were closed down).

The anti-Dreyfusards bided their time. During the 1930s, their political descendants organised into far right, fascist parties like Action Française (French

THE STORYBOOK ENDING

On 13 July 1906 the French government reinstated Dreyfus in the army as a lieutenant-colonel and Picquart as general (he was to become Minister of War). A week later Dreyfus was made a Chevalier of the Legion of Honour in the same courtyard of the Ecole Militaire where he had been degraded eleven years before. At his 'Rehabilitation' ceremony and to enthusiastic yells of "Long Live Dreyfus!", he shouted back: "No, gentlemen, no, I beg of you. Long Live France!". This storybook ending is soured by an incident that occurred when Dreyfus attended the funeral of his greatest supporter Emile Zola. He was shot in the arm by a fanatical anti-Dreyfusard journalist. His attacker, pleading "provocation", was acquitted by a Paris court.

Action). When the Germans invaded, they enthusiastically collaborated to stamp out their rivals. Left-wing intellectuals were assassinated by the *Milice* (the Vichy police) and others put under house arrest. Jewish Dreyfusards were put on trains to the death camps.

In turn, the left-wingers got their own back after 1944, getting the National Writers' Committee to blacklist their old enemies and putting collaborator anti-Dreyfusards on trial. One of them, the 77-year old writer Charles Maurras, who had invented the theory of "the patriotic forgery", was dragged from the dock to serve his sentence of life imprisonment for collaboration, screaming: "*C'est la revanche de Dreyfus!*" ("It's Dreyfus' revenge").

A HUNDRED YEARS ON

"*In sometimes surprising ways, the long reach of France's history still intrudes on the nation's conscience. How else to explain the scene on September 7 when 1,700 people, invited by France's Central Consistory of Jews, turned out to hear General Jean-Louis Mourrut, head of the army's historical service. The subject was Captain Alfred Dreyfus. Mourrut's mission on this occasion was to acknowledge more than a century later that the French army had been wrong Mourrut's appearance, in fact, was prompted by an article in the army historical journal last year that questioned Dreyfus' innocence, suggesting it was merely 'the thesis generally accepted by historians'. Such was the outcry in the French Jewish community that Mourrut's predecessor, Colonel Paul Goujac, in charge of the history division was fired for casting doubt on Dreyfus' innocence. The French never lack for new quarrels, but they never quite forget the old ones.*" Time magazine, 25 September 1995.

In 1985, the French Ministry of Culture commissioned a statue of Dreyfus. What followed was comical, as a game of pass-the-statue was played out. It took almost three years to agree where it would be placed. The obvious site, the *Ecole Militaire* where Dreyfus was publicly honoured was rejected by the army. The *Ecole Polytechnique*, which Dreyfus attended, was rejected by the Ministry of the Interior. Finally, the statue was erected in 1988 in the Tuileries Gardens in Paris.

In February 2002, Reuters news agency reported that the statue had been vandalised. Witnesses said a yellow star of David had been painted over the plaque at the foot of the statue, which had "Dirty Jew" scrawled on it.

THE PERFORMANCE YET TO COME
"*The Dreyfus Affair is the culmination of the anti-semitism which grew out of the special conditions of the nation state. Its violent form foreshadowed future developments, so that the main actors of the Affair sometimes seemed to be staging a huge dress rehearsal for a performance yet to come.*" Hannah Arendt, political philosopher, 1951.

The Horrifying Fraud

Why The French Think the U.S. Was Behind 9/11

A new urban legend is sweeping France: that the U.S. itself organised the attacks of September 11. One man has become rich and famous by pandering to France's national paranoia – Thierry Meyssan.

O n 11 September 2001 nineteen men affiliated to al-Qaeda, a militant Islamist organisation, hijacked four commercial aircraft. They flew one into each of the two tallest towers of the World Trade Centre in New York. The third plane smashed into a field near Shanksville, Pennsylvania when passengers attempted to retake the plane.

The fourth aircraft, American Airlines Flight 77 was flown into the U.S. Department of Defence headquarters, the Pentagon, in Arlington County, Virginia, just outside the capital, Washington, D.C. at 9:37:46 a.m. local time. Sixty-four people on the plane and a further one hundred and twenty-five in the building were knifed, burned, crushed or suffocated to death.

In March 2002, Thierry Meyssan published his book *L'Effroyable Imposture (The Horrifying Fraud)*. The 44-year old theology student is the founder and president of his own think-tank, *Réseau Voltaire* (Voltaire Research), named after the Enlightenment free-thinker, François-Marie Arouet de Voltaire.

His 235-page book claims that the planes that struck the World Trade Centre were not flown by bin Laden fanatics but stooges programmed by right-wingers inside the U.S. government who were planning a coup unless President Bush agreed to invade Afghanistan and Iraq to promote their oil interests. The bulk of the book centres on claims that the Pentagon was hit not by a plane but by a guided missile or a truck bomb.

The real craziness of Meyssan's book is not that it was written or published – after all, there are plenty of books in circulation by holocaust deniers and U.F.O. abductees – but that in one month after publication the French bought 200,000 copies of the book at around €15 ($19) each, making him a millionaire.

MEYSSAN'S RATIONALE

"America is severely ill and needs healing. America used to be a tremendously attractive country, the embodiment of democracy, but since 9/11 that has changed. The idea of an 'axis of evil' involving Iraq, North Korea and Iran poses a grave threat to world peace. Now this theory is a direct result of 9/11. I felt I had an obligation to investigate the September attacks and see whether the military campaign launched by the Bush administration was justified." Thierry Meyssan, interview on Chinese news website, Sina.com.

MEYSSAN'S TRUTH

"The official explanation of the 9/11 tragedy is a loony fable patched together by the White House and the Defence Department as one lie called forth another. If the energy lobby was the main beneficiary of the war in Afghanistan, the biggest victor of September 11 was the military-industrial lobby. Its wildest dreams have now been fulfilled." Thierry Meyssan, quoted in Time magazine.

The book became the fastest-ever seller in French publishing, breaking the record held by Madonna's *Sex*. It shot to the top of Amazon France's best-seller list and made it to second place in the sales list in the booksellers' weekly *Livres Hebdo*. The book and its sequel, *Pentagate*, have been riding high in French best-sellers' lists ever since.

Meyssan claims that he used an investigation team of twenty experts to put together his case. These include his French publisher, Pierre Krebs, president of a pagan sect, called the "Thule Seminar", together with other unnamed authorities in "Switzerland, Britain and Pakistan". He gathered further evidence by working from statements mostly sourced from the Internet. He did not travel to the United States to interview any witnesses. Indeed, he dismisses the accounts of witnesses to the crash of the American Airlines Boeing 757 into the Pentagon:

"Far from believing their depositions, the quality of these witnesses only underlines the importance of the means deployed by the United States Army to pervert the truth," he says.

The Horrifying Fraud is a masterpiece of constructive reasoning, literally a textbook example of how a conspiracy theory can be built around unclear official statements, unnamed "experts", unverified published facts, references to past United States policy in Cuba and Afghanistan, use of technical jargon, "revelations" about secret oil-industry manoeuvres and plonking, rhetorical unanswerable questions intended to sow doubt.

The core of Meyssan's allegations regarding the Pentagon disaster centre on his analysis of photographs of the disaster area immediately after the event. From this, he has created a set of "unanswerable questions" on which his theory is based. The questions, as the "conspiracy debunkers" at www.snopes.com have proved, turn out to be eminently answerable.

The "Unanswerable Questions" Answered:

1. *Can you explain how a Boeing 757-200, weighing nearly 100 tons and travelling at a minimum speed of 250 miles an hour only damaged the outside of the Pentagon?* Despite appearances in exterior photographs, the Boeing 757-200 did not "only damage the outside of the Pentagon". It caused damage to all five rings (not just the outermost one) after penetrating a reinforced, 24-inch-thick outer wall. As C.B.S.' *60 Minutes II* reported in its "Miracle of the Pentagon" episode on 28 November 2001, the section of the Pentagon into which the hijacked airliner was flown had just been reinforced during a renovation project that had been underway since 1993.

2. *Can you explain how a Boeing 14.9 yards high, 51.7 yards long, with a wingspan of 41.6 yards and a cockpit 3.8 yards high, could crash into just the ground floor of this building?* As eyewitnesses described and photographs demonstrate, the hijacked airliner dived so low that it hit the ground in front of the Pentagon first, thereby dissipating much of its energy that might otherwise have caused more extensive damage. However, as described by *The New York Times*, the plane still hit not "just the ground floor" but between the first and second floors because, even while disintegrating, this large object was able to plough forward and upward into the Pentagon itself.

3. *Why can we not find debris of a Boeing 757-200 in the photographs?* Because the plane disappeared into the building's interior after penetrating the outer ring, it was not visible in photographs taken from outside the Pentagon. Moreover, since the airliner was full of jet fuel and was flown into thick, reinforced concrete walls at high speed, exploding in a fireball, any pieces of wreckage large enough to be identifiable in after-the-fact photographs taken from a few hundred feet away burned up in the intense fire that followed the crash (just as the planes flown into the World Trade Centre towers burned up, and the

intensity of their jet-fuel fires caused both towers to collapse). Small pieces of airplane debris are plainly visible on the Pentagon lawn in other photographs.

4. *Can you explain why the Defence Secretary deemed it necessary to sand over the lawn, which was otherwise undamaged after the attack?* The claim that the Defence Secretary ordered the lawn to be sanded over is false. A path of sand and gravel was laid on the Pentagon lawn because the trucks and other heavy equipment used to haul away the debris would have been slipping and sliding on the grass and become mired in the Pentagon lawn otherwise.

5. *Can you explain what happened to the wings of the aircraft and why they caused no damage?* As the front of the Boeing 757 hit the Pentagon, the outer portions of the wings snapped during the initial impact, then were pushed inward towards the fuselage and carried into the building's interior; the inner portions of the wings penetrated the Pentagon walls with the rest of the plane.

6. *Can you explain why the County Fire Chief could not tell reporters where the aircraft was?* This is what he actually said to in answer to a question from a journalist: "Is there anything left of the aircraft at all?". He replied: "First of all, the question about the aircraft, there are some small pieces of aircraft visible from the interior during this fire-fighting operation I'm talking about, but not large sections. You know, I'd rather not comment on that. We have a lot of eyewitnesses that can give you better information about what actually happened with the aircraft as it approached. So we don't know. I don't know." The fire chief wasn't asked "where the aircraft was?"; he was asked, "Is there anything left of the aircraft at all?"

7. *Why can't we see find the aircraft's point of impact?* Immediately after Flight 77 smashed into the Pentagon, the impact was obscured by a huge fireball, explosions, fire, smoke and water from fire-fighting efforts. Within half an hour, the upper stories of the building collapsed, thereby permanently obscuring the impact site. It simply wasn't possible for photographs to capture a clear view of the impact site during that brief interval between the crash and the collapse.

When the book was published even the French press, which can swallow just about anything, found its wildfire appeal in France hard to stomach. The newspaper *Libération* slammed the book as "a tissue of wild allegations", marvelling at its quick rise to fame, from internet chat-rooms, via television chat shows, to best-seller.

"The pseudo-theories of *The Horrifying Fraud* feed off the paranoid anti-Americanism that is one of the permanent components of the French political cauldron", wrote Gérard Dupuy in a *Libération* editorial. Edwy Plenel, news editor at *Le Monde*, wrote: "It is very grave to encourage the idea that something which is real is in fact fictional. It is the beginning of totalitarianism".

Guillaume Dasquié and Jean Guisnel, the authors of *The Horrifying Lie*, a book that responds directly to Meyssan's *The Horrifying Fraud*, favour a different explanation for the book's success. They write of France's "profound social and political sickness", which leads people to embrace the idea "that they are victims of plots, that the truth is hidden from them, that they should not believe official versions, but rather that they should demystify all expressions of power, whatever they might be".

Meyssan is not unusual in France. *Time* magazine has reported polls that find that two out of five French people believe the U.S. government was behind the attacks and the murder of its own citizens. Those appalled by Meyssan's enrichment at the expense of the Pentagon dead and the eager credulity of the French public who so believe him will take no comfort from a comment from Meyssan's inspiration, Voltaire, who wrote in 1767:

"Anyone who has the power to make you believe absurdities has the power to make you commit injustices."

Continues overleaf

THE PENTAGON RESPONDS

"I think even the suggestion of it is ludicrous. And finally, it is just an incredible, incredible insult to the friends and the relatives and the family members of the almost 200 people that got killed here on September 11 and the thousands who were killed in New York." Victoria Clarke, Department of Defense news briefing, 24 April 2002.

THE REBUTTAL.

"I was in my Washington office when one of the secretaries told me that an aircraft had hit the World Trade Centre. We brought the news up on the projection screen in our darkened conference room and watched the coverage A short time later a friend of mine called, an Air Force officer, and we spoke awhile about the strikes in New York. I was standing, looking out my large office window, which faces west and from six stories up has a commanding view of the Potomac and the Virginia heights. The Pentagon is about a mile and half distant in the centre of the tableau.

"I was looking directly at it when the aircraft struck. The sight of the 757 diving in at an unrecoverable angle is frozen in my memory There was a silvery flash, an explosion, and a dark, mushroom-shaped cloud rose over the building.

"So, of course, I take it personally when a half-wit like Meyssan comes along saying it did not happen. The history of the twentieth century should show that no idea is so absurd that it cannot take destructive hold and play havoc with societies. When such ideas are allowed to stand, they take root among the impressionable or those predisposed to think the worst. I was there. I saw it. That is my entire rebuttal." James S. Robbins, National Review Online.

Tick Tick Tick

Countdown to Murder in the South Pacific

In the mid-'80s, the Greenpeace ship, *Rainbow Warrior*, was interfering in nuclear tests in French Polynesia. France's solution was simple: terrorism, murder and blackmail.

In 1985, the world learned that a team of "rogue agents" from France's secret service, the D.G.S.E. (*Direction Générale de la Sécurité Extérieure* – General Directorate for External Security) had sunk a civilian ship in a friendly port. As the affair unravelled, it was revealed not only that the operation was personally authorised by President François Mitterrand but that he would go to any lengths, including the direct blackmail of an allied government, to cover up the affair.

15 MAY 1985
Admiral Charles Lacoste, head of the D.G.S.E. meets President Mitterrand for an intelligence briefing. They discuss possible Greenpeace interference in upcoming nuclear tests at Mururoa Atoll. "I asked the President if he would authorise me to conduct the project of neutralisation that I had studied at the request of [Defence Minister Charles] Hernu. He gave me his consent while emphasising the importance he placed on the nuclear tests."

23 APRIL

Christine Huguette Cabon, aged 33, a lieutenant in the French Army and working for the D.G.S.E., arrives in Auckland, New Zealand, under the name of Frédérique Bonlieu, to infiltrate the Greenpeace Organisation and gather data on harbouring arrangements for a planned visit of the *Rainbow Warrior*.

22 JUNE

Major Alain Mafart, aged 34 (alias Alain Turenge of Switzerland), and Captain Dominique Prieur, aged 36 (alias Sophie Turenge, also of Switzerland), arrive in Auckland Airport from Paris via Honolulu. Both are French Army and Mafart is a graduate of the Combat Frogman School at Asporetto, Corsica.

29 JUNE

The yacht Ouvea arrives from New Caledonia and enters Whangarei Harbour, 130 miles north of Auckland. Its crew includes three French Navy frogmen and a doctor, all D.G.S.E. operatives.

7 JULY

Alain Tonel, aged 33, and Jaques Camurier, aged 35, arrive at Auckland Airport. Claiming to be physical training instructors at a girls' school in Papeete, they are the D.G.S.E. agents who will plant the charges on the ship.

7 JULY

The *Rainbow Warrior* arrives in Auckland Harbour and ties up at the Marsden Wharf. At 23:50 a bomb blast rips open the ship. A photographer, Fernando Pereira, aged 36, the father of two young children, tries to retrieve his equipment. A second bomb explodes. As the *Rainbow Warrior* sinks, Pereira drowns.

12 JULY

"In no way was France involved," says Charles Montan, political counsellor at the French Embassy in Wellington. "The French Government does not deal with its opponents in such ways." As Montan is talking, the police swoop on a French-speaking couple returning a hired campervan. Their Swiss passports identify them as Sophie and Alain Turenge. Britain's MI6 identifies them as French spies Mafart and Prieur.

15 JULY

A squad of Auckland detectives fly to Norfolk Island to interview the crew of the Ouvea. The police lack evidence to hold the crew and the Ouvea sails away, purportedly for Noumea. The yacht never arrives and is presumed to have been scuttled at sea.

9 AUGUST

President Mitterrand condemns the *Rainbow Warrior* bombing as a "criminal attack" and promises stern punishment if allegations that French agents were involved prove to be true. In a letter to New Zealand Prime Minister, David Lange, the President writes: "I intend that this affair be treated with the greatest severity and that your country be able to count on France's full co-operation". With great fanfare, Counsellor of State, Bernard Tricot is appointed to enquire into the allegations.

26 AUGUST
The Tricot Report says there is no evidence that the French Government ordered the sinking of the *Rainbow Warrior*. The report says the five agents were authorised to "observe" Greenpeace and to consider ways to counter its activities but not to carry out any actions. Tricot declares the two agents held in Auckland are "innocent". The report makes him an international laughing stock. Mr Tricot defends himself to reporters: "I have not excluded the possibility I was deceived". French prosecutors in Paris say the three Ouvea crew members will not be extradited to New Zealand.

28 AUGUST
The French Prime Minister, Laurent Fabius, says: "Our condemnation is not, as has sometimes been rumoured, a condemnation against the poor execution of a questionable project. It is an absolute condemnation against a criminal act. The guilty, whoever they be, have to pay for this crime." Fabius orders a fresh investigation into French links with the bombing.

21 SEPTEMBER
The French Defence Minister, Charles Hernu, resigns and D.G.S.E. head, Admiral Pierre Lacoste, is sacked after refusing to answer questions about the affair.

23 SEPTEMBER
Fabius calls an urgent press conference and announces: "Agents of the D.G.S.E. sank the boat. They acted on orders."

4 NOVEMBER
As their trial begins, Mafart and Prieur change their pleas and admit lesser charges of manslaughter and wilful damage. They are sentenced to ten years' imprisonment in New Zealand. Paris newspapers immediately call for an early extradition of the pair. In passing the sentence, the Chief Justice, Sir Ronald Davidson, says: "People who come to this country and commit terrorist activities cannot expect to have a short holiday at the expense of our Government and return home heroes."

30 JANUARY 1986
Talks between the French and New Zealand Governments about compensation for the bombing reach a stalemate as the French Government presses for the return of the agents.

21 FEBRUARY
France bans €6.9 million ($8.5 million) lamb imports from New Zealand. Further New Zealand products are banned from France including fish, canned kiwi fruit, fertiliser and lamb.

17 JUNE
United Nations Secretary General, Xavier Perez de Cuellar, agrees to mediate between the French Government and New Zealand.

JULY 1986: A year later, de Cuellar rules that France must pay the New Zealand Government $10.5 million ($13 million) in compensation but Prieur and Mafart are to be transferred from New Zealand and spend three years confined to the island of Hao in French Polynesia. Joel Prieur, Dominique's husband is made Head of Security at Hao Atoll.

14 DECEMBER 1987: Mafart is repatriated to France due to a mysterious stomach ailment, which cannot be treated on Hao. He is immediately appointed to the *Ecole de Guerre* (College of War) for a two-year course before taking on a staff position.

6 MAY 1988: Dominique and Joel Prieur are repatriated to France. Dominique's father is reportedly suffering from terminal cancer.

26 NOVEMBER 1991: Swiss authorities arrest Gerald Andries, one of the Ouvea's crew in Basle, Switzerland, on the warrant issued in 1985, and advise the New Zealand police. He is to be held while New Zealand police assemble a case for extradition.

5 DECEMBER: Pressure is again applied from France, aimed at crippling New Zealand exports. The French claim the settlement covered all the agents, not just Mafart and Prieur. They aim to stop the attempt to extradite Gerald Andries.

18 DECEMBER: Eighty-five affidavits have been sworn to the New Zealand police and witnesses are ready to testify. Under intense political pressure, the New Zealand Government drops the attempt to extradite Gerald Andries for trial in Auckland. He, like the rest of the thirteen-strong murder team, go free.

10 JULY 2005: *Le Monde* newspaper in France publishes extracts from D.G.S.E. reports written in 1986 that show that former President Mitterrand (now dead) authorised the *Rainbow Warrior* bombing to prevent the vessel intervening in France's scheduled nuclear testing. The same day, a commemoration is held on the coast north of Auckland where the *Rainbow Warrior* has been placed to form an artificial reef. The ship's skipper at the time of the bombing, Pete Willcox, dives 25 metres to place a memorial sculpture on the bridge while above Pereira's daughter Marelle casts flowers into the water.

Bad Faith

Why Hell Is Jean-Paul Sartre

France loves its intellectuals, and the more argumentative, outrageous and absurd the better – and the archetype of them all was Jean-Paul Sartre.

A NAUSEATING LIFE

Jean Paul Sartre, born Paris 21 June 1905. His father, a minor naval officer, dying when he is 15 months, his mother moves in with his grandfather, the priest and teacher Karl Schweitzer. Attends the Lycée Henri IV in Paris, then the prestigious Ecôle Normale Supérieure. While studying to be a teacher, meets Simone de Beauvoir, forming a long-term relationship. In 1938, publishes his first novel, Nausea. *During the war, serves in a meteorological unit, is interned and later returns to Paris to continue his literary career, which includes publication of his major philosophic work,* Being and Nothingness *(1943). Becomes recognised as a leading European exponent of "existentialism". Founds the literary magazine* Les Temps Modernes *with himself as editor-in-chief. Develops into a political activist, supporting ever more radical causes. Refuses the Nobel Prize for Literature in 1964. Offers "moral support" to the students of Paris during the 1968 riots. Dies 15 April 1980 of smoking-related illness.*

When he died in 1980 a crowd of twenty thousand turned up at Jean-Paul Sartre's funeral. President Giscard d'Estaing had already been photographed by the deathbed, brooding in a cream-coloured safari-suit. In Montparnasse cemetery film stars and politicians jostled with students, radical journalists, independent film-makers, social activists, psychotherapists, folksingers, cafe philosophers, Soviet diplomats and many pale, thin, adoring young girls.

Sartre's long-time companion, Simone de Beauvoir, put in an appearance. Though she missed the actual interment, she sat in front of the open grave for ten minutes, looking suitably pensive, while the press got their snaps. A photographer from *Paris-Match* even fell in. Oh, they couldn't have enjoyed themselves more.

Only in France would this swivel-eyed, totalitarian dwarf have merited a rock star's funeral. But Sartre wasn't a rock star, he was a philosopher, called by one newspaper "the secular messiah of existentialism", his own religion of miserableness.

WHAT'S IT ALL ABOUT, JEAN-PAUL?

"Existentialism is more a trend or attitude than a coherent philosophy. It emphasises the isolation of man in a hostile or indifferent universe, regards human existence as inexplicable, and stresses freedom of choice and responsibility for the consequences of one's acts. This responsibility, according to one of the few self-declared existentialists, Jean-Paul Sartre, leads to anxiety and 'bad faith', a refusal to accept freedom. Sartre's main philosophical work, Being and Nothingness *(1943), did much to 'popularise' the radical individualism of Existentialism in the two decades after World War II and remains influential in world philosophy."* Austin Cline, Council for Secular Humanism, 2005.

His childhood was so dingy that he almost could have made it up himself (and considering the inaccuracies in his 1964 autobiography, *Les Mots*, that wasn't beyond him). He was brought up in a small apartment in the Paris suburbs by a doting mother, who often dressed him as a little girl, and a domineering grandfather, a pastor who routinely seduced women in his congregation. Sartre's father died just after his birth, of a lingering disease.

SARTRE ON FATHERHOOD

"It is not the men who are at fault but the paternal bond which is rotten. There is nothing better than to produce children, but what a sin to have some! The death of Jean-Baptiste [his father] was my greatest piece of good fortune. Had he lived, my father would have laid down on top of me with all his weight, and squashed me." Les Mots (Words), 1964.

At the age of three, an infection caught by the seaside left him with only ten percent vision in his right eye and a brutal squint that he framed or rather accentuated with thick rimmed glasses. He grew to be 5' 2" tall. His teeth were bad ("He was scornful of even the most basic conventions of bourgeois dental hygiene", says the historian Leland de la Durantaye, " 'mossy' is a word that comes easily to mind"). He smoked heavily. He studied to be a teacher but initially failed the qualifying exam, the *agrégation*. The second time, he was luckier. His new girlfriend, a pinched, serious student from the Sorbonne, Simone de Beauvoir, coached him through the exam. He called her "The Beaver".

SARTRE ON SMOKING

Sartre's cafe regimen was fuelled, according to de Beauvoir's autobiography, by a daily intake of between three and four litres of alcohol and coffee, a dozen corydrane tablets (a mixture of amphetamine and aspirin then available over the counter; the recommended dose was two) and forty Boyard cigarettes. Sartre called smoking "the symbolic equivalent of destructively appropriating the entire world". Once he tried to give up in typical existential fashion. "In truth," he wrote, "I did not care so much for the taste of tobacco that I was going to lose, as for the meaning of the act of smoking. [I had to reduce] tobacco to being only itself: a leaf that burns; I cut [its] symbolic links with the world. Suddenly my regret was disarmed and quite bearable."
Bearable – for about a week. Sartre went on to smoke for another 40 years and died of a lung tumour that turned his body gangrenous. British philosopher A. J. Ayer commented: "Existentialism really only works on paper".

From the 1940s onwards, the couple gained a weird hold over French cultural life for nearly half a century, becoming a kind of anti-Bogart and Bacall of the *rive gauche*. They hung out in the fashionably seedy St. Germain-des-Pres quarter, at the café *Les Deux Magots* or the *Café de Flore*, drinking scotch, mocking their rivals and holding court over tables full of adoring youngsters until three or four in the morning, the air blue with cigarette smoke.

Sartre's secret was existentialism, the philosophy he laid out in *l'Etre et le néant* (*Being and Nothingness*). Life is meaningless, a "futile passion", he said in six hundred and thirty-two pages, and only a few individuals, like him, are intellectually serious enough to reject its falsities. This pessimistic message was champagne for the ears of the post-war French, especially the young (those under forty out-numbering those over in France after 1950). It provided a better, nobler reason to be depressed. Existentialism became France's first post-war youth fad. Existentialists wore black, they listened to moody jazz, they had tortured affairs, they ironed their hair (girls) or grew stringy beards (boys). To do anything else was "*mal foi*" (bad faith), the kiss of death for any existentialist. Basically, you did as Sartre did. And why not? He was a war hero, resistance fighter and original thinker.

SARTRE ON REALISING HE IS ALIVE
"The thing which was waiting was on alert, it pounced on me, it flows through me. I'm filled with it. It's nothing: I am the Thing. Existence, liberated, detached, floods over me. I exist." La Nausée (Nausea), 1938.

Or not. Sartre as war hero is pure myth. He served in a meteorological unit, tending a weather balloon. He wasn't captured, he turned himself in and was interned for a year. Nor was he a leading light of the Resistance like another famous existentialist, Albert Camus, who edited an underground newspaper, *Combat*, and had to spend the Occupation years lugging his printing press around Paris, one step ahead of the Gestapo.

"Instead", said Sartre, "I took up arms in the theatre". He put on two plays. One of them, *Les Mouches* (*The Flies*, 1943), he claimed was a coded attack on the Nazis themselves. It was so heavily coded that it got an admiring review in *Das Reich* magazine edited in Berlin personally by Goebbels. In August 1944 Sartre did write one blazing attack on the Germans that appeared in *Combat* but by this time the Americans were already in Paris. "Jean-Paul Sartre and Simone de Beauvoir entered the Resistance", concluded his English biographer, Ronald Hayman, "at the same moment as the Paris police".

SARTRE ON THE NATURAL SCIENCES
"Slime is the agony of water. It presents itself as a phenomenon in the process of becoming; it does not have the permanence within change that water has. Nothing testifies more clearly to its ambiguous character as a substance between two states' than the slowness with which the slimy melts into itself." L'Etre et le néant (Being and Nothingness), 1943.

SARTRE ON THE NAZIS
"We were never more free than in the Occupation." A typical paradox from the old word-twister. Perhaps he wasn't trying to be paradoxical; under the Nazis, Sartre managed to get two smash hit plays put on and finish off his major philosophical work, Being and Nothingness.

Perhaps none of this really matters.In philosophy, it really is the thought that counts. Then again, the core of Sartre's philosophy was not original but lifted from less showy German philosophers, including Martin Heidegger. "Sartre's *Being and Nothingness*", wrote critic Jim Holt in *The New Yorker*, "is just Heidegger's *Being and Time* with some racy passages thrown in about the anus and Italian love-making". Heidegger gave a lecture suggesting that Sartre did not actually understand existentialism. Sartre, who never refused a grudge, responded with a torrent of essays, lectures and articles, claiming it was *Heidegger* who did not understand existentialism. The spat dragged on for years.

Sartre's influence over France's intellectual life was immense. He expounded – endlessly – his ideas in two huge philosophical works, four novels (including the famous *La Nausée* (*Nausea* – described by British philosopher A J Ayer as "a title that reviews the book"), seven plays and literally thousands of articles, essays and lectures. He started his own literary magazine to publish them, *Les Temps Modernes,* and when that turned out not to be big enough to carry his output, he founded *Libération*, a newspaper that continues today as the mouthpiece of the French left. On average, he wrote twenty pages a day. Quality control was poor since he refused to edit or even read anything once written.

SARTRE ON OTHER PEOPLE
"Hell is other people."

By the mid-'50s, Sartre realised that however huge he might be in philosophy, in the real world he was just a short man with a big mouth. It was then he began his career as perennial political activist. At first this began with vocal opposition to France's war in Algeria, so vocal in fact that at one stage five thousand ex-servicemen marched past his apartment in the rue Bonaparte, chanting "mort à Sartre" ("death to Sartre"). In 1961, the right-wing terror group O.A.S. (*Organisation de l'Armée Secrète*, the Secret Army Organisation) tried to blow him up, twice, and failed. This seemed to show Sartre that he was on the right track and he began espousing causes even further to the left, like Stalinism.

The fact that the radical individualism of existentialism was illogical beside Marxist totalitarianism seems to have passed him by. When even his fellow leftist, Camus, broke with the Russians after their invasion of Hungary in 1956, Sartre turned on him: "an anti-Communist is a dog. I don't change my view on this. I never shall." Then Stalin died and Russia seemed to go soft so Sartre switched to Maoism just at a time when millions were dying in the Chinese cultural revolution. He went on to defend the massacre of Israeli athletes by Black September terrorists at the 1972 Munich Olympics.

SARTRE ON COMMUNISM
"Freedom of speech is complete in the USSR, and the Soviet citizen is constantly improving his way of life in the midst of a society that is making constant progress."

The political attitudes of an unkempt eccentric (perhaps slightly more than an eccentric; an experiment with mescaline so altered his brain that Sartre laboured under the hallucination for more than a year that he was being chased by a giant lobster) are usually insignificant but thousands of French teachers, journalists, lecturers and artists followed him on his intellectual pilgrimage into the ultra-left. One of them was a young journalist who acted as Sartre's driver on a jaunt to Germany to protest against the imprisonment of the Baader-Meinhof Group. He was Joachim Klein, who went on to take part in the attack on an O.P.E.C. summit in Vienna in 1975 as part of Carlos the Jackal's terror gang.

Sartre was not responsible for Klein's rampage but he was responsible in part for giving intellectual weight to the bombs, murders and kidnappings that rocked the world in the 1970s. "Mistaken ideas always end in bloodshed', Albert Camus once remarked, "but in every case it is someone else's blood. That is why some of our thinkers feel free to say anything". He was thinking of Sartre.

Eventually his star waned. Existentialism went out of fashion, superseded by another French philosophical trend, deconstructionism. Even Sartre's appeal to young people petered out. During the 1968 événements, when the streets of

SARTRE ON THE NOBEL PRIZE

Sartre's refusal of the Nobel Prize for Literature in 1964 was true to his idea of what being an existentialist was all about. As he said in an interview with Canadian T.V. in 1976: "To have accepted it, would have given me a little badge of distinction, a little symbol of power, which would have separated me, a worker of the mind, from other members of the proletariat". What he didn't tell the interviewer, and what wasn't known until after his death, is that while Sartre publicly and loudly rejected the prize, he then wrote to the Swedish Academy asking to have the 53,000 Kroner prize money sent on to him in secret. The Academy's reply was along the lines of: "Ha ha. No".

Paris were full of youngsters tearing up paving stones and having punch-ups with the riot police, he cut rather a ridiculous figure, standing outside a car factory and handing out a Maoist newsletter urging the workers to shoot random policemen. At one major rally, as he rose to speak, the organisers handed him a terse note: "Keep it short".

SARTRE ON THE FUTURE
"One is still what one is going to cease to be and already what one is going to become. One lives one's death, one dies one's life."

But Simone de Beauvoir stayed with him to the end, almost. Her intellectual credentials were as prominent as his. Her book, *The Second Sex* (1949), had become the bible of gender politics and the French writer and philosopher Raymond Aron, in view of her stern demeanour and light moustache, dubbed her "the father of modern feminism". A more sympathetic author, Angela Carter, asked, "There is one question that every thinking woman in the western world must have asked herself at one time or another. Why is a nice girl like Simone de Beauvoir sucking up to a boring old fart like Jean-Paul Sartre?".

The answer is, they were about as nice as each other. Sartre had stopped having sex with her after the war, his decision rather than hers, and they agreed to an open relationship so long as each told the other about their affairs, in crude detail as it turned out from their letters. Sartre went on to have a string of affairs with thin, nervy young women sufficiently intimidated by his intellect to overcome any possible distaste for his physical appearance and habits; de Beauvoir, a bisexual, did much the same. The letters reveal that in later life de Beauvoir would seduce her students and then pass them on to Sartre, consoling them with the information, "he cannot have conventional relations any more but likes to have someone in bed to talk to about himself".

SARTRE ON THE TOILET

"Sartre felt most at home in cafés and restaurants where he could annex space by dominating the conversation and exhaling smoke. To reassure his mind that it had nothing to fear from sibling rivalry with his maltreated body he constantly ignored all messages [that his body] sent out He resented the time he had to spend on washing, shaving, cleaning his teeth, taking a bath, excreting and he would economise by carrying on conversations through the bathroom door." Ronald Hayman, Sartre: a Biography,

SARTRE ON GOD

The basis of Sartre's existentialism is that man must recognise that there is no God. "The absence of God is more divine than God." He was known as one of the world's most famous and argumentative atheists. However, near the end of his life, his nerve faltered. He told Pierre Victor: "I do not feel that I am the product of chance, a speck of dust in the universe, but someone who was expected, prepared, prefigured. In short, a being whom only a Creator could put here; and this idea of a creating hand refers to God." His fellow existentialist and long-time companion, Simone de Beauvoir, had by this time had quite enough of him: "How," she asked, "should one explain the senile act of a turncoat?"

In the last years, Sartre and de Beauvoir's famous relationship soured but they found themselves locked together by their mutual fame, though heartily sick of one another. Sartre determined to cut her off from any access to the burgeoning royalties of his life's writings. To make a will or to marry one of his girlfriends would have been unthinkably bourgeois. Instead, he adopted one of his girlfriends, the nineteen-year-old Arlette Elkaïm, making her automatically his sole heir when he died in 1980. Not to be outdone, de Beauvoir also adopted a young girl, Sylvie le Bon, a student aged sixteen, who inherited her estate in 1986.

Twenty years after their deaths, their literary estates are locked in constant legal battle to prevent the publication of work by one which might possibly have been contributed to by the other. Dearly loving a feud, both Sartre and de Beauvoir would surely have been delighted.

Continues overleaf

THE NEW SARTRE?

The French have a fetish for philosophers like Jean-Paul Sartre. Entirely without practical use, philosophy is a compulsory part of the school curriculum from an early age. In France, the best known philosophers have the status of celebrity footballers however spurious their philosophy – in fact, the more spurious the better.

Jacques Derrida *(1930 – 2004), the father of deconstructionism, a philosophic approach stressing the importance of language – and non-verbal communication – in the formulation of thought. Unusually for a specialist in language, Derrida was usually unintelligible. Here he discusses the terrorist attacks of 11 September 2001:*

Interviewer: "Was September 11 [le 11 septembre] an important historical event?

Derrida: "Le 11 septembre, as you say, or, since we have agreed to speak two languages, 'September 11'. We will have to return later to this question of language. As well as to this act of naming: a date and nothing more. When you say 'September 11' you are already citing, are you not? Something fait date, I would say in a French idiom, something marks a date, a date in history. To mark a date in history' presupposes, in any case, an ineffaceable event in the shared archive of a universal calendar, that is, a supposedly universal calendar, for these are – and I want to insist on this at the outset – only suppositions and presuppositions. For the index pointing toward this date, the bare act, the minimal deictic, the minimalist aim of this dating, also marks something else. The telegram of this metonymy – a name, a number – points out the unqualifiable by recognizing that we do not recognize or even cognize that we do not yet know how to qualify, that we do not know what we are talking about."

In 1992, Cambridge University in the U.K. awarded Jacques Derrida an honorary doctorate, a courtesy often provided automatically to academics at sister universities. The university's Philosophy Department, notoriously argumentative in its own right, came together to issue a formal letter protesting against the award and accusing Derrida of charlatanism.

Similarly, the US linguist and activist Noam Chomsky has called Derrida typical of the Parisian intellectual community "that acts as an elite power structure for the well-educated through difficult writing designed to exclude others".

The Nobelest Profession

Hell Is Other Writers

Why does France dominate the ranks of Nobel Laureates for Literature? And yet feature so poorly in all the other categories?

WRITE ON

"In North America, the first thing people ask when they hear we are writing is how we earn a living. To avoid this question, we usually present ourselves as journalists. But in France, as we discovered, journalists are only of secondary interest. When we understood this attitude, we introduced ourselves as writers, and the invitations to parties, conferences, and round tables started flowing in". Jean-Benoît Nadeau and Julie Barlow, Sixty Million Frenchmen Can't Be Wrong, *2004.*

In a country with as many social, political, regional and class hatreds, and hatreds within hatreds, as France, only one profession commands universal respect: writer. This is partly due to the enduring national love affair with "*les intellectuels*" and partly because French writers rarely fail to sell out to one or other of the prevailing factions, the more fashionably radical the better. Jules Verne, for example, was a frothing anti-Dreyfusard, while Jean-Paul Sartre was variously a Stalinist, a Maoist and finally a groupie for the Baader-Meinhof terrorist group.

The rewards are huge for a French writer. Colette, an early twentieth century writer of what would now be called soft-porn but who was also a strip-tease artist, lesbian call-girl and Nazi collaborator, was made a *Grand Officier* of the Legion of Honour and got a state funeral on her death in 1953.

Ironically, many of the authors the French love the most are unknown outside France. While quite a few of their characters and ideas have crossed national borders, from Verne's Captain Nemo to Victor Hugo's Quasimodo, the "classics" of French literature, even the modern works, are usually incomprehensible to most foreign booklovers whether in the original or in translation. If you are not up to speed on formal French traditions of rhetoric and imagery, the writing can often seem as dense and turgid as the "serious" ideas they must contain to be taken seriously by a French readership. "Reading Sartre", said Ernest Hemingway, "is like eating lead".

For all this, there are more French winners of the Nobel Prize for Literature – twelve – than from any other nation. Then again, unlike other the Nobel categories of Chemistry, Physics, Medicine and even Economics where achievement is scientifically verified, or Peace, where success is judged by popular acclaim, the Literature category is based only on the opinion of the eighteen members of the Royal Swedish Academy.

Not only is the Academy modelled on the *Academie Française* (French Academy) but its members have traditionally had close ties to Gallimard, the famous and long-established French publishing house, home of many of the French Nobel Laureates and their back catalogue. Even today Gallimard publishes the French translations of the works of Lars Gyllensten who was Permanent Secretary of the Academy between 1977 and 1986.

The Nobelest Of Them All
French Nobel Literature Laureates include

1901 *René Sully-Prudhomme* (1839-1907)

The first ever winner of the Nobel Prize for Literature. A clinical depressive, his mood was not lightened by a career as a notary's clerk, an unsuccessful love affair and a stroke that paralysed his lower body. His melancholy poems are now mostly forgotten, including *Le Zénith* (1876) about three balloonists falling to their death. Even famous grouch August Strindberg was horrified by Sully-Prudhomme's award, calling it "contrary to statutes and will".

"You who will help me in my anguish,
Don't speak to me;
Play me some music,
And I will die a bit happier.

"Music heals, enchants and unties
Things of the deep.
Rock my pain; I beg you,
But mostly just shut up".
L'agonie (Anguish)

1915 *Romain Rolland* (1866-1944).

Novelist, musicologist, dramatist, essayist, mystic and pacifist. Left war-torn France in 1914 to live in Switzerland, only deciding it was safe to return in 1938. His fame rests on his ten-volume novel *Jean-Christophe* (1904-12) about a heroic novelist, musicologist dramatist, essayist, mystic, and pacifist, pronounced by Nancy Mitford to be "France's answer to the sleeping draught".

"The greatest book is not the one whose message engraves itself on the brain – but the one whose vital impact opens up other viewpoints, and from writer to reader spreads the fire that is fed by the various essences, until it becomes a vast conflagration leaping from forest to forest. It must also sell beyond three printings. Magazine publication helps."
Letter to Malwide von Maysenbug

1921 *Anatole France* (1844-1924).

France's greatest man of modern letters. Born Jacques Anatole François Thibault, he changed his name for better brand recognition. Compulsive womaniser and atheist, he was outraged whenever one of his books, usually satirical social novels or poorly researched histories, was not banned by the church. On his death, his rival Paul Valery was unwisely invited to deliver the eulogy which he turned into a ninety minute lecture on why France's writing was so bad.

"A woman without breasts is like a bed without pillows."

"Of all sexual aberrations, chastity is the oddest."

"We have drugs to make women speak, but none to keep them silent."

"All the historical books which contain no lies are extremely tedious."

1927 *Henri Bergson* (1859-1941).

Philosopher and superintellectual. His *Matière et mémoire* (*Matter and Memory*, 1896) and *L'Evolution créatrice* (*Creative Evolution*, 1907) mixed Darwinism with psychology and physics. His ideas were so impenetrable that they were lauded by both the Left and the Right who knew they must be good because they were banned by the church. Einstein himself intervened publicly to establish that Bergson's

Michael Miles: " Well your question for the blow on the head this evening is: what great opponent of Cartesian dualism resists the reduction of psychological phenomena to physical states?"
Woman: "I don't know that!"
Michael Miles: "Well, have a guess."
Woman: "Henri Bergson".
Michael Miles: "Is the correct answer!"
Woman: "Ooh, that was lucky. I never even heard of him."
Monty Python's Flying Circus

scientific theories were gibberish. While his 800-page examination of humour, *Le rire* (*Laughter,* 1900), is still rated as one of the dullest books on the subject, his philosophical work is today largely dismissed.

1947 *André Gide* (1869-1951).

The Liberace of French writing. Gide's fame rested on his ability to find a convention then flout it. His novels focused on child-molesting priests and dark, young boys who'd do anything for drugs. One of the first advocates of gay rights in books like *Corydon* (1924), his 27-year marriage to his cousin was, not surprisingly, unconsummated. Gide left for North Africa in 1942 to continue research into dark, young boys who'd do anything for drugs. In 1952, in a backhanded tribute, the church posthumously banned all his works.

"10 May 1927: Many opium smokers and cocaine addicts in Zurich. Some of them, Rychner tells me, began to inject themselves during their last year at the Gymnasium; that is, when aged sixteen or seventeen. He knows one of the naughty boys whom the professors caught using a syringe in a final examination. Cornered, he confessed that he had got his habit in class. 'Do you think anyone could endure the dullness of X's teaching without shooting up?' he asked." *Journals*

1957 *Albert Camus* (1913-60).

French author and philosopher and one of the principal luminaries (with Jean-Paul Sartre) of existentialism, the attitude that life is not simply meaningless but miserable. His novel, *L'étranger* (*The Stranger,* 1942), was hailed as a masterwork by droopy, duffel-coated students everywhere. As royalties and fame rolled in, he changed his mind, concluding life was worth living after all. Almost immediately afterwards, he died in a car crash.

"There is only one really serious philosophical question, and that is suicide. Deciding whether or not life is worth living is to answer the fundamental question in philosophy. All other questions follow from that." *Le Mythe de sisyphe* (*The Myth of Sisyphus*), 1942.

1964. *Jean-Paul Sartre* (1905-80)

(refused "in protest at the values of bourgeois society").

The archetype of the post-war French intellectual. Politicised, competitive and dismissive of opposition, he was the focal point in partnership with his lover, Simone de Beauvoir, of New Left thought. He glossed over the contradictions between his existentialist ideas about self-determination and his long-time communist principles to become the bespectacled, toadish poster-boy of the 1968 Paris student disturbances.

"The bad novel aims to please by flattering, whereas the good one is an exigence and an act of faith. But above all, the unique point of view from which the author can present the world to those freedoms whose concurrence he wishes to bring about is that of a world to be impregnated always with more freedom."

Qu'est-ce que la littérature? (What Is Literature?)

1985 Claude Simon (1913-)

Perhaps the most utterly unintelligible of all French writers ever. A convinced *nouveau roman* (new writing) author, he throws out fuddy-duddy concepts of plot, character and narrative and, in works like *Leçon de choses* (*Lesson of Things*, 1975), punctuation (except brackets, which he loves). His sentences can run to a thousand words or more which makes following the action difficult since what little action there is is also non-chronological.

"The description (the composition) can continue (or be continued) indefinitely according to the meticulousness with which it is brought to its execution, the drive of its metaphors, the addition of other visible objects in their entirety or fragmented by use, time, shock (that is to say, if they appear only partly within the framework of the whole), without counting the various assumptions from which the scene is generated, etc, etc ".

(The works of all these authors are published in whole or part by Gallimard, Paris).

France has a lot to be proud of in the field of literature, according to the Nobel Committee. But according to the same Committee, it lags badly in the other, objective categories. The French education system – especially at higher levels – is old-fashioned, emphasising rigid principles of Cartesian logic and enquiry. These help sustain a continuing if rather repetitive stream of artists, including writers, but they are not so productive in making world-beating scientists, mathematicians and chemists if France's performance in the Nobel sciences is anything to go by. It is no coincidence that Marie Curie, France's famous winner of the Nobel Prize for Physics in 1903 and for Chemistry in 1911, was born and bred in Poland.

NOBEL COUNTRY RATINGS ACROSS ALL PRIZES SINCE 1901

1. United States   261
2. United Kingdom 79
3. Germany   61
4. France   28
5. Switzerland   22
6. Sweden   18
7. Russia   11

Country of Citizenship Nobel Prizes in Science	Chemistry Nobel Prizes	Physics Nobel Prizes	Medicine Nobel Prizes	Total Nobel Prizes In Science, 1951-2002
	96	117	123	334
1. United States	45 (47%)	70 (60%)	70 (57%)	185 (55% of all Prizes)
2. Great Britain	19 (20%)	7 (6%)	19 (15%)	45 (13%)
3. Germany	10 (11%)	12 (10%)	9 (7%)	31 (9%)
4. Russia	1 (1%)	9 (8%)	2 (2%)	12 (4%)
5. **France**	0	4 (3%)	5 (4%)	9 (3%)

Trente-Neuf

The Arrow. . .

France's Flights of Fancy No. 1: Concorde

Vanity comes before a fall. Despite hundreds of millions of taxpayers' money, Concorde came to earth as a commercial failure....

LACK OF CONCORD
"It rises like a rocket but sells like a stick." British Minister of Aviation, Julian Amery, cursing the international deal that got his country entangled in one of France's most costly vanity projects.

As pure engineering (mostly British), Concorde was a dream. It cruised at around 1,350 mph at an altitude of up to 60,000 ft (11 miles). A crossing from Europe to New York took less than three and a half hours – less than half the normal flying time for other jets. "The Americans may have their missiles," said President Charles de Gaulle smugly, "but France has her Concorde".

Concorde, whatever the implications of its name, was born out of international diplomatic wrangling. In 1962, de Gaulle vetoed Britain's entry into the E.E.C., a serious economic blow, so to keep him sweet while it tried again the British government ordered B.A.C. (the British Aircraft Company) to partner

CONCORDE: YESTERDAY'S PLANE OF TOMORROW

Passenger capacity:	*100 seats*
Range:	*4,300 miles (6,880 km)*
Speed:	*Mach Two (2,150 kph)*
Length:	*62.1 m*
Engines:	*4 x Rolls-Royce / Snecma Olympus 593 engines provide more than 38,000 lbs of thrust each.*
Fuel consumption:	*5,638 imperial gallons every hour.*
First supersonic flight:	*1 October 1969*
Last commercial flight:	*24 October 2003*
Heyday:	*At its most popular, Air France Concordes flew only 23,000 passengers a year at a loss of approximately €240 ($300) a head.*

with France's Sud Aviation to make a supersonic airliner, a pet project of the ever-touchy French leader.

As far as the British were concerned, the deal was a loss-leader from the start. The minuscule French aviation industry was far less advanced than its neighbour over the Channel. Not only did B.A.C. have to share its advanced avionics knowledge with Snecma, its smaller French equivalent, but also much of the job-creating construction of the plane's body (which the French justified by claiming that the weather around their Toulouse plant was better for test flights).

Almost immediately, costs spiralled upwards. The project, funded by the French and British taxpayer, was initially budgeted at £100 million. By the time the first production models rolled onto the tarmac in 1969, the real cost had risen to £1.1 billion (£11 billion in today's money). Appalled by the overruns, British ministers had been desperate to pull out but were soothed by the assurances of their counterparts in Paris, responsible for marketing Concorde, that seventy-four orders for the aircraft had been received from sixteen airlines, half of them American.

It was all pie in the sky. By the time the aircraft was ready to fly in 1976, none of the orders had been signed and, with oil prices rising, who wanted a plane that consumed four times more fuel than a 747? The then state-run airlines, Air France and British Airways, had to take the planes, seven and five respectively, which were given to them at a nominal price of £1 and 1 franc each by their gov-

FOR THE SAKE OF AN E
One of the least of the arguments about Concorde was how to spell its name. Without an "e" (as in the English spelling) or with (as in the French)? When the British announced they preferred the English spelling, the French protested and threatened to withdraw from participating in the design and writing of all materials associated with the aircraft (from technical manuals to press releases). With the aircraft's launch imminent, the British conceded the point .

ernments. The earthbound British and French taxpayer was lumbered with the write-off.

With only twenty ever built, Concorde became an expensive toy for the super rich flying the Atlantic to New York (since Concorde's sonic boom broke both European and U.S. noise regulations, it was never allowed to fly over land). British Airways, which was privatised in the mid-'80s, just about made its service pay by charging £8,000 a ticket but Air France, with a smaller fleet, was never allowed by the French state to make its prices economic, reportedly so that government ministers could continue travelling the Atlantic in style without voters becoming enraged by sky-high travel expenses appearing in the public accounts.

CONCORDE'S DEATH KNELL

In July 2000 an Air France Concorde, carrying 100 German tourists on a package trip to New York, crashed on take-off. A metal strip, fallen from another plane, caused a tyre burst and the debris ruptured the fuel tanks at high speed. The plane crashed into the Hotelissimo hotel in the town of Gonesse, north of the capital, killing another ten people two minutes after take-off from Charles de Gaulle airport. All Concordes, British and French, were immediately grounded. After a safety review, it was announced that protective adjustments to the aircraft would be necessary, at a price of €50 million ($62 million). It was decided to retire the plane rather than meet this prohibitive cost.

By the end of the century, the "plane of tomorrow" was looking rather old-fashioned. Air France could attract only enough business for one transatlantic flight a day (instead of the previous two), and even then the aircraft was often carrying only a couple of dozen paying passengers. Extra seats were often filled by upgrading subsonic first-class and business-class customers.

Vanity, like pride, has its fall. In July 2000 an ageing Concorde, carrying a charter flight of German tourists, crashed on take-off at Charles de Gaulle airport. With 113 dead and faced with an astronomical bill for revamping its planes to twenty-first century safety standards, Air France finally pulled the planes out of service for good.

THE END OF CONCORDE

A BRITISH VIEW: *"The economics of Concorde were nonsense from the start, even with the hypothetical 'hundreds' of sales. It was far too small, and the trail of destruction left on the ground when it flew supersonic meant that it could only do so over the sea: and the only ocean it had the range to cross was the Atlantic. Really, a 10-year-old could have worked out how unviable this project was but, of course, 10-year-olds are short on testosterone and high on common sense."* Daily Telegraph newspaper, 2003.

A FRENCH VIEW:
"Not only did it embody a certain conception of a victorious France but above all it symbolised modernity – triumphant in all the refined elegance of its curves." Libération *newspaper, 2003.*

. . . And the Elephant

France's Flights of Fancy No. 2: Airbus A380

Will Concorde's successor, the Airbus A380, be the new white Elephant of the Skies?

Any way you look at it, the Airbus A380 is big. Above all, it is a big French gamble using European money for the bet. In January 2005 the new 555-seat superjumbo was unveiled in an all-singing, all-dancing ceremony in Toulouse. Not elegant by any means, looking rather like a super-sized maggot, the giant plane – the first full double-decker – has a 262 ft wing-span, a tail as high as a seven-storey building and room for the equivalent of seventy cars on its wings.

Airbus believes that bigger is better. The A380 will have nearly 50% more space than the Boeing 747, the current largest airliner, and can carry a third more passengers (up to 800, if they are packed in tight and use the cargo hold).

FRENCH AIRBUS

Airbus is no ordinary company. From start-up in 1969, its natural parents were the national governments of France, the U.K., Germany and Spain using state-owned or -influenced defence or engineering concerns as proxies. Over the years, each government stepped away from Airbus, leaving it controlled by public companies – except France. Today, the dominant owner of Airbus is E.A.D.S. (European Aeronautic Defence and Space Company), holding 80% of its shares, and the dominant owner of E.A.D.S. is the French government, which controls its stake through French state-owned companies within the partnership.

U.K. Prime Minister Tony Blair, Spanish Prime Minister José Luis Zapatero and German Chancellor Gerhard Schröder all attended the 2005 launch of the A380 – but the day belonged to the fourth and, on paper, equal partner, President Jacques Chirac of France.

In an emotional speech, Chirac touched on previous French-driven triumphs in aviation including, to the raised eyebrows of the international press corps, the first powered flight. He ended: "A new page of aeronautical history has been written. It is a magnificent result for European industrial co-operation and an encouragement to pursue this path of building a Europe of innovation and progress". For "European", Chirac surely means "French".

Airbus may be a European consortium registered in Amsterdam but its main office is in Paris, 20,000 of its 49,000 employees work in France and, thanks to one of those "informal" agreements which the French demand for participation, the most senior executives must have a strong French presence.

But the progressive thing about Airbus, as far as the French government is concerned, is that the company is effectively underwritten by the taxpayer. Over the last four decades, Airbus has got subsidies worth €32 billion ($40 billion) from both national governments and the European Union, mostly in the form of

THE AIRBUS A380

Flight crew:	2
Passengers:	*560 in 3 classes*
Length:	*73 m*
Wingspan:	*80 m*
Height:	*24.1 m*
Empty Weight:	*280,000 kg*
Maximum takeoff:	*560,000 kg*
Powerplant:	*4 x Rolls-Royce Trent 900 or Engine Alliance GP7200 turbofans, 302 kN (67,890 lbs) thrust each*
Cruise speed:	*0.85 Mach (approx 902 kph or 487 kts)*
Range:	*9,400 nautical miles*
Ceiling:	*13,100 m (43,000 ft)*

government loans with utterly uncommercial repayment terms. When projects go wrong, like the poorly received A300 (which only had fifteen orders on its 1972 launch), taxpayers around Europe foot the bill.

The Airbus A380 did not come cheap. Airbus has ploughed €10 billion ($13 billion) into the plane's development, 33% of which comes from below-market rate loans from European governments. Each aircraft has a list price of €224 million ($280 million) a pop. Rainer Hertrich, outgoing co-chief executive of Airbus, announced his company would have to sell 300 A380s (an upgrade of the original estimate of 250) to break even – and 750 of the planes if Airbus intends to repay its government loans.

This is where the A380 becomes a gamble. The Superjumbo – and Airbus itself – have only ever had one real competitor: the Americans, in the form of the giant aero-engineering company, Boeing. One plane has dominated the skies for the last thirty years, the Boeing 747 jumbo jet. The A380 has been specifically designed by Airbus to replace its ageing rival. It can carry a third more passengers, it flies 9,000 miles (5% further than a 747) and it burns 12% less fuel with half the take-off noise and needs shorter runways. All in all, a magnificent French (apologies, European) flip-off to the Americans. No wonder President Chirac calls it: "The unstoppable flagship of Europe".

But how stoppable is it? If Boeing knows one thing, it is the airliner marketplace. The company never made planes for a successor to the jumbo because it saw the market was changing. The plane on which Boeing has pinned its hopes is the new 787 Dreamliner. This is a mid-sized, twin-aisle plane that will carry between 200 and 350 passengers depending on the seating configuration. Because it will eventually be made of 80% composite materials, it is lighter than all other passenger carriers, and 30% more fuel efficient. It goes further with a range of 11,000 miles. Each one only costs €92 million ($120 million).

The theory behind the 787 Dreamliner is based on the "hub-and-spoke" reality of the world's airports. In each country, there are only one or two major airports with facilities large enough to take giant carriers. That said, countries

---

FARE COMPETITION?
Boeing has continually complained about the plentiful "launch aid" that Airbus gets from the partner governments in the consortium. Airbus has to pay back this money and its interest but only if the plane is a commercial success; 33% of the A380's €10 billion ($12.4 billion) cost is met through government loans which are held at interest rates far below market rates. On 31 May 2005 the United States filed a case against the European Union for providing illegal subsidies to Airbus. A day later, the European Union filed a tit-for-tat complaint against the United States protesting against support for Boeing in the form of military contracts for the company's defence divisions. Boeing pointed out that this action was rather rich since Airbus is owned by Europe's two largest defence consortia, E.A.D.S. and BAe, both awash with government money.

---

have smaller regional airports, sometimes many hundreds of miles distant from the main hub. To travel long distance, a passenger has to fly in from their spoke, catch the carrier from the hub, fly to another hub and then perhaps take another plane to their final destination if it is not close to that hub.

The 787 is designed to fly "spoke-to-spoke" to the approximately 20,000 airports already able to take it – and do so cheaply and frequently. The A380 flies "hub-to-hub" – and, for the sake of profitability, can only do so when its huge passenger decks are full; that means fewer flights and only at rigorously scheduled times. Right now, there are only sixty airports in the world with the entry and debarking facilities to handle the A380 – and some of those are having to undergo costly refits to handle the giant plane. (London's Heathrow, for example, is having to invest £580 million to enlarge Terminal 3 to take it).

SUPERDUMBO

"One thing was not mentioned: the A380 is a superlative also in aesthetical terms, since it is one of the ugliest airplanes of modern times. The plane is too short, too thick, too high. It looks like a flying liver sausage the end of which got out of place – or like an elephant, whose trunk is sadly hanging down. The A380 – a sad elephant? More importantly, in economic terms, will it be a white elephant?" Sybille Haas, Süddeutsche Zeitung newspaper, April 2003.

If Boeing is right, then the Airbus, designed and directed by a French desire to put one over the Americans is riding for a massive financial fall. Luckily, the European taxpayer will cushion the fall.

Not tonight Josephine

Are The French Just Not Sexy Anymore?

50% of the French do not associate sex with "pleasure". Just how do they really perform against their reputation for bed-hopping sexiness – or is it a case of all mouth and no trousers?

There are some things the world just accepts that the French do best in the world. Like make wine, snub tourists, sell arms and, most famously of all, make love. The achievements of all the great French heroes seem to go hand in hand with

IT'S GOOD TO BE ON TOP
"Anyone who doesn't have a mistress is a nincompoop."
Francis I, King of France,
1494-1547.

their sexual accomplishments. Henri IV not only had two wives but over fifty mistresses on his books, not counting over a thousand "day companions". Louis XIV had fewer lovers, perhaps only fifty, one of them being Marie Mancini, the niece of Cardinal Mazarin, his chief minister, who, keeping things cosy, was also sleeping with Louis' mother. Napoleon's "official" lovers numbered around a hundred though historians speculate that with the Emperor exhausted by constant campaigning, many were just for show (one of his girlfriends, Marguerite Josephine Weimer, also slept with the Duke of Wellington and was disappointed with Napoleon's lovemaking, complaining that: "*Monsieur le Duc était de beaucoup le plus fort*" – "The Duke was far more vigorous").

Probably the only French hero not setting records in bed was Joan of Arc but her image as an hysterical, armour-clad, teenage virgin gives her prominence as a sexual archetype amongst psychotherapists everywhere.

Even today, the movers and shakers of French society take a not-so-discreet pride in their sexual conquests. President Jacques Chirac's much reported dalliance with Italian B movie actress, Claudia Cardinale, is in the tradition of President Giscard d'Estaing's relationship with French B movie actress, Sylvia Krystel. President Mitterrand, who well understood that in matters of sex quantity is more important than quality, told his psychiatrist that he himself could be compared to fabled lover, Don Giovanni, with about the same score, "*mille e tre*" (one thousand and three) attributed to the seducer in Mozart's opera. Of recent French politicians, only Charles de Gaulle seems to have been comparatively undersexed. (The British press speculated that this might have been the reason that his widow, when asked what life held for her after her husband's death, replied: "A penis". Prime Minister Harold Wilson chipped in quick: "Madame de Gaulle obviously means 'happiness'").

Yet elites everywhere are notoriously delinquent when it comes to keeping their underwear on, not only in France. Bill Clinton's escapades in the United States prove that. What is different is the reaction of the ordinary French, a reaction best summed-up by one woman in the street interviewed by an American reporter about the Monica Lewinsky scandal: "So what? It was only about sex."

Having spent centuries circumventing a once repressive Catholic church, the modern French invest the same moral significance in the subject as shaving their armpits or tearing up traffic tickets; in other words, not much. While France's state brothels were closed down in 1947 and the legendary *cinq à sept*, that period spent with someone other than your spouse between the close of business and supper time, may be a thing of the past, one look at their newspapers shows that the French are laid back to say the least about sex. For three weeks during the summer of 2005, *Libération*, the high-minded Left-wing daily founded by Jean-Paul Sartre, devoted its centre pages to articles on fetish sex, illustrated by giant close-ups of genitalia. "Let's not be hypocritical", said Mathieu Lindon, editor of the series, "most adolescents [in France] have seen porn films by the time they are thirteen".

This kind of blasé attitude has given the French a reputation for sex and sexiness that is as cast-iron as the Eiffel Tower, and they are just as proud of it. Recently Marie-Hélène Colson, a doctor working for the *Société Francophone de Médecine Sexuelle* (the French-Speaking Society of Sexual Medicine), was asked whether French lovemaking was qualitatively better than those of other nationalities. "We don't have that much data but I have heard it is a bit quicker in Anglo-Saxon and northern countries", she replied. "It is unthinkable for French people to rush these things".

But is such self-satisfaction really justified by the, er, satisfaction delivered? Recent studies suggest that the French reputation as the world's greatest lovemakers doesn't quite stand up.

Do the French really have a better sex life than the rest of the world? Only 23% of French people are happy with their sex lives compared to 27% in the United States and 26% in Mexico. Even the repressed British managed to come in at 25%. For the record, Venezuelans seem to be having the best time in bed, scoring 46%. (Starch Roper Worldwide, 2000).

How much do the French enjoy sex? Not as much as you would think. A disappointing 50% of French people do not associate sex with pleasure and 23% said they would be "relieved" not to have sex for several months on end. (*Journal of Sexual Medicine*, 2006).

How many times do the French make love a year? Here, the French beat the world. They make love, on average, 137 times a year. The Greeks come next with 133 times. The phlegmatic Brits make love 119 times a year and Americans are not far behind with 111 times. The Japanese trail with 74. (Durex.com, 2004).

Do the French think they are getting enough sex? Only 5.6% of French men (and 8% of French women) expressed satisfaction with the "frequency of intercourse in their lives". (*Journal of Sexual Medicine*, 2006).

How good is sex with a French person? When it comes to the crunch, orgasms per bout, the French perform weakly. 61% of Italians will have an orgasm each time they make love (figures averaged between men and women). Only 31% of their neighbours in France can say the same. (Durex.com, 2004).

How many lovers do the French have? The average French person has 8.1 sexual partners in their lifetime. The Danes score the highest in Europe, with 12.5. The U.S. and the UK come in with 10.3 each. (Durex.com, 2004).

Why are the French not so hot in bed? Perhaps it's because they only spend an average 19.2 minutes on foreplay. The British, on the other hand, take their time at 22.5 minutes, followed closely by the Germans (22.2), the Irish (21.8) and the Spanish (21.7). Even Americans, usually eager to get down to business, spend 19.7 minutes on the prep work. (Durex.com, 2004).

But maybe the French are, you know, *filthier* in bed? If we're speaking metaphorically, no. When it comes to rating perversions in Europe, the British come out on top. More than 38% of Britons say they have used bondage to enhance sex while the next most likely to do so are the Dutch on 27%. The French lag well behind with a docile 11%. Britain also had the highest rates in Europe for using sex toys and pornography though the Dutch were out in front when it comes to lingerie with 52% claiming that they had donned a posing pouch or leather gear. (Policy Exchange, 2005).

Well then, surely the French still lead the world in *ooh la-la*, Feydeau farce-style adultery? Again, no. The spark seems to have gone out of French philandering. 69% of French men and 85% of single French women report fidelity to one single sexual partner – and that compares unfavourably (or favourably depending on your moral compass) to 48% of American men and 66% of American women. (*The Journal of Sex Research*, 2001).

The Crucifixion of Alain Hertoghe

France's Unfree Press

During the war in Iraq, the French press revealed its ugly anti-Americanism. What one reporter discovered, to his cost, was that it also exposed its corruption, incompetence and blatant disregard for the truth.

A READER WRITES
"I am unable to understand how a man of honour could take a newspaper in his hands without a shudder of disgust." Charles Baudelaire, 1821–67, widely banned poet, chronic opium abuser and necrophile who knew "disgusting" when he read it.

A free press, however horrible, stupid and crass its opinions, is ultimately the first guarantor of an individual's freedoms. But France, as Alain Hertoghe found out with a shock, really has no free press at all.

Hertoghe should have known better. He is a Belgian, educated in France, and a seventeen-year veteran staffer on *La Croix*, a respected Catholic daily where he is, or was, a senior editor.

During the recent war in Iraq, Hertoghe was very much onside with the 87% of French public opinion and 100% of the French media that opposed the conflict. All the major newspapers not only opposed the war, which was simply a question of their opinion, but they also predicted a savage, swift defeat for the Americans and the British, which they presented as a matter of fact.

Hertoghe happily mucked in, leading with graphic pictures of American casualties when they arrived, subbing the copy coming in from the heavily censored French correspondents in Baghdad and headlining the op-ed pieces highlighting the Iraqi people's hatred of the coalition and the heroic struggle of Saddam (always referred to as M. le Président de l'Irak).

Then, after three weeks, it was all over. Baghdad was taken, the regime fell and, a little later, Saddam was found hiding in a hole. Hertoghe just could not understand it. Neither could the rest of the French media.

"Five days into the campaign the press was already talking about a quagmire, then about Vietnam", Hertoghe remembers. "They said the Pentagon's plan was wrong, there weren't enough soldiers, the military equipment was too sophisticated for this kind of campaign and the Americans were stuck 80 km from Baghdad. Of course what happened is that the Americans were at the gates of Baghdad by the 2nd or 3rd of April. The French press didn't explain why this happened; they began to announce that the battle of Baghdad would be a new Stalingrad. And of course that didn't happen either."

In fact, Hertoghe had already begun to question the systematic misrepresentation of objective fact by the French media. He had been made uneasy about cartoons showing U.S. troops stamping on dead babies and by editorials accusing President Bush of racism. As a journalist he had read the wires coming in from Associated Press and Agence France-Presse services and

REPORTING THE ARROGANT, IMPERIALISTIC SUPERPOWER

"The war has been dreamed up by the Pentagon strategists as a war of world domination through the occupation of Iraq and the control of the Middle East. The real question now is the withdrawal of U.S. troops because for the United States, military victory has already lost any rational political possibility." Jean-Pierre Chevènement, former Defence Minister Le Monde, 7 April 2003.

"Before Baghdad has even fallen, the Americans are preparing the energy future of the country. After having invented the concept of 'preventive war', the Americans have now inaugurated the concept of 'lucrative peace'." Le Figaro, editorial, 7 April 2003.

"This victory for Bush means that America will remain an arrogant, imperialistic superpower which will worsen the international anti-American hatred which has grown spectacularly under his presidency." Libération, editorial, 10 May 2003.

FRENCH PRESS: BUSH VS. SADDAM
"Reading French dailies, you are under the impression that America, apart from a handful of admirable pacifists, is full of unpleasant brainless, selfish and violent 'patriots'. Most editorials even put Mr Bush on a par with Saddam." Alain Hertoghe, La Guerre à outrances, 2002.

become confused at the disparity between their information from the spot and the stories that were appearing in Paris. He realised the story was not about the Coalition's victory in Iraq but about the defeat of the French media.

So he wrote a book about it. In October 2002, he published *La Guerre à outrances: Comment la presse nous a désinformés sur l'Irak* (rough translation: *War of the Wor(l)ds; How the press lied to us about Iraq*). It explored how the major French newspapers covered the three-week war. His survey took in his own paper, the Catholic *La Croix*, the centre-left *Le Monde*, the conservative *Le Figaro*, the communist *Libération* and the regional daily *Ouest-France*, which has the largest circulation in France.

The book is a damning compilation that confirms not only the press' systemic anti-Americanism (for example, during the three weeks of war, the five papers carried 29 headlines condemning Saddam's dictatorship

HOW THE FRENCH STATE BUYS ITS NEWSPAPERS.
"France's press is subsidized in one way or another by an estimated €55 million [$68 million] annually. Prices of newspapers are controlled by the government. They were fixed in 1963 at 30 centimes a copy, except for Le Monde *and* Paris Presse, *which were permitted to sell at 40 centimes. The others were raised to that level on 1 August 1967. Subsidisation takes several forms. For example, a journalist in France phones, cables, or telexes his story at half the ordinary rate, and newspapers are mailed to subscribers for only a fraction of the cost for other material of the same weight. If a reporter has to travel anywhere in France on a story, he pays half fare on French railways. Sometimes the subsidy is direct. If a publisher desires to build a new printing plant, the government will pay up to 15% of its cost, and in the important budget item of paper cost it will pay the difference between the French price for newsprint and the world price, which is lower. The state also subsidises overseas sales of French newspapers. It does not require publishers to pay a purchase tax, and it exempts them from the corporation tax on profits if the money is reinvested within five years." Print Media – Newspapers, Magazines, www.discoverfrance.net*

and 135 condemning Bush and Blair) but its systematic disregard of basic fact.

Simply put, the French press was dishonest and incompetent across the board. "When Baghdad fell, the readers couldn't understand how the Americans won the war," Hertoghe wrote, "because the French press was so carried away. The journalists dreamed of an American defeat."

Hertoghe attributes this deception – and self-deception – by the press to two core reasons. The first is an intellectual and therefore, by French reasoning, moral anti-Americanism. Fair enough, that is really a political decision which any newspaper is free to make. The second reason is more ominous: the French press followed the anti-war line of the French government because it was essentially controlled by that government through massive pay-offs (€400 million – $494 million – in 2004 alone).

In essence, the French press is not only unable to report the Iraq war with balance, even if it had the will to do so, but *any* issue because it is subsidised by the state. Prices of newspapers are controlled by the government. If a publisher wants a new printing plant, the government pays up to 15% of its cost. Working journalists get an automatic 30% deduction on their income taxes as an expense allowance.

The relationship between the government and the state is even more incestuous, as Dennis Boyles, a long-time journalist and U.S. expat in France reports in his book *Vile France: Fear, Duplicity, Cowardice and Cheese* (2004).

"It turns out that journalists were routinely helped by the government, to find cheap apartments, fix traffic tickets, get free transportation, gain entrance for their kids into prestigious schools. That relationship hasn't changed in the last thirty years."

Stanley Hertzberg, a retired director of *Wall Street Journal Europe*, agrees that the daily press, including the qualities like *Le Monde*, have no tradition of independent reporting. "The problem is, they are afraid. Journalists here are afraid to do good journalism because they could lose their jobs, their credentials, their contacts. It's hard to get a good job in the French press. They know that if they break a story, they will get into trouble."

FRENCH JOURNALISM GETS INTO BED WITH THE GOVERNMENT
"Most of them [journalists and politicians] use the familiar form 'tu' when they address each other. These people lunch together, take holidays together, have affairs with each other. Once you've established this kind of relationship, it's much harder to be critical." Daniel Schneidermann, former senior editor at Le Monde.

And trouble is what Hertoghe got. Just before Christmas 2003, he was confronted by his editor, Bruno Frappat, who told him that he had "committed an act of treason" and fired him.

Hertoghe's silencing was not a one-off. The French media has a tradition of silencing those who pipe up about its institutional bias and corruption. In 2002, *La Face cachée du Monde* (*The Hidden Face of Le Monde*) was brought out by Pierre Pean and Philippe Cohen, respectively France's leading freelance investigative reporter and a business editor at the weekly *Marianne*. This investigation into the journalistic and editorial practices of the 400,000-circulation newspaper uncovered business malpractice, government control and flamboyant campaigns designed to pay off old scores. (The authors recount how *Le Monde*, followed by the rest of France's media, trumpeted a highly dubious accusation of sexual harassment against a prominent intellectual, brought by a close friend of one of the paper's directors).

Daniel Schneidermann, an editor at the paper who is also a prominent television personality, submitted a piece on the book and was immediately fired by the editors, who reacted furiously. "We have to know where you stand,

DÉJÀ VU ALL OVER AGAIN

The French government – and the French establishment – recently lost its massive campaign to persuade the French people to vote "Yes" in a referendum to accept the proposed European Constitution. Their most fervent cheerleaders were, of course, the French press.

"In the fraught, passionate and sometimes frenzied debate in France over the referendum the spotlight has now been turned full beam onto the role and conduct of the media. A group of journalists from French state T.V. and radio are so angered by what they see as one-sided propaganda campaign on behalf of the government and the Yes campaign that they have set up an online petition, signed by more than 15,000 people since 1 May. They presented it to President Jacques Chirac, the heads of French T.V. and radio and to the director of the C.S.A. French broadcasting standards authority, Dominique Baudis. 'This is a grotesque situation,' says Jacques Cotta, a well-known T.V. correspondent for France 2 who is one of the leaders of the campaign for fair coverage. 'Publicly-owned media in France are broadcasting sheer propaganda to the public, and this absence of any pluralism or any attempt to represent and discuss the point of view of those who want to vote No to the Treaty is profoundly undemocratic.' Both centre-right ruling party and Socialists campaigned for a Yes vote. During the campaign French T.V. and radio gave 71% of its time to the Yes campaigners, and devoted a mere 29% to the No campaign between 1 January and 31 March." Caroline Wyatt, B.B.C. News, May 2005.

Schneidermann", he was told. "Are you in or out?" Then they fired him. Schneidermann at least was able to defend himself on his own T.V. show.

As for Hertoghe, his removal from *La Croix* was met with absolute silence in the French press. His book was not reviewed by a single mainstream newspaper and he was unable to get any other job in the French media. The rest of the world media was more disturbed and his sacking was reported by the *International Herald Tribune*, the *Wall Street Journal*, the B.B.C., the *Guardian* and the *Daily Telegraph*. *Fox's* Bill O'Reilly even tried to get Hertoghe for an interview, which he declined ("I thought it would be just about French bashing", he said).

"The message was clear", concludes Dennis Boyles. "The elite French press had lied to their readers and when someone called them on it and blew the whistle, they buried him in silence and public ridicule, all of which adds more tarnish to the cheap metal pot that constitutes journalism in France."

NOTHING BUT BAD

"A free press can, of course, be good or bad, but, most certainly without freedom, the press can be nothing but bad." Albert Camus (1913-60), *French intellectual, author and depressive.*

Secrets of the Sphinx

The Secret Life of François Mitterrand

One man represents the spirit and reality of modern France –
two-time president, François Mitterrand, still revered today
as statesman, author and resistance fighter. Was he also a
crook, fraud, spy, collaborator and murderer?

MITTERRAND ON MITTERRAND
"I am the last great president. After me will be only financiers and accountants."
President François Mitterrand, articulating his own obituary and, quite possibly,
the well-founded wish that his accounts be audited only after his death.

The Mayor of Paris, Bertrand Delanoë, recently organised a series of city walks in honour of a former French president and named a street after him. It runs along the banks of the Seine, between the leafy Tuileries gardens and the splendour of the Louvre palace in whose cobbled forecourt now stands a giant glass and steel pyramid placed there by the great statesman. At the same time, the municipality of Jarnac bought the house where the president had been born and turned it into a museum. Such veneration of safely dead politicians happens in democracies all the time. Imagine though, the outcry not just in the United States but around the world, if the president in question had been Richard Nixon.

TONTON'S TALE.
*François Mitterrand (1916 –1996), born Jarnac, Charente. His father was a
stationmaster. As a youth, joined the ultra-nationalist Croix de Feu (Cross of Fire),
a far-right Catholic organisation. Enrolled during WWII, captured in 1940.
Became a high-ranking official in the Vichy government though in late 1943
secretly joined de Gaulle's Free French Forces. Held office in the Fourth Republic as
deputy and minister (with eleven portfolios), before resigning in 1957 over the the
Algerian war of independence. In 1958, one of the few to object to Charles de
Gaulle as head of government. During the 1960s, turned to the French Socialist
Party (P.S.), becoming leader by 1971. Ten years later, became the first socialist
President of the Fifth Republic in alliance with the Communist party. Domestically,
his policies were blunted by financial crises, and then by a conservative parliament
(1986-88 and 1993-95). Initiated various "great projects", including the Channel
Tunnel, the pyramid at the Louvre (1988), the Grande Arche at La Défense (1989),
and the Bibliothèque Nationale de France (1995). Because the Socialists had lost so
many elections before his election in 1981 – and re-election in 1988 – Mitterrand
was regarded as the saviour of the Left, perhaps to the point of ridicule (generating
the so-called tontonmania, from "tonton", or "uncle", one of his many nicknames.
This also led many to overlook the numerous scandals and rumours surrounding
both his early career and his presidency. His term as President ended in May 1995,
having served longer in the post than any other. He died of prostate cancer eight
months later at the age of 79.*

Nixon left office after being caught bugging his Democrat opponents in the
Watergate Hotel. Beside François Mitterrand, the man whose memory the French
are now honouring with utterly straight-faced esteem, Nixon was a butter-
fingered amateur.

Not only did Mitterrand regularly, even compulsively, bug his political
opponents, he bugged anyone who caught his interest, including good-looking
actresses. He, was also, it seems mad, a Nazi collaborator, a Communist spy, a
multi-million dollar fraudster, a murderer, bewitched by Margaret Thatcher and
twice-elected President of France.

Notoriously secretive (he was nicknamed "le Sphinx"), only now are the more
unsavoury details of his career coming light. Yet France doesn't seem to care.
According to one 2005 Sofres poll, nearly two-thirds of the French have a
positive memory of the Mitterrand years, and a similar proportion say he will
have a "great" place in history. Another poll makes him France's most popular
leader of the last half-century, according to 35% of respondents. One of
Mitterrand's loudest cheerleaders is former Culture Minister Jack Lang, who
describes "Mitterrandisme" as "the power of the will and the certainty that one
can move mountains by force of spirit". Here are some lesser-known aspects of
"Mitterrandisme" in action.

1930s: MITTERRAND THE "HOODIE"

Before the Second World War, the fragile French democracy was beset by street terrorism carried out by gangs and secret societies of the extreme right and left. One of the most violent was fascist "La Cagoule" ("The Hood") which made a practice of targeting Jewish public figures for attack and assassination. Despite many accusations, the young Mitterrand, then a student at the prestigious Institute of Political Science ("Sciences-Po") in Paris, always denied he was a "Cagoule" activist although two contemporary photos have since come to light. One places him at a demonstration against "l'invasion métèque" (the mixed race, ie, Jewish, invasion); the other shows him in the middle of a street disturbance targeting a Jewish professor at his college. The daughter of "La Cagoule's" leader married Mitterrand's older brother. After the war, Mitterrand used his politicial connections to protect the organisation's leading financier, Eugène Schueller (the founder of international cosmetics brand, L'Oréal), from prosecution.

1940s: THE FRANCISQUE

Mitterrand's supporters focus on the important work he did for the Resistance during World War II. As a high-up official in the puppet Vichy government, Mitterrand was able to arrange travel and identity papers for those opposing Nazi rule. What has only become clear recently is that Mitterrand was not simply posing as a loyal Vichy official, he was one. He did not join the Resistance until late in 1943, by which time it was obvious that the Allies would win the war. De Gaulle professed that he never trusted the ambitious young civil servant. A photograph from this time shows a beaming Mitterrand shaking the hand of Marshal Pétain, the rabid anti-semite heading the Vichy government, as he received the Francisque, the highest civilian honour that Vichy could bestow. Mitterrand routinely denied receiving this medal until hard evidence emerged during the late '50s. As President, Mitterrand tried to prevent the trials of his Vichy colleagues, Maurice Papon, Paul Touvier and René Bousquet, all of whom were wanted for crimes against humanity during the Occupation. Every year until his death, Mitterrand would lay a wreath upon Marshal Pétain's grave.

1954: THE MILITARY SECRETS SCANDAL

Mitterrand, rising rapidly, was Interior Minister in one of the many governments of the Fourth Republic. The Paris police chief, Jean Baylot, was a hardline anti-Communist, a kind of French Edgar Hoover but more paranoid, if possible. Two weeks into his term at the Ministry, Mitterrand fired him. Baylot had been working on a case that suggested somone in the National Defence Council was leaking its minutes to the U.S.S.R., and the evidence, he said, was pointing to Mitterrand. After his dismissal, the investigation was closed, and when Mitterrand became President, the files on the case were destroyed.

1958: THE OBSERVATORY AFFAIR

On the night of 15 October Mitterrand was returning home after a dinner in the Boulevard Saint-Germain when his car was machine-gunned by members of the right-wing terror group O.A.S. (l'Organisation de l'Armée Secrète, the Secret Army Organisation). Mitterrand told police that the attack had been carried out after a furious car-chase and that he had escaped only by jumping over a hedge into the gardens in the Avenue de l'Observatoire. Later, to general derision, he was forced to admit that he had set up the whole incident himself to gain public support at a time when he was shifting from the Gaullist right to the Socialist left. His own revised explanation was limp: the gunman, Robert Pesquet, had been threatened with death by the O.A.S. if he didn't kill Mitterrand so Mitterrand had stage-managed the event because he felt sorry for Pesquet.

1982: BUGS AND THE BOND GIRL

In 1982, one year after taking office as President, Mitterrand set up a private secret service, the Elysee Cell. Originally conceived as a specialist anti-terrorist unit answerable to the President, the team carried out secret operations for Mitterrand and bugged journalists, lawyers and businessmen. One target was the Chanel model and Bond actress, Carole Bouquet, to whom Mitterrand was attracted. Another was the editor of Le Monde newspaper, who at the time was investigating claims – since shown to be true – that the Cell had framed evidence against alleged Irish terrorists in the early 1980s. Also bugged was the writer Jean-Edern Hallier who was investigating the story of Mitterrand's illegitimate daughter, Mazarine. On one occasion the Elysee learned that Hallier was to appear on a television chat-show and had the programme cancelled. Others were journalists and lawyers looking into the 1985 Rainbow Warrior affair. The existence of the secret listening-room was not revealed until 1993 along with the names of the 150 people tapped in this bizarre operation.

1988: ELF OF THE NATION

The French state oil company, Elf, France's largest enterprise was robbed of over 2 billion francs – €305 million ($377 million) – by its top executives during Mitterrand's second seven-year term, and much of it was on his behalf . Elf's boss, Loïk Le Floch-Prigent later justified his misappropriation of company funds with the defence: "I was only answerable to one man" – Mitterrand. As a state enterprise, Elf had its executives appointed by the President of the Republic. Le Floch-Prigent operated the Elf slush fund, "caisse noire", according to Mitterrand's instructions: "This system existed essentially for the Gaullist party, the R.P.R.; I informed President François Mitterrand, who told me that it would be better to spread it about a bit, without leaving out the R.P.R. all the same". In this way, all of France's major parliamentary parties, left and right, benefited from Elf's, or, more exactly, Mitterrand's patronage and payroll. Under Mitterrand's directions, for example, Elf funds were used to buy a magnificent chateau at Louveciennes from one of the President's friends at a vastly inflated price so that Mitterrand could take occasional golfing outings at a nearby links. Elf cash was also allegedly used to set up Anne Pingeout, mother of his secret daughter Mazarine, in her own business. A further €10 million ($12.5 million) was passed on to his great friend and ally, former German Chancellor Helmut Kohl, to help him win the elections of 1994, a matter now under investigation by the German police.

1980S: MURDER ET CIE?

In 1985, President Mitterrand personally ordered France's secret service, the D.G.S.E. (Direction Générale de la Sécurité Extérieure, General Directorate for External Security) to place the mine on the Greenpeace ship, the Rainbow Warrior, that killed the photographer, Fernando Pereira. What is not known – or at least not yet proven – is whether Mitterrand used the secret service to silence embarrassing personalities closer to home. Chief amongst them was Pierre Bérégovoy, who served as Mitterrand's Prime Minister during a time of ever-intensifying investigation into political corruption. On 1 May 1993, having left office, he was found by a canal in a coma with a bullet in his head. Police investigators ruled his subsequent death as a suicide while depressed. This confirmed his bodyguard's deposition that the former Pinister was with him when he grabbed the guard's gun. The bodyguard later retracted the statement that he was present at Bérégovoy's death and submitted that the gun was taken from the glove compartment of the official car. Bérégovoy left no note and Mitterrand took possession of his diary, which was never returned to the family. A senior police official did inform the family that one theory under investigation was that the politician had been murdered by frogmen who emerged from the canal while Bérégovoy waited to meet a representative from the Elysee Palace. This theory, for which no evidence was found, was also voiced by François de Grossouvre, a senior advisor to the Mitterrand presidency with responsibility for the secret services. He was found dead in his office in the Elysee in April 1994, killed by a self-inflicted gunshot.

1990S: A VERY SICK MAN – MITTERRAND AND MARGARET THATCHER

In October 1994 President Mitterrand gave a surprise interview in Le Figaro newspaper. He revealed that he was suffering from prostate cancer, an illness for which he had first been treated from the first years of his presidency. From November 1981, all the health bulletins issuing from the Elysee Palace had been faked. What effect the heavy load of drugs he took to control his illness had on his judgement and his mental well-being can only be guessed at. However, in 1982, on the advice of his personal astrologer (that's right, astrologer) the President began seeing a psychiatrist, Ali Magoudi. In the super-secret sessions that followed, Mitterrand laid bare his soul. He suffered, according to Magoudi's book Rendez-vous: The psychoanalysis of François Mitterrand (2005), from paranoid tendencies, anxiety attacks and, it seems, a peculiar yen for the then British Prime Minister, Margaret Thatcher. She had, he mused, "the eyes of Stalin, the lips of Marilyn Monroe". During the Falklands War, he announced that "she threatens to launch the atomic weapon against Argentina – unless I supply her with the secret codes that render deaf and blind the missiles we have sold to the Argentinians. Margaret has given me very precise instructions on the telephone". (Admiral Henry Leach, chief of the British naval staff at the time, has already recorded: "We did not contemplate a nuclear attack and did not make any even potentially preparatory moves for such action"). Magoudi asked if Mitterrand felt "symbolically emasculated" dealing with the Iron Lady. "Of course it is only her power that matters", Mitterrand mused, " but that's why I admire Thatcher so much". Sadly, the passion seems not to have been reciprocated. Thatcher's own memoirs remember him as "a self-conscious intellectual bored by detail and possibly contemptuous of economics" but, she ends charitably, "oddly enough, I quite liked [him]".

Quarante-Quatre

The Forbidden Scarf

The Blazing Riots of 2005

In 2005, 28,000 vehicles were burned in riots that spread across fifty French cities as the country's aggrieved minorities rioted. How much of this was due to a ban on, of all things, a headscarf?

O n 1 November 2005, a Wednesday night, forty cars and two buses were set alight in nine towns in the suburban département of Seine-Saint-Denis. When firefighters arrived, they were pelted with stones and bottles. The police, following soon after, were shot at. When a T.V. broadcast van was attacked, France's national networks announced, as one, that they would not film this kind of news until the trouble was over. When it was over, or at least had ebbed, 28,000 vehicles had been destroyed in a year of riots spread over fifty cities.

Was this all for the sake of a scarf?

A year earlier, in February, the French parliament passed a law by 494 votes to just 36 banning "obvious religious apparel" from schools. It prohibited pupils from wearing "ostentatious" Christian crosses, Jewish skullcaps, Sikh turbans and the one item that the law was really directed against, the hijab, the headscarf worn by young Muslim women. The politicians hardly debated the issue at all. Just five minutes for each party to sum up their position. That was to be expected. The National Assembly does not have a single black or Muslim *député* from the sixty million plus population of Metropolitan France.

CHIRAC AND THE
FORBIDDEN HEADSCARF
"In all conscience, I consider that the wearing of dress or symbols which conspicuously show religious affiliation should be banned in schools. For that, a law is necessary. I want it to be adopted by parliament and in force before the return to school next year."
President Chirac, Elysée Palace, 2003.

To observers abroad, the law might appear petty. Aside from a deep intrusion into its citizens' personal life, it was so heavy-handed, the kind of thing best dealt with at local, even school board, level rather than by the central government.

In fact, Chirac was scoring points off the National Front, the extreme right wing party that won 17% of the popular vote in the 2002 presidential election on an anti-immigration ticket. He knew well that no one ever lost votes cracking down on Islam in France, a country that the Council of Europe's European Commission Against Racism and Intolerance warned in 1998 still maintained systemic discrimination against its minorities.

LES HARKIS

By 1962, 236,000 Algerian Muslims were fighting for the French army in the Algerian War. At independence, Charles de Gaulle ordered that the Harkis be prevented from fleeing to Metropolitan France. Some French officers disobeyed and helped Harki families reach France, around 91,000 in all. Of those that remained in Algeria, between 50,000 and 150,000 were killed by the F.L.N. or by lynch mobs. The government refused to recognise their right to stay in France. They were held in "temporary" internment camps, surrounded by barbed wire, for twenty years. General outrage finally led the French government to free them from the camps in the 1980s.

It so happens that Islam is the primary religion of France's largest non-European ethnic group, *les Maghrebins*, the six million-strong Arab and African community. When France gave independence to its colonies, many North Africans came to France as economic migrants, especially from Algeria, a country ruined after a bitter war that ended in 1962 (not counting the many *harkis*, pro-French Algerians who fought for the colonial government and were abandoned when France evacuated, 100,000 of them being killed by their vengeful fellow-countrymen).

Today *les beurs* (slang for "Arabs", the term under which most immigrant French are lumped), now represent around 10% of the overall population. Their parents and grandparents were hidden away in *cités* ("cities", Americans would say "the projects"), clusters of towering high-rises like Savigny-sur-Orge and Raincy in the suburbs of Paris but also ringing other cities. Often there was only just enough public transport provided to take their communities directly to their jobs in the factories of the *périphérique* (the industrial outskirts circling the larger towns) but little or none linking the ghettos to the city centres themselves.

THE PROPHECY

"What hope does a young person have who's been born in a quartier *without a soul, who lives in an unspeakably ugly high-rise, surrounded by more ugliness, imprisoned by gray walls in a gray wasteland and condemned to a gray life, with all around a society that prefers to look away until it's time to get mad, time to forbid.*" President François Mitterrand, *making a bid for the ethnic vote whose problems he then studiously neglected, 1990.*

Fifty years later, these *cités* are run-down, frightening sprawls. The high-rises are served by broken elevators, heating systems don't work in winter, dirt and dog mess pollute the hallways. Violence is unexceptional. Even on a normal weekend, between twenty and thirty vehicles are regularly burned by rioters. Joblessness is endemic. France's unemployment rate has hovered around 10% for a decade; in the *cités*, it is around 50%.

Despite the lip service paid to the unity of France, or perhaps because of it, the country is more discriminatory than almost any other western nation. There are rarely black or Arab faces on T.V., none in the government. Job applications from candidates with North African names go unanswered. Telemarketers must use names that are obviously *français de souche* (those of "real" French stock, code for white). The police stop Arab and African drivers fifteen times more often than white drivers. The *Institut Montaigne*, one of France's proliferating think-tanks, has issued reports on the country's "rampant ethnic segregation" and "veritable ghettos". France, one report says, "scarcely recognises the reality of minorities".

IT *IS* RACISM

"Immigrants are blamed by a majority of French citizens for *unemployment, crime and decreasing educational standards. They are seen by nearly three-quarters of the population as more likely to commit crimes than the average French person is. Nearly 40% of the population supports forcible repatriation of unemployed immigrants, and 22% supports forcible repatriation of all immigrants.*" Vernellia R. Randall, *Human Rights Documentation Center, 2001.*

The ban on headscarfs was just another indication to *les beurs* that some French were more equal than others. Their situation was not helped by scare stories in the newspapers about radical Muslim preachers setting up shop in the ghettoes and stirring up trouble amongst the young with their "Islamic gangrene" (as one otherwise impeccably P.C. newspaper put it).

So despite the fact that only about 1,200 Muslim girls regularly turned up to school in a headscarf anyway (of a school population of three million), the law was passed. Some 456 girls did go to school in their *voiles* (veils) and 45 were expelled (along with two sikhs). That, it seemed, was that.

IT'S *NOT* RACISM

"Our problem is not foreigners, but there's an overdose, the Muslims and the Blacks. The French worker who toils, along with his wife, earns about 15,000 francs, and sees across the next door landing of his council flat, all packed together, a father with three or four wives, and a score of children, who are receiving 50,000 francs in welfare benefits, naturally without working If you add the noise and the smell, well, the French worker goes mad. It's not racist to say this." Jacques Chirac, speech in Orleans, 19 June 1991.

A year later, Paris and the major cities of France were rocked by a wave of race riots. The spark was an incident on 27 October 2005 when two teenagers, Zyed Benna and Bouna Traoré, were electrocuted after climbing into an electrical sub-station in the Paris suburb of Clichy-sous-Bois in what locals say was an attempt to hide from pursuing police. News of their deaths triggered riots in the area. Only a couple of days before, the Interior Minister, Nicolas Sarkozy, had been pelted with stones and bottles on a visit to the Argenteuil suburb to see how new measures against urban violence were working. Obviously not very well. In a rage, he declared that the neighbourhoods should be "cleaned with a power hose", describing the violent elements as "gangrene" and "rabble".

Riots spread quickly to every major city and town in France. Trouble was reported in Strasbourg in eastern France, in Rennes, Rouen and Lille in the northwest and Nice, Toulouse and Avignon in the south. In the Paris region, two nurseries, one in Yvelines and another in Brétigny-sur-Orge, were set on fire along with a school in Seine-et-Marne. Rioters turned over a police station in Aulnay-sous-Bois. In Meaux, Arab kids threw Molotov cocktails at paramedics, In the Normandy town of Evreux, rioters torched 50 vehicles, a shopping centre, a post office and two schools; live rounds were fired but no one died.

At the height of the violence, more than 1,400 vehicles were destroyed in a single night. Badly panicked, the government used a 1955 law imposing curfews and restricting people's movements. Three thousand were arrested and almost all came from the dispossessed Arab-African community. The destruction was estimated at €230 million ($286 million) though the European Union, ever accommodating to its chief member, chipped in with a €50 million ($59 million) grant to the French.

The higher-ups were at a loss to explain the explosion of violence and looting. One right-wing deputy, François Grosdidier, headed a group of parliamentarians that proposed banning French rap music on the grounds that it incited the violence. Another, from the left, Manuel Valls, called the riots "the consequences of territorial apartheid", combined with the "bankruptcy of the model of integration". The Foreign Minister, Philippe Douste-Blazy, argued that it was all due to a "very deep crisis due to the crisis of immigration and the failure of our minorities to integrate".

Perhaps the answer lies in a comment from Samia Amara, 23, a youth worker near Paris, interviewed for the B.B.C. "People always talk of the need to 'integrate' Muslims. But these youths are French. It is a hundred small things every day, like the ban on the hijab, that show them France does not consider them French".

THE RIOT OF 1961

France's treatment of its Arab-African population has rarely been sensitive. However, the police response to the 2005 riots was gentler than its treatment of disturbances in 1961, when as many as two hundred Algerian protestors were killed. On the evening of 17 October about 30,000 protesters from among some 200,000 Algerians, ostensibly French citizens, marched on central Paris to demonstrate against an 8:30 p.m. curfew imposed only on Muslims.

They were met by about 7,000 police and members of special Republican Security companies, armed with heavy truncheons or guns, who attacked them. One shocked foreign reporter counted at least thirty corpses in several piles outside his office near the city centre. Another correspondent reported seeing police backing unarmed Algerians into sidestreets and clubbing them at will. Later eyewitness reports recounted stranglings by police and the drowning of Algerians in the Seine, from which bodies would be recovered downstream for weeks to come. "Drowning by Bullets", a British T.V. documentary, alleged that scores of Algerians were murdered in full view of senior police officials in the courtyard of the central police headquarters.

The prefect of police was Maurice Papon, who was later tried for deporting French Jews to Auschwitz during World War II while he was part of the Vichy government. The full horror of this 1961 episode was largely covered up at the time. Oficial figures state that only five people died in the riots . Journalists were warned away from coverage of the demonstration and were not allowed near the detention centres. French newspapers reporting the massacre were seized by the police. As recently as October 1996, on the 35th anniversary of the massacre, copies of the Algerian daily Liberté – which examined Papon's role in the slaughter – were confiscated by customs officers at Lyons airport.

Quarante-Cinq

Spitting
In The
Soup

Seven Truths About French Wine

French wine has a special status – but not perhaps for the reasons the French think. We look at the legends of French viticulture and uncover the truths behind them, including systematic fraud and chronic alcoholism.

THE FRENCH AND BOOZE
"Other countries drink to get drunk, and this is accepted by everyone; in France, drunkenness is a consequence, never an intention. A drink is felt as the spinning out of a pleasure, not as the necessary cause of an effect which is sought: wine is not only a philtre, it is also the leisurely act of drinking." Roland Barthes, French – typically French – critic (1915-80).

1. THE FRENCH INVENTED WINE
"Only France," said Alexandre Dumas, famous novelist and drunk, "could have the genius to create wine". It hadn't and didn't. Scientists from the University Museum, Pennsylvania have identified wine residue in ancient pottery jars excavated at Hajji Firuz Tepe in Iran's Zagros Mountains that date back to the Neolithic (5400-5000 B.C.) period. The first known reference to a specific vintage

occurs in the diaries of Pliny the Elder who rated 121 BC as a vintage "of the highest excellence in Italy". Wine was introduced into France as the beverage of choice of its new Roman overlords after Julius Caesar's invasion of 58 B.C.

2. FRANCE MAKES THE BEST WINE

Not if you go by taste. (And what else would you go by? Its radioactive weight?). The world woke up to this truth after an incident still rocking the world of wine – the Paris Wine Tasting of 1976. Parisian wine merchant, Steven Spurrier, organised a prestige "blind" tasting before a jury of nine tasters consisting of the *crème de la crème* of France's wine snobs. To their horror, they found that they had rated Californian wines as winners in both the red and white wine categories. One judge demanded her ballot back and, when she didn't get it, refused to speak to Spurrier again. The French wine industry banned him from the nation's famous wine-tasting tours – with one famous producer accusing him of "spitting in our soup". The French press first denied any tasting had happened and then implied that Spurrier had fixed the results. It was all too late, the story was around the world that wines from other countries were the equal and often better than France's most famous wines. The story dramatically encouraged wine production in the U.S., Australia and South America for the next 30 years.

3. FRANCE HAS THE WORLD'S MOST SUCCESSFUL WINE INDUSTRY

France produces the most wine by value in the world, exporting €5.6 billion ($6.9 billion) worth of wine products in 2004 (2% of its total exports). However, world consumers are recognising that French wine is not only amongst the most expensive but that its quality can be rivalled by better-priced wines from elsewhere. Between 1994 and 2003, the French share of imported wine fell from 37% to 23% in Britain (the world's largest importer of wine) and from 26% to 16% in America, to be replaced by domestic products and imports from new wine-producing regions like South America, Australia and New Zealand. Meanwhile, in France, the unsold surplus from the 2004 harvest stands at 213 million bottles, 23% of production.

4. FRANCE OFFERS THE MOST DIVERSE RANGE OF WINES IN THE WORLD

True, but that doesn't mean all or even most are any good. Bordeaux alone has over nine thousand different château labels (which is odd, since the French Ministry of Culture lists only 158 actual châteaux in the region). Of these, there are 14 châteaux labels with "Belair", 22 with "Corton" and 151 with "Figeac" in their names. This proliferation is down to the official French classification system which labels a wine by its location as opposed to its grape (the latter being the way it is done in most of the world). The regional committees of the *Appellation d'Origine Contrôlée*, the system that is supposed to guarantee wine quality, are packed with local winegrowers who rarely fail to approve each others' wines (and thus become eligible for state and European Union funding). In 1995, the then head of the A.O.C. himself protested that many of the wines being passed for consumption were "scandalously bad", not unexpected since the committees pass 98% of all local wines put before them.

5. YOU CAN TRUST FRENCH WINES

No you can't. French vintners have a long and rich tradition of wine fraud. Veteran journalist and France-watcher Jonathan Fenby mentions "the many real or apocryphal stories about tanker lorries filled with cheap southern (or North African) plonk turning up in Beaujolais and Burgundy to add strength to the produce of up-market vineyards in thin years". The French wine anti-fraud squad employs only 45 inspectors and they only catch the tip of the iceberg. In 1973, Henri Cruse, a reputable wine shipper for centuries, was caught blending Spanish Rioja wine into Bordeaux. His company was bankrupted by the €6 million ($8 million) fine. More recently, Jacques Hemmer, a Bordeaux négociant, was caught blending cheap wines from southern France into 4,000 hectolitres of much more expensive Bordeaux. He was fined a million euros in 2002 and served a year-and-a-half jail sentence.

6. BECAUSE THE FRENCH DRINK WINE, THEY SUFFER FEWER DRINK-RELATED ILLNESSES

Untrue. French commentators like to point at American dopeheads or English and Dutch soccer hooligans befuddled with beer when discussing substance abuse. Because wine is the "totem drink" (in the words of Roland Barthes, ever ready with nonsensical terminology) of France, they argue its people drink far more wisely and suffer fewer effects. In fact, the French consume more alcohol (the equivalent of 10.91 litres of pure alcohol a year) than anyone in the world except the Mexicans. In 2005 journalist and former alcoholic, Hervé Chebalier, was commissioned by the French Health Ministry to write a report, *Alcoholism – The Simple Truth*. He found that alcohol was directly responsible for 23,000 deaths a year in France, and indirectly responsible for a further 22,000. "A third of all custodial sentences in this country, half of all domestic violence, a third of all handicaps are due to alcohol", he says. "One French person in 10 is ill as a result of alcohol, and every day five French people die after an accident linked to alcohol." He also found that 5 million drink too much (2-3 units of alcohol per day), and 2 million French people are dependent on alcohol (over 5 units per day).

7. THE FRENCH REALLY *KNOW* WINE

Not true – what they do know is how to *talk about* wine. The entire language and terminology of wine "appreciation" was invented by the French and then adopted wholesale by wine snobs the world over. Whereas the ordinary tippler only tastes slightly watery alcohol with a wood-ish afterburn (that comes from the barrel), the wine connoisseur speaks of "tones" and "hues"; he or she looks for "opalescence"; they discuss its "angularity" and whether it has "bigness". This jargon is designed only to disguise the basic fact that it's all a matter of opinion and that, as a recent experiment showed, even French wine experts can be very wrong indeed. In 2001, French researcher Frédéric Brochet asked 57 of Bordeaux's greatest wine experts to a red wine tasting. Among the reds was one bottle of white wine, to which he'd added a flavourless red dye. Not one of the experts noticed. He then asked them to taste two bottles of Bordeaux, one fancily labelled as a *grand cru* and the other clearly marked as a ho-hum *vin de table*. In fact, the same wine was in both bottles. But the experts gushed over the "*grand cru*" and dismissed the "*vin de table*" as weak. His conclusion: "People talk a lot of garbage about wine and we French are the worst."

France's Fruit Machine

The E.U. and the Common Agricultural Policy

From the start, the European Union has been a French-dominated affair. For all the talk of "organic unity" and "common interest", it often seems to be an instrument for the interests of France alone.

Few subjects are as soul-corrodingly dull as the European Union. It was supposed to be an engine for European unification but, precisely because no normal person can contemplate its bureaucratic mazework and legal convolutions without coughing up their own skull, it has been engineered into a fruit machine that pays off for really just one country, the French.

THE REAL MASTERS
"Europe is the way for France to become what she has ceased to be since Waterloo: the leading power in the world." General de Gaulle to Alain Peyrefitte, 1962.

The basis of the E.U. was the European Coal and Steel Community (E.C.S.C.) of 1951. This was formed of six countries: France, Germany, Italy, Belgium, Holland and Luxembourg. On paper this was supposed to be a club for the free trade of basic industrial materials between its members. From the

THE NATURE OF THE BEAST

The European Union (E.U.) is an inter-governmental union of 25 mostly European countries established in 1992 by the Treaty on European Union (the Maastricht Treaty), although many aspects of the Union existed before then through a series of predecessor agreements, dating back to 1951, most of them trade agreements initiated by the traditional driving force of European integration, France. Today, the E.U.'s activities cover all areas of public policy from health and economic policy to foreign affairs and defence; however, 40% of the E.U.'s annual budget is devoted to agricultural subsidy even though agriculture represents only 12% of the continent's G.D.P.

Member States: *Austria, Belgium, Cyprus, Czech Republic, Denmark, Estonia, Finland, France, Germany, Greece, Hungary, Ireland, Italy, Latvia, Lithuania, Luxembourg, Malta, Netherlands, Poland, Portugal, Slovakia, Slovenia, Spain, Sweden, United Kingdom.*

Official centres: *Strasbourg (official seat), Brussels (executive), Luxembourg (administrative)*
Area: *3,976,372 km?*
Population *(2005): 459,500,000*
G.D.P. *(2005): €9,961,516 million ($12,329,110 million)*

---

start, the French had other ideas. Robert Schumann, the French Foreign Minister of the time, said as the treaty was signed: "Through the consolidation of basic production this proposal represents the first concrete step towards a European federation, imperative for the preservation of peace".

That phrase, "preservation of peace", was code for "keep Germany on a leash". Twice in the previous fifty years, the Germans had attacked France. After the Second World War, it was in France's interests to tie its larger neighbour down with as many treaties of co-operation, co-ordination and cultural friendship as possible.

THE BEGINNINGS.
Between 1951 and 1961, the value exchanged between the member countries under the ECSC was estimated at 62% to France, 16% each to Italy and the Benelux countries, and just 6% to Germany. The first two presidents of the E.C.S.C. were French, the third was Belgian. Two-thirds of its budget was devoted to agriculture. Germany contributed 65% of the budget and France 8%.

THE CODE

"In France the language of federalism, on the lips of political traders, has become a code. French nationalists, listening to their president recommending federalism, are expected to think: 'We will outsmart them because we are so much cleverer, and we will run Europe as well as our own country'." Conor Cruise O'Brien, Irish politician, 1974.

IF THE C.A.P. FITS

The Common Agricultural Policy (C.A.P.) is a system of European Union agricultural subsidies which represents about 44% of the E.U.'s budget (€43 billion – $53 billion – in 2005). These subsidies guarantee a minimum price to producers through direct payment. The reason is set out in Clause 2, Article 39 of the Treaty of Rome: "to ensure a fair standard of living for the agricultural community". Over the years, the social and financial value of this clause, especially to the French, has seen it outweigh the importance of other clauses in Article 39, including Clause 5: "to provide consumers with food at reasonable prices". C.A.P. price intervention causes artificially high food prices throughout the E.U. Europeans pay about 25% more for their food than they would without the C.A.P. (the Timbro Research Institute has counted figures reaching over 80%). European sugar alone costs more than three times the global market price. This subsidy costs each E.U. citizen, on average, €24 ($30) per week.

The E.C.S.C. now gave France a high level of influence over the industrial and economic policy of the burgeoning Federal Republic – especially since of its six members, three and a half of them were French-speaking. What post-war Germany got out of the deal, according to one commentator, was re-admission to the human race.

Of course, as far as successive French governments were concerned, the Germans had to pay a pretty hefty admission fee. The deal was that France would open its market to German exports in return for German taxpayers subsidising French farmers who were the basis of its largely agricultural economy in the years after the war. That deal solidified into the Common Agricultural Policy in 1957 when, with great fanfare, the E.C.S.C. became the European Economic Community, the forerunner of the European Union.

Ever since, the C.A.P., as it became known, has been passionately defended against all comers by successive French governments. Two-thirds of its budget was devoted simply to French agriculture. Very simply, it allows the French to pay off their farmers, traditionally one of the country's most vociferous and frequently violent interest groups, with cash from the taxpayers of other countries. In 1965, when the Germans suggested some timid reforms that might have led to a cut

"NON"

"The entry first of Great Britain and then of the other states will completely change the series of adjustments, agreements, compensations and regulations already established the cohesion of its members would not hold for long and in the end there would appear a colossal Atlantic Community under American dependence and leadership, which would soon swallow up the European Community. That is not at all what France wanted to do and what France is doing, which is strictly a European construction ." President de Gaulle, vetoing Britain's entry into the E.E.C. in 1963.

in the C.A.P. budget, President de Gaulle ordered his delegates out of all E.E.C. bodies, freezing all decision-making in the Community until the other members caved in six months later.

Over the years, the European Community has been enlarged – often in the face of vigorous French opposition (the country vetoed the U.K.'s application for membership twice). It now numbers twenty-five. It is no longer quite so easy for the French to fix the fruit machine so that the jackpot comes up every time.

Nevertheless, since 1994 France has paid in €10.53 billion ($13 billion) into the E.U. budget while taking out €68.6 billion ($84.9 billion), almost all of it in agricultural subsidy. A 2003 economic report commissioned by the E.U. Commission described the C.A.P. as "an historic relic" and recommended that it be scrapped. The recommendations were ignored.

Today, the C.A.P. accounts for 40% of the total annual E.U. budget even though agriculture accounts for just 5% of E.U. jobs and 1.6% of economic output. The biggest beneficiary remains France which, though only one member out of twenty-five, takes a quarter of the budget, amounting to €10.4 billion ($12.9 billion) in 2003.

HOME FROM HOME

A telling example of France's influence over the E.U. can be seen in the European Parliament whenever it meets in Strasbourg, a middle-sized city in the east of France. The Parliament itself has very little say about how things are run but it gives a little democratic sheen to the organisation. When the Parliament was set up, it was due to sit in Brussels, where the European Commission meets. However, the French objected, demanding that the hugely expensive parliamentary apparatus be moved to Strasbourg to give that city's economy a boost. In 1979, a compromise was agreed. The Parliament would go to Strasbourg but for only 48 days a year. The rest of the time it would meet in Brussels while two-thirds of its staff and its library would be sited in Luxemburg . A new parliament building was constructed at a cost of €404 million ($500 million) in Strasbourg. This back and forth of members, secretaries, translators and general hangers-on costs 20% of the Parliament's €1.3 billion ($1.6 billion) budget each year.

The French argue that Europe must support their farmers because their standard of living is essential to the culture of the entire continent. The beret-wearing, wise old man (Gérard Depardieu), tending his vines while his winsome daughter (Juliette Binoche) draws water from the well and the apparently hundreds of thousands of peasant farmers living the *Manon des Sources* lifestyle across France must be preserved if the world is to enjoy those cottage-made cheeses that smell like mud or those tasty thrush pies or that local brandy that can eat through a ceramic beaker.

Except that this image of French agriculture is completely false. Only 4.5% of

HITTING THE JACKPOT. *This is how the E.U. system of contributions and subsidies works for France. By comparison, the figures for the U.K., a country of comparable economic size and G.D.P. are also included.*

	France	U.K.
Net contribution to E.U. (2003)	€0.081 bn	€7.95 bn
Total net contribution to E.U. since 1994	€15.272 bn	€34.638 bn
Total C.A.P. receipts since 1994	€99.2 bn	€41.1 bn
C.A.P. receipts per head (2003)	€169.0	€65.0

It should be noted that the largest overall contributor to the E.U. budget and the C.A.P. is Germany (though Holland pays more per head). If it were not for the budget rebate negotiated by U.K. Prime Minister Margaret Thatcher in 1984, the U.K. would be paying 14 times the contribution of France. In 2005, President Chirac launched a diplomatic campaign in the E.U. to reduce this rebate.

the French workforce are employed in agriculture, and 80% of the C.A.P. subsidies paid go to just 20% of French farmers, mostly corporations, who run the industrial-sized beef, cereal, dairy and beet operations for huge French *hypermarché* chains.

France's control of the C.A.P. within the structures of the European Union is very tight. In 2005, the British proposed reforming the agricultural budget. President Chirac responded by demanding that the rebate paid by the E.U. to the British be cut, which it was – in return for a pledge that the French would review the national weighting of the C.A.P. "sometime in 2012".

This issue is about far more than a nice little bribe to a sector of the French electorate that President Chirac wants to keep sweet. The C.A.P. might be run for the benefit of France but it inflates food prices across all of Europe by roughly €83 billion ($103 billion) a year (in the U.K., one of the richer E.U. members, that's an additional £1,500 a year on the food bills of a family of four). More destructively, the huge C.A.P. leads to vast agricultural surpluses in farm goods, like sugar beet, that have been over-produced but no-one in Europe can buy because that would lower prices. Instead, they are dumped below cost in the markets of the Third World, effectively kicking the floor out from

THE WHINERS WIN
France's influence throughout the E.U. and its institutions is pervasive. Many diplomats from member countries complain about France's "presumption of ownership". In 2005, almost the entire political establishment of France were desperate that their citizens should vote in the new – French-written – European Constitution. To help them out, in April 2005, the European Commission bowed to French pressure and deferred the imposition of a new duty on wine already agreed by all the other member states. "France is very sensitive and we are very sensitive to France", the London Times *quoted one European Commissioner as saying.*

under the feet of the real peasant farmers of Asia, Africa and South America.

Even enthusiastic pro-European, anti-free market observers like tubby film-maker Michael Moore understand the poisonous implications, which he describes as "literally killing people in the Third World. In fact. it is killing more people than all of Dubya's bombs". According to the *Human Development Report 2003*, the average dairy cow in the E.U. received €739 ($913) in subsidies in 2000, compared with an average of €6.5 ($8) per person in Sub-Saharan Africa.

"NO" TO EUROPE

French politicians got a taste of their own obstructionist medicine in 2005 when, to the amazement of the rest of Europe, the French public voted "Non" to a mooted European Constitution. This Constitution had been written by a former French President, Valery Giscard d'Estaing (who, after losing an election when it was revealed that he received regular gifts of diamonds from General Jean-Bedel Bokassa of the Central African Republic, had typically been appointed Chairman of the Convention on the Future of Europe). It was a step closer to making the European Union into a "super-state", giving its institutions new powers in the domestic and economic lives of its citizens. French politicians led by Jacques Chirac were so confident that the Constitution would consolidate French power in Europe, that they made the treaty's ratification subject to a national referendum. But on 29 May 2005 the French public voted "Non", despite a prolonged, partly government-funded campaign that was supported by all the major political parties and the media in France. Paradoxically, the voters rejected the treaty by 55% to 45% because it didn't give enough influence to France and potentially threatened to dilute their much-valued subsidies.

Quarante-Sept

The Holocaust
to Liberty

The French Revolution
and "The Terror"

The French are proud of their Revolution, claiming it to be the prime example of a people seizing and protecting liberty for itself. In reality, it was a frenzied, paranoid bloodbath.

THE HOLOCAUST 1792
"Once more, citizens to arms! May all France bristle with pikes, bayonets, cannon and daggers Let us clear the ranks of vile slaves of tyranny. Let the blood of traitors be the first holocaust [literally, le premier holocauste] to Liberty." Fabre d'Eglantine in September 1792, revolutionary poet and leader, himself executed in 1793 when his political faction fell out of favour and he was judged "counter-revolutionary".

On 14 July 2005, President Chirac motored down the Champs Elysées in a polished-up army jeep. A column of tanks rumbled past, cheered on by flag-waving crowds. Fighter jets roared overhead. In the evening, there was a spectacular firework display centred around the Eiffel Tower. In a televised address, the President reminded viewers that the day's celebrations commemorated a moment in history when "the world looked to France as she proclaimed *liberté, egalité, fraternité* for all".

Bastille Day is a national holiday celebrating the French Revolution. Regarded as a central event in Western civilisation, the Revolution is usually cited by historians, both French and foreign, as a blazing example of a nation granting

281

itself political and social liberty. Since the Revolution actually introduced industrialised killings, systematic repression, military dictatorship and world war, this view seems skewed. But it does reveal the Revolution's true significance in history; as the first occasion in which quite obvious terror was justified because it was on behalf of "the people", a thumbs-up previously reserved for "God" and "The King".

From the start, the Revolution was built on such delusions. The storming of the Bastille in July 1789 was not, as legend has it, a triumphant battle in which a crowd of Paris' poor overran a fortress to free the prisoners of a cruel king. The 'crowd' was several thousand strong and armed with canon seized from military depots around Paris, and it was opposed by 110 soldiers. Only seven inmates were inside, not one of whom was a political prisoner. Moreover, the jail was more like a white-collar, country-club facility; prisoners brought in their own furniture, servants and even sexual partners. All the soldiers were massacred after they had surrendered. "Gracious God", said one American observer, Gouverneur Morris, "what a people".

The fall of the Bastille, regarded as the beginning of the Revolution, was not really out of the ordinary. It was just one in a long cycle of riots and civil disturbances which ebbed and flowed across France, provoked by poor harvests and a wartime

REVOLUTION TO DICTATORSHIP: STEP-BY-STEP

1789
May 5	Meeting of the Estates-General
June 17	National Assembly declared
July 14	Storming of the Bastille
August 4	Feudal rights abolished
August 27	Declaration of the Rights of Man

1790
July 14	Constitution signed by the king
July	Growing power of the clubs
June 20-25	Royal family tries to flee France but is arrrested
September 30	Assembly dissolved

1792
April 20	War declared against Austria
September 2-7	September Massacres

1793
January 21	Execution of Louis XVI
February 1	War declared against Britain, Holland, Spain
March	Royalist revolt in the Vendée
April	Power centered in Committee of Public Safety
June 2	Arrest of 31 Girondist deputies (moderates)
September 17	Establishment of food controls
October 31	Execution of Girondists
November 10	Replacement of Christianity by "Cult of Reason"

1794
March 24	Execution of Hébertists (extremists)
April 6	Execution of Danton and the Montagnards (moderate extremists)
June 10	Law of 22 Prairial (allowing arbitrary arrest and execution)
July 27	Execution of Robespierre and the Jacobins (extreme extremists)

1795
April 1	Bread riots in Paris
October 5	Napoleon Bonaparte's troops fire on Paris crowds, showing them once and for all who was boss.

"LIBERTÉ"

During the Revolutionary period, liberty was a meaningless word to the 500,000 slaves working the French sugar plantations on Sainte Domingue (later Haiti). In 1790, the National Assembly decreed to exempt the colonies from the constitution and French troops co-operated with planter militias to disperse anti-slavery demonstrations on the islands. On 22 August 1791 the slaves rose in rebellion and, after a bitter war, succeeded in establishing Haitian independence in 1804 at the cost of 75,000 French and 200,000 Haitian dead.

economy. On the same day the Bastille fell, crowds had sacked the nearby convent of Saint-Lazare, which acted as a charity hospital. A month before, the Paris mob had destroyed a wallpaper factory. It was the same in the provinces, with noble houses occasionally being burned and barns looted. It was like a day out.

The reason that this was allowed to go on was that the king, the pudgy, vague Louis XVI, was far from an absolute autocrat. None too bright, his ministers had already persuaded him to call a parliament which had evolved into France's first representative government, the National Assembly. It took some prodding but he signed over power peaceably enough. The Assembly promulgated the document that turned France into a constitutional democracy and a beacon of liberty, on paper. This was the famous *Declaration of the Rights of Man and of the Citizen*, based on the three principles of *liberté, égalité, fraternité*.

None of these principles was put into practice from the off. The constitution of 1791 with its press censorship and right of arbitrary arrest would not have been out of place, observed Tom Paine, American revolutionary and freelance troublemaker, "in the enslaved domains of the Tsar of Muscovy". The French jailed him for uppitiness.

What the Revolution did provide was talk, and plenty of it. For months, speaker after speaker in the Assembly (which evolved into the National Convention), echoed outside by wave after wave of pamphlets and posters, worked themselves into a froth trying to out-Revolution all the other revolutionaries. "A huge conspiracy is taking place against the liberty not only of France but of the whole human race", said one parliamentarian, Hérault de Sechelles, in a piffling debate on whether priests should be compulsorily

"EGALITÉ"

Equality was not even applied in France itself, since the poor were not allowed to vote in elections. The Constution of 1791 imposed a property qualification which left around four-fifths of French male adults without the vote. The Constituion of 1793 (there were many such constitutions) proposed universal male suffrage but it was immediately suspneded by the Jacobins in favour of "revolutionary government until the peace". However, there never was any peace.

"FRATERNITÉ"
Obviously this didn't apply to half of France's population, its women. They had been promised a political voice and economic indpendence by the new regime. By the end of the Revolution, a woman could not even attend the Assembly as a visitor unless she had a signed pass and was accompanied by a male adult. One law stipulated that groups of more than five women gathered together in public should be broken up by troops. Such new restrictions caused an outcry amongst the many articulate female supporters of the Revolution until one of them, Olympe des Gouges, was stripped naked, whipped on the street and eventually guillotined for "obstructionism".

married. "The enemies of the people", suggested another in the same debate, the self-named Anacharsis Cloots, "must be smothered in their own blood". Soon the Convention talked itself into declaring a revolutionary war on Austria and, when it went badly, began a witch hunt against anyone who was, in the words of Maximilien Robespierre, a lawyer from Arras and leading light in the new Committee for Public Safety, "against freedom in our pure republic". Such words keyed up the populations of France's cities, especially Paris, to an hysterical pitch.

The Reign of Terror (*la Terreur*) began. The first big massacres of the Revolution kicked off in September 1792. The prisons of Paris were filled with priests who had protested when the Revolution had confiscated Church land. With them were members of the old Royalist army suspected of being politically unsound, shopkeepers accused of price gouging and reporters caught by the censorship laws. Under the direction of the Paris Commune, which had taken control of the city, gangs entered the gaols on the evening of 2 September. The lucky prisoners were shot, the rest were bayoneted or clubbed to death and, in some cases, chopped up with a butcher's saw. Official figures record that 1,400 were killed over the next few nights. The authorities took over responsibility for exterminating the real or imagined enemies of the Revolution. A guillotine was set up in the Place de la Révolution in front of the Tuileries Palace. King Louis was rushed through a show trial and executed.

His queen, Marie Antoinette, soon followed. An indication that even the most *enragé* Jacobins thought the treason charges against Marie-Antoinette were weak, she was additionally accused of lesbianism and incest with her own infant son, the *Dauphin*. After their deaths, he was kept in darkened solitary confinement in the Temple prison where he died two years later either of disease or strangulation, aged ten.

In terms of revolutionary logic, killing off the head of the old regime made a kind of spiteful sense, although the revolutionaries had bafflingly failed to prevent 150,000 aristocrat families fleeing France and into the arms of its increasingly hostile neighbours. What followed was a frenzied, paranoid bloodbath.

Political cliques, one after the other, seized control of the government and

SIX DEGREES OF (CRANIAL) SEPARATION

A defining feature of the Revolution was that the governing clique invariably had the clique it succeeded sent to the guillotine before being guillotined in turn by the clique that would replace it. This pattern can be seen most plainly by examing the fates of six representative personalities involved in the Revolution.

KING LOUIS XIV *(1754 – 21 January 1793). Monarchist.*
Vague, fumbling French king, unlucky enough to be the symbol of autocratic repression in France at the start of the Revolution though really about as dictatorial as a wet sheep. Accepted the position of constitutional monarch but eventually tried to flee Paris. Arrested for treason. Among the members of the National Convention voting to execute him was:

PHILIPPE EGALITÉ *("Philip Equality"). Constitutional monarchist. The "street-name" of Louis Philippe II, Duke of Orléans (1747 – 6 November 1793). A favourite cousin of King Louis but a prototypical limousine liberal who joined the National Convention and voted for his death. Alway suspected that he himself wished to replace Louis as king. His eventual arrest and execution on general charges of being a filthy aristocrat were warmly supported by:*

MADAME ROLAND, *the name used by Vicountess Jeanne Manon Philipon Roland de la Platière (1754 – 8 November 1793). Whilst holding no political position, she was the wife of a senior Constitutional republican politican (called* Girondins*) though it was recognised that she was the brains of the partnership (she was arrested, he wasn't). A journalist, activist and general busybody, her execution was fixed by:*

JACQUES HÉBERT *(1757 – 24 March 1794). Extreme republican (called* Cordeliers*), one of the nastiest personalities of the Revolution, editor of obscene political newspaper* Le Père Duchesne *and police chief He said of Mme. Roland's death "She asked for it, the bitch". Was himself led screaming and begging to the block having fallen foul of:*

GEORGES JACQUES DANTON *(1759 – 5 April 1794). Moderately extreme republican (called* Montagnards*). Toad-faced compulsive orator and notably corrupt Minister of Justice. Proudly created the notorious Revolutionary Tribunal which purged the National Convention of his political enemies but then ordered the execution of its creator when it fell under the control of:*

MAXIMILIEN FRANÇOIS MARIE ISIDORE DE ROBESPIERRE *(1758 – 28 July 1794). Ultra-extreme republican (called* Jacobins*). Colourless, periwigged administrator in silk knee breeches. Abolished religion and appointed himself high priest of the "Cult of the Supreme Being". Architect of the Terror, made the mistake of announcing a new wave of arrests was imminent but without listing names. He was arrested and executed himself by those fearful he was talking about them, chief amongst them being etc, etc.*

immediately ordered their predecessors to the guillotine until it was their own turn for the chop. The government itself became a centralised police administration which wasn't above using paid mobs from the streets to beat up or kill its opponents. (When it was realised that a famous beauty of one of the few remaining aristocrats, the Princesse de Lamballe, might gain sympathy if she were publicly guillotined, the authorities had her released from La Force prison and straight into the arms of a pre-hired gang waiting outside who stripped her, raped her, cut off her head and breasts, mutilated her genitalia and stuck the parts on pikes which they paraded around Paris).

NOTHING PERSONAL
The horrors of the Revolution are generally excused because at least those who committed them were acting impartially. Not exactly. For the French, it proved to be a wonderful opportunity to pay off old scores. Before the Revolution, the great chemist Antoine-Laurent Lavoisier turned down a chemical treatise as worthless. The writer was Jean-Paul Marat who became one of the most radical revolutionaries. He saw to it that Lavoisier was made increasingly unpopular. In 1794 Lavoisier was guillotined. When pleas were made that such a distinguished scientist should be saved, the judge declared: "The Republic has no need for men of science".

For nearly a year, the guillotine worked away as busily as a sewing machine. All dissent of any kind was classified by the Revolutionary Tribunals as "counter-revolutionary" and became punishable by death (one unlucky farrier lost his head for blowing his nose on a red rag, considered to be the colour of the revolution). Residents living in the streets close to the Place de la Révolution, where the executions took place, complained that the stench of blood was lowering their property prices. The chief executioner of Paris, Charles Henri-Sanson, became so adept at his job that, at the height of *La Terreur*, he was able to despatch twelve victims in thirteen minutes. Not until the advent of the gas chambers was political killing so efficiently automated.

The number of people who died in Paris is still fiercely debated by historians. The officially sanitised records show that only 2,800 were executed in the capital over eight months; however, Sanson's diary mentions that in just one three-day period, he himself despatched 300 victims. Modern historians like Simon Schama estimate that 10,000 died in Paris alone.

Another 30,000 died in the provinces as revolutionary commissioners set out to purge the major towns. In Lyon, Collot d'Herbois used cannon for his mass executions; Carrier drowned his prisoners in boats at Nantes; while Fouché in Toulon liked, among other methods, to herd them into cavernous wine cellars and then wall the places up. "Tonight we will execute 1,213 insurgents", he wrote to a friend. "Adieu – tears of joy flow from my eyes".

"MADEMOISELLE GUILLOTINE"

The guillotine, the Revolution's most dramatic symbol, is named after the "humanitarian" physician, Joseph Ignace Guillotin. A member of the French National Assembly, he recommended that executions be performed by a beheading machine rather than by hanging since it was quicker. In 1791 the Assembly adopted a design by Dr Antoine Louis, secretary of the College of Surgeons, and it was first used on 25 April 1792, to execute a highwayman named Pelletier. During the Terror, executions by guillotine were a popular entertainment attracting great crowds of spectators. Vendors would sell programmes listing the names of those scheduled to die. Regulars would come day after day and vie for the best seats. Parents would bring their children. Audiences to guillotinings told numerous stories of blinking eyelids, moving eyes, mouth movements, even an expression of "unequivocal indignation" on the face of the decapitated Charlotte Corday (executed for assassinating the extreme Jacobin, Jean-Paul Marat) when her cheek was slapped by an executioner playing up to the crowd. These symptoms may be only random muscle twitching or automatic reflex action. Technically, the massive drop in cerebral blood pressure caused victims to lose consciousness in 5-10 seconds. The device was called a louisette *or* louison *after its inventor's name, but because of Guillotin's famous speech, his name became associated with the machine. Toward the end of the Terror, the good doctor only just avoided ending up on his own device. After his death in 1814, his children tried to have the device's name changed. When their efforts failed, they had to change their name instead.*

The revolutionaries did not have it all their own way. A royalist counter-revolution sprang up in the Vendée region, the Deep South of France, and pitchfork-wielding peasantry eagerly took their revenge on their snotty revolutionary cousins in the local towns in what is now called the "White Terror". This outbreak was followed by bloody repression, with massacres aplenty on both sides during 1793 and around 100,000 fatalities.

Mercifully, it didn't last. The Revolution ended the way that revolutions usually do; with a military dictator. Fearful that their own heads might be the next to bounce into the basket, government

THE KINDLY COMMISSIONER

The revolutionary commissioner sent to purge Nantes, Jean-Baptiste Carrier, considered the guillotine too slow. He preferred to have his victims packed into barges which were then towed into the river Loire and capsized. To add a sexual frisson, young couples were stripped naked and tied face-to-face before drowning. The water became so polluted with corpses that fishing was banned. Carrier also held that the guillotine was an unsatisfactory method of beheading children under six, tending to chop their heads in half since their necks were too small a target for the blade. One executioner collapsed and had a heart attack after beheading four little sisters. Considerate to the feeling of his staff, Carrier refused to allow five hundred further youngsters scheduled for execution to go to the guillotine – instead, he had them shot in a field.

officials engineered an army coup. They hoped that at least a little of the freedom that the Revolution had been supposed to provide could now be delivered. Some hope. The man they chose to lead their coup was a certain General Bonaparte. He had no doubt what the high talk and deaths of the last few years had been all about: "Vanity made the [French] Revolution; liberty was only a pretext".

The final outcome of the Revolution was Emperor Napoleon I and a totalitarian regime far more revolutionary than the Revolution ever was – and its cost to France and the world not tens of thousands but millions of lives.

ROBESPIERRE EXPLAINS WHY TERROR IS NOT REALLY AS BAD AS IT SOUNDS
"Terror is nought but prompt, severe, inflexible justice; it is therefore an emanation of virtue; it is less a particular principle than a consequence of the general principle of democracy applied to the most pressing needs of the fatherland." Maximilien Robespierre, Address to the National Convention, 1794.

CHILDREN OF THE REVOLUTION
"We need the real, nation-wide terror which reinvigorates the country and through which the Great French Revolution achieved glory." Vladimir Lenin, Russian revolutionary and dictator, 1920.

Quarante-Huit

Enarques

Masters of le Grand Oral

For years, France's political institutions, civil service and
leading businesses have been run by specially trained, super-
intelligent *Enarques*. Who are they? What do they do?
And why are so many facing criminal charges?

"Enarque *is the colloquial name for a graduate of the* Ecole Nationale
d'Administration *or one of the other elite French institutes of higher education
dedicated to preparing young people for careers in public administration.* Enarques
of all ages call each other tu *and expect to run the great departments of state;
many now go on to high positions in industry or the European Commission."*
Rodney Leach, A Concise Encyclopedia of the European Union, *2000.*

More than in any other western country, political, economic and
administrative power in France is in the hands of a tiny elite – the
énarques. All are graduates of Paris's celebrated *Ecole Nationale
d'Administration* (E.N.A., National School of Administration) and its sister
institutions, the *Ecole Polytechnique* or the *Institut d'Etudes Politiques de Paris* (the
Paris Institute of Political Sciences) still better known as "Sciences Po".

The roll call of modern French government reads like a graduation class from E.N.A.: six of the past nine prime ministers; usually the bulk of the cabinet; two of the past three presidents, including the current incumbent, Jacques Chirac; and just over half of the top 17 ministers in the last government (the present-day Minister of the Interior, Dominique de Villepin is an *énarque*).

The sheer exclusivity of their education keeps the *énarques'* old-boy network going. Each year E.N.A. produces a mere hundred or so graduates (of whom a quarter to a third are women). There are only 5,000 living *énarques*, against some 100,000 current graduates of Oxbridge and over half a million more Ivy Leaguers.

LIKE FATHER LIKE SON
General de Gaulle founded ENA in 1945 to break the upper classes' control of the civil service and prevent nepotism. But while 29% of E.N.A. students came from working-class backgrounds in 1950, the figure has shrunk to 9% today. 2004 research by the Ecole Normale Superiere shows that parents are typically C.E.O.s or senior civil servants with 6% being énarques *themselves.*

Candidates, selected from within the civil service or snaffled from the country's most academic universities, spend up to two years preparing for the gruelling E.N.A. entrance examinations. Spaced out over three months, these culminate in *le Grand oral* – a 45-minute interview where questions on any imaginable subject are fired at the candidate. The secret to success here is apparently the ability to argue a point from both sides

Only 120 are granted a place but once accepted they receive around €1,500 ($1,850) a month from the state to cover living expenses. The curriculum is narrow, mostly dealing with case studies in international relations and administrative law. Not much else is taught. A recent E.N.A. graduate currently working in the Ministry of Finance and interviewed in 2004 by the *Economist* magazine says that he didn't learn much academically at the school. "There were some great extracurricular activities – I took Arabic lessons and sport – but as for the actual academic subjects, it was mainly rehashing what I already knew from my political science studies."

The prize makes it all worthwhile. All graduates are automatically given five years employment in the French civil service with the ability to pick and choose from top government postings available. One graduate summed this up: "There is a lot of pressure to succeed, because

DEADLOCKED
"Today France is directed by a group of irresponsible public servants who have seized both political and economic power – deadlocked the system – and are driving the country into a wall. Some members of this nomenklatura *are heading the state (Chirac, de Villepin, Juppé, Jospin, Hollande), others are in charge of its businesses (Messier, Jaffré, Bilger, Seillière)." Jean-Christophe Mounicq, French political writer and* Washington Post *contributor, 2003.*

the results so determine what you will end up doing if you do poorly, you risked being stuck in some *trou* (one-horse) regional state department for the rest of your life".

After their stint of public service, graduates then tend to move into politics or the private sector, getting the best jobs at the best salaries. No students have to look for jobs after the course, an E.N.A. brochure explains – "the jobs come to them".

Finally, more than a few end up in the civil or criminal courts.

Like *énarque* Jean-Marie Messier, former head of French media group Vivendi Universal. In 2003, when the giant French media group collapsed with crushing debts, the Paris Commercial Court had to authorise a freeze on the €20.5 million ($25 million) severance approved for Messier by Vivendi's Chief Operating Officer, *énarque* Eric Licoys. The court then froze a similar pay-off to Licoys approved by Messier. The ex-chairman is now on bail of €1 million ($1.25 million) while French courts investigate share price manipulation, misuse of company funds and publication of misleading information.

Like *énarque* Pierre Bilger, ex-chairman of Alstom. In his two years at the helm he crippled the engineering firm, maker of the prestigious T.G.V. high speed train, with €4.9 billion ($6 billion) debts and saw its shares drop by 90%. His severance package was €3.9 million ($4.8 million). He currently faces a formal inquiry by the U.S. Securities and Exchange Commission into accounting irregularities at its U.S. transport unit.

Like *énarque* Roland Dumas, head of the Constitutional Court, who in March 2002 took "temporary leave" pending inquiries into gifts allegedly received from the then state-owned Elf oil company when he was Foreign Minister.

Like former Prime Minister, *énarque* Alain Juppé, convicted of presiding over illegal party funding while Secretary-General of President Chirac's Union for a Popular Majority (U.M.P.) during the '80s.

NOT SO TOUGH AT THE TOP
A study from the C.N.R.S., Centre National de Recherche Scientifique *revealed that half of the chairmen of France's top 200 companies are* énarque *or* polytechniciens *including* Ernest-Antoine Seillière (boss *of Wendel Investissement),* Henri de Castries (), Bernard Arnault (boss of L.V.M.H.) *and Bertrand Collomb (head of Lafarge).*

ENA=MAFIA?
"Ireland has the I.R.A., Spain has E.T.A., Italy the mafia, but France has E.N.A." Alain Madelin, new leader of the free-market Liberal Democracy party (formerly the Republican Party).

Like *énarque* Bernard Bonnet, former prefect of Corsica, accused of burning down a restaurant so he could blame it on Corsican nationalists.

Like the *énarques* amongst the six former or current leaders of political parties, the thirty ex-ministers, over a hundred former or serving members of parliament or mayors, and a quarter of the heads of the forty biggest companies (some of whom have since left), who are or have been subject to official investigations into corruption.

But not like the current Prime Minister Jean-Pierre Raffarin, a blokeish provincial not in the *énarque* mould at all. His cabinet only has two *énarques* (the last one had eight with two-thirds of the ministerial *directeurs de cabinet* being *énarques* or *polytechniciens*).

E.N.A. has been lambasted for being socially selective and anti-free market. Bernard Zimmern, author of a recent book, *Les profiteurs de l'Etat* (*They profit from the State*), is not alone in complaining about *énarques* being indoctrinated with "statist propaganda to the glory of the public service". Raffarin seems to have listened.

Prompted by a growing outcry in the French parliament and the press, he is pushing through reforms to E.N.A., which include uprooting the school from Paris and placing it in Strasbourg. However, his reforms have been mild; the guarantee of high-flying civil service posts for all graduates, much demanded by anti-E.N.A. campaigners, has not been abolished.

BLOCKING THE PATH
"Half a century on, we cannot avoid the conclusion that E.N.A. has produced nothing more than an omnipotent 'caste' capable of only one thing: planning its members' career-paths." Jean-Michel Fourgous and Herve Novelli, members of the French National Assembly, 2003.

And the move to Strasbourg may not be as innocent as it seems. After all, the city is home to the world's fastest burgeoning, highest paid civil service – the European Commission. The current French European Commissioner is Jacques Barrot, a close ally of Jacques Chirac and a former minister convicted in 2000 of embezzling party funds (a fact he did not reveal at his appointment hearings before the commission in 2004).

Barrot is, obviously, a graduate of the *Institut d'Etudes Politiques de Paris*.

Perfidious Albion Non Plus

France Faces Facts About Its Neighbour

For a thousand years of history, the French have hated the British. But now, as the world enters the twenty-first century, is France throwing in the towel on its age-old rivalry?

"PERFIDIOUS ALBION"
The insult traditionally thrown at Britain by its so sadly unfulfilled friends over the English Channel (the name France is officially forced to call this sea by the 1763 Treaty of Paris, ending another unsuccessful war against its neighbours) has a long history. It originates in a ballad from the Hundred Years War by Eustace Deschamps, bailiff of Senlis, after Henry V's men burned his castle down. He bewailed the destruction of "this crude island of the giants / Which we must call Albion" (a medieval term for England dervided from the Latin word albus *(white), said to have been given by Julius Caesar, alluding to England's white cliffs seen from France). The term "la perfide Angleterre" (perfidious England) was used in 1702 by Jacques-Bénigne Bossuet, bishop of Condom (and incidentally father of three), in his* Sermon on the Circumcision. *During the Napoleonic wars, the Marquis de Ximenès called hopelessly for the French fleet to "Attack in its very waters, that perfidious Albion". The phrase caught on and was used in an 1809 poem by Henri Simon celebrating a French victory at Essling: "Quiver, tremble, you perfidious Albion". In 1842, British author William Thackeray noted while travelling in Paris that almost every news from over the Channel "evokes ferocious yells of hatred against perfidious Albion uttered by the French press". The epithet has stuck and even today almost every discussion in the French media about the comparative status of the two countries works as a kind of stock joke. French humour, eh? Not for export, really.*

It's like some terrible dream. You run through a wood, shadowed by a relentless, hateful thing. You hear mocking laughter, smell breath rotten with beer and poor dentistry at your neck. It's going to leap! You jolt awake but, *calmes-toi*, you're in bed at home and, why, here is *maman* with your *café au lait* and your blue blankie. Wait, that's not ma It's the *thing*. It's back and you're still trapped in a dream. It's *déjà vu* all over again! The French have a word for this kind of nightmare: the British.

For a thousand years, Britain was at almost perpetual war with France, blocking Europe's domination by the Sun King, the Jacobins or Napoleon, or at the least stopping France escaping into the outside world.

Between 1689 and 1815 alone, Britain took her on in seven major *world* wars. Peace, even when France was nominally an ally, was like a cold war. Various British justifications were given at different times. Sometimes it was god, gold, the flag, the slave trade or the anti-slave trade

BRITAIN VS. FRANCE
Major conflicts between France and the U.K. over the last 1,000 years (smaller wars excluded)

Date	Winner
Norman Conquest *(1066)*	*France*
Wars of Henry II *(1152-89)*	*Britain*
The Hundred Years War *(1337-1453)*	*France*
The Italian Wars *(1542-59)*	*France*
War of the Grand Alliance *(1688-97)*	*Britain*
The War of the Spanish Succession *(1701-14)*	*Britain*
The War of the Austrian Succession *(1740-48).*	*Draw*
The Seven Years War *(1754 and 1756–63)*	*Britain*
The American Revolutionary War *(1775–83)*	*France*
The French Revolutionary Wars *(1792-1802)*	*France*
The Napoleonic Wars *(1802-15)*	*Britain*
World War II *(1939-45)*	*Britain*

(though initially an ally of France, Britain sank France's Mediterranean fleet and invaded Vichy North Africa)

or the basic belief that the principles of "Liberté, Egalité et Fraternité" were the same in practice as "Arbeit macht frei" or "Workers of the world, unite!". The underlying geostrategic theme remained consistent; screw the French.

As a result, French is not the common language of modern Germany, Italy, Holland, Spain, India, America, the workable parts of Africa or (despite a persistent sore on its north-west side) nearly all of Canada. "If it had not been for you English," said Napoleon, throwing in the towel at last to a Royal Navy captain, "I should have been Emperor of the East; but wherever there is water to float a ship, we are sure to find you in our way". He was then carried off to perpetual exile on a rock in the middle of the Atlantic.

In the twentieth century, the rivalry faded away. In the real world wars, as far as the French were concerned, the United Kingdom proved a useful but not

THE FRENCH ON THE BRITISH

AND THE BRITISH ON THE FRENCH

"The English people believes itself to be free; it is gravely mistaken; it is free only during election of Marliament; as soon as the members are elected, the people is enslaved." Jean-Jaques Rousseau, Swiss-French philosopher and chronic masturbator, 1702.

"Britain is always the Machiavellian Albion." Honoré de Balzac, hugely prolific French author, died of addiction to espresso one-shots, 1844.

"Impious England executioner of all that France holds divine – murdered grace with Mary, Queen of Scots, inspiration with Joan of Arc, genius with Napoleon." Alexandre Dumas, historical novelist, lover, syphilitic and writer of an estimated 25% of his own books, 1855.

"France must always be at war with England." President de Gaulle, 1963.

"The land across the channel is in danger of becoming an underdeveloped nation." Jacques Attali, former advisor to President Mitterrand and disgraced former president of the European Bank for Reconstruction and Development, 1983.

"The only thing [the British] have ever given European farming is mad cow disease. You can't trust people who cook as badly as that. After Finland's, it's the country with the worst food." Jacques Chirac, French President, promptly provoking the Finns to switch their vote from Paris to London as the preferred venue for the 2012 Summer Olympics, July 2005.

"Being French amounts to a farcical pomp of war, parade of religion, and Bustle with very little business. In short, poverty, slavery and insolence with an affectation of politeness." William Hogarth, artist, cruel cartoonist and much-loved hater of everything, 1750.

"Frenchmen are like gunpowder, each by itself smutty and contemptible, but mass them together and they are terrible indeed!" Samuel Taylor Coleridge, poet, radical and originator of the all-opium diet, 1815.

"France is and must always remain Britain's greatest enemy." Marquess of Salisbury, nobleman, eccentric, borderline autistic and British Prime Minister (1885-86 1886-92, 1895-1902), 1890.

"Perfect – without the French." D H Lawrence, chippy British author of provincial art-porn, 1922.

"There's always something fishy about the French." Noel Coward, actor, playwright and professional pantywaist (amended in 1941 by Ivor Novello, another actor, playwright and professional pantywaist, to: "There's something Vichy about the French"), 1936.

"The rulers of France hate the British, and our freedom-loving ways, because they consider us, and our example, as an insidious threat to their grip on the French masses." Paul Johnson, thunderous commentator, journalist, moralist and spanking aficionado, 1989.

In 1984, the E.E.C. (as the European Union was then known) set quotas for the amount of produce that any one one member nation could export to another without tariffs. French farmers, used to a closed market, began violent attacks on British trucks carrying Welsh lamb into their country, burning the vehicles and their – live – contents by the roadside. The French police were often present when these acts occurred but did nothing, despite fierce British protests. In 2002, the French decided to use the excuse of "Mad Cow Disease" to ban U.K. lamb as well. The British were ready. Rather than making futile protests to the French government, they immediately hauled France before the European Commission for breaching E.U. law. Faced with heavy fines, the French "delayed" the ban and then diplomatically forgot about it. One interesting argument cited by British lawyers was that the risk of human B.S.E. contracted from tainted lamb was so small that it was the equivalent of to the chance of death by autoerotic asphyxiation in all European countries except France, where it was lower.

decisive ally and, after them, it was all played out. With its domination of the European Union, for France to worry about what the British did or thought would be to acknowledge them as some kind of equal, like comparing a noble Alpine eagle to a bluebottle.

From time to time, naturally, some slaps had to be administered to the British. President de Gaulle happily vetoed the U.K.'s entry into the European Union twice and even when it finally got in, in 1973, Margaret Thatcher had to negotiate until 1983 to get a rebate on the British payments made to the Union (which, if left alone, would have left the country, then the third poorest member, paying fifteen times more than France). Even so, the French felt confident enough to ignore E.U. laws when it suited them to remind the British who was boss, allowing its farmers to hijack trucks coming into France in the 1980s carrying Welsh lamb while the gendarmerie looked on bemused.

And yet, as the millennium dawned, France began to wake up from its deep dream of neighbourly superiority to find perfidious Albion not only level but ahead in every field about which France cares.

For a start, the French have discovered that the E.U. doesn't belong to them any more. As soon as the wily Brits finally got through the gates they threw the

JUNE 2005: MELTDOWN

"He wanted to safeguard his entire rebate and that led to other countries to overplay their hand to the detriment of Europe It is pathetic and tragic." President Chirac at the Brussels E.U. Budget Conference on being outmanoeuvred by Prime Minister Blair "I'm not prepared to have someone tell me there is only one view of what Europe is Europe isn't owned by one country. Europe is owned by all of us," Prime Minister Blair replies.

keys over the wall to other nations still waiting outside. The U.K.'s quiet but concerted campaign for enlargement has seen the French-speaking majority of the original seven founding nations diluted into a polyglot twenty-six.

Just how diluted became clear in June 2005, at a grand summit in Brussels, when the French proposed that Britain's €3 billion ($3.7 billion) annual rebate be cut. Britain agreed but only so long as the French renounced their 22% share of the total European agriculture budget, a far heftier €12 billion ($15 billion) payoff. To its fury, France found the Brit-led majority agreed. Chirac stormed out to tell reporters how "pathetic and tragic" it all was that France's vote now counted only as much as, say, Estonia's.

These budget squabbles are a sign of the bigger struggle for the soul of Europe, the confrontation between Britain's free-market economy and France's "social model" with its high taxes, big spending welfare and tight regulation. And France appears to have lost the upper hand to those dirty fighters over the Channel. Despite its smaller population and landmass consisting mostly of rocks, the free-wheeling U.K. now outweighs its neighbour not just in domestic product but in economic growth. Most of the continent, emerging from decades of central planning and creaky welfare states, no longer considers France as a good model with its 10% unemployed and the highest tax rates in mainland Europe despite the pleas of President Chirac: "I do not think the British example is one we should envy". "If the French model is working so well", snapped back one E.U. Commissioner referring to the recent economic unrest that broke out across the country in late 2005, "why are their cities on fire?".

Anyway, the French shrug, who cares about vulgar money? We may be poor (and France is the only country where "peasant" is actually a compliment) but at least we have "*l'art de vie*", while all *les sales anglos* have, according to one recent Parisian newspaper, is "knitting jumpers and breeding rabbits".

The French government has quoted figures produced by itself and its British opposite number in Westminster comparing poverty levels; only 7% of the French live in "poverty" to 17% of the British. Poverty is measured in different ways either side of the Channel: the British calculate integers such as two household televisions and a cell phone as placing you above the poverty line while the French set the marker at in-door plumbing.

The French themselves feel they are failing in comparison with their bumptious next door neighbours – except in taking anti-depressants, at a rate out-consuming Britain by five times. In May 2005 the conservative newspaper *Le Point* summed

FRANCE IN TWO MINDS ABOUT BRITAIN. "*I admit that I have not understood whether Europe was supposed to be British already or we have to stop it becoming so. Of the two options, however, there is one thing we must not do [according to the government]: admire Great Britain In truth the British miracle should serve us as an example, provided we have the courage to cross the Channel and seek answers to the anaemia of our economy.*" Stéphane Denis, editorial, Le Figaro, 2005.

up what a whole wave of French books, articles and media programmes have been insinuating since the turn of the millennium: "Albion, for the moment, is causing us envy rather than pity. Britain is displaying insolent economic health and British diplomacy is exerting its influence over a Europe increasingly shaped to its wishes". The lament was developed by its counterpart on the left, *Le Nouvel Observateur*, touted as the weekly bible of the thinking classes, in a series of articles called simply: "Why are the British better than us?".

HOW THE CONTENDERS WEIGHED IN 2005

	France	U.K.
Population	*60.95 m*	*60.44 m*
Landmass	*547,000 km²*	*244,000 km²*
G.D.P.	*£1.1 trillion*	*£1.2 trillion*
Income per head	*£12,517*	*£13,600*
2004 G.D.P. growth	*2%*	*3.5%*
Foreign direct investment	*£13.8 bn*	*£44.6 bn*
Unemployment	*10.2%*	*4.2%*

In July, Nicolas Sarkozy, a senior government politician, deliberately needled his bitter rival President Chirac by summing up the comparison by asking: "Who would have thought in thirty years, Great Britain would have become a leading light in the world? They have modernised the country, fundamentally revised their values, abandoned taboos and achieved great ambition".

Chirac made no answer but flew out to Singapore to finish off the four-year French campaign to persuade the International Olympic Committee to make Paris the venue for the 2012 Summer Olympics, not only to provide a much needed commercial boost but also to help restore the morale of the country. "We think our country needs the Olympic Games for its development, for lasting development, to make it attractive," he schmoozed. "We have presented the assets of France but also the desires of France." Paris was the obvious choice. Where else could they possibly hold the games?

The I.O.C. deliberated and then decreed:

London in 2012.

THE FRENCHMAN'S FRENCHMAN DECIDES!
"[The British] are people [who] have a great sense of humour. It is the French who are cretins." Dirty, drunken yet iconic French actor Gérard Depardieu makes his choice, 2005.

Cinquante

Senator-*for*-Life

Chirac's Get Out of Jail Free Card

The moment Jacques Chirac leaves office as President of France, he also leaves behind its immunities to civil and criminal prosecution. But one group of his supporters are lobbying to change the constitution to put their champion beyond the reach of the law forever.

THE SUPERLIAR
During the 2002 elections, it was so widely accepted that Jacques Chirac was deeply involved in major political and financial frauds that it became almost his trademark. The French equivalent of the U.K.'s satirical Spitting Image *puppet show,* Les Guignols, *has cast the President as a Superman-style figure, dressed in the right outfit, but known as* Supermenteur *(Superliar). It caught on so well that children chant the name during presidential visits.*

In 2001, the Secretary of State for Northern Ireland, Peter Mandelson, was ejected from the British cabinet for ringing up his opposite number in the Home Office to enquire about a business friend's application for citizenship. In 2002 U.S. Senator Trent Lott was hurriedly obliged to resign as Senate Majority Leader after making congratulatory remarks at the 100th birthday party of an elderly racist colleague.

Such are the casualties of politics in almost every liberal political democracy. The slightest shade of sleaze can be fatal for a politician. In France, the supporters of President Chirac regard it not only as a plus but are lobbying to change the constitution so their *patron* can never be touched by the law again.

In 2002 Jacques Chirac swept back into power after the second round of the French presidential elections gave him 82% of the popular vote, thrashing his National Front opponent, Jean Marie le Pen. On the streets, Chirac's breezy unofficial election slogan was: "Vote for the crook, not the racist".

Allegations of chicanery have pursued Chirac throughout his career. Now, if his parliamentary supporters have their way, they will never catch up with him.

And it may be just in time. In February 2004 the former Prime Minister, Alain Juppé was convicted of illegal party-financing high-jinks. Unusually in France, his position as serving Mayor of Bordeaux and president of the ruling U.M.P. political party did not help him. If the appeal process is exhausted, the suspended jail term and ban on holding elected office may actually be carried out. The sentence, intimated the presiding judge, would have been more severe except that evidence showed that the guiding genius behind the fraud had not been Juppé at all but the man for whom he worked at the time, the then Mayor of Paris.

APPLEGATE

In 2002 incumbent Paris Mayor, Socialist Bertrand Delanoë, filed a civil complaint about Chirac's huge food bills during his tenure in the Hôtel de Ville. The affair was dubbed Applegate after journalists worked out that the Chiracs' personal grocery bill meant they could have afforded 100 kilos (220 lbs) of apples a day. Audits revealed Chirac and his wife spent €2.2 million ($2.7 million) on wine and food for private consumption (not official dining) between 1987 and 1995, more than half of it in cash. It also revealed €1.4 million ($1.7 million) in cash was given to the Chirac's personal cooks, without any control. The audit pointed to bills which had been paid several times and others which appeared to be for fictitious items.

Between 1977 and 1995, Chirac was Mayor of Paris. Chirac's uniquely enriching career will on his retirement enable this son of a bank clerk to take his ease in any one of his many properties including an agreeable sixteenth-century chateau in Corrèze. However, despite "Applegate" and "Travelgate", it may be his party activities that finally crimp his style and even his liberty – simply because they are being driven by his political enemies rather than the police and the investigating magistrates whose inquiries are much easier to derail in France.

During his stint as Mayor, Chirac set up his own political party, the R.P.R., (*Rassemblement pour la République*, Rally for the Republic) to provide him with a powerbase against his old mentor-turned-rival Valéry Giscard d'Estaing and his U.D.R. party (*Union des Démocrates pour la République*, Union of Democrats for the Republic).

Setting up political parties costs money and Chirac was not choosy about how he got it. Among much evidence currently untested in any judicial court is a notorious video secretly filmed by businessman Jean-Claude Méry, now dead. It details the kickback schemes he operated in the Paris region, thanks to a 5 million franc payment he personally made in cash to Jacques Chirac.

So long as he is President, none of this matters. In 1999 the *Conseil Constitutionnel* (Constitutional Court) ruled that a serving president (which at the time was Chirac) enjoys total immunity from any kind of civil or criminal prosecution. On that basis, he flatly refused to testify before Eric Halphen, the investigating magistrate looking into the massive frauds that had rocked the City of Paris during Chirac's tenure as Mayor. He argued that testifying would be "incompatible with his presidential function".

Chirac's immunity is far broader than that of most of his counterparts. The American president can, as Bill Clinton famously discovered in the Paula Jones case in 1997, be called to answer even civil lawsuits. Most European heads of government are subject to normal prosecution for criminal (and sometimes also civil) offences. Indeed, Italy's Silvio Berlusconi is due to return to court soon –after his attempt to give himself the immunity that Chirac enjoys was thrown out by Italy's constitutional court.

TRAVELGATE
While he was Mayor of Paris, Chirac made a string of lavish trips around the world. In 2001 a committee of deputies from the Office of the National Assembly (the parliament's regulatory body) handed over data regarding the financing of these jaunts to investigating magistrates. Chirac refused to be questioned about this "Travelgate" scandal, claiming that the money came from "special funds", a discretionary salary top-up, which is reported to have never appeared as income in any tax declaration. He has also refused to discuss the source of these "special funds".

FRIENDS OF JACQUES (1):
So far, a number of prominent politicians have been convicted for crimes associated with Jacques Chirac's tenure as Mayor of Paris.

ALAIN JUPPÉ. *Former Prime Minister, former secretary-general of the R.P.R. and former Deputy Mayor in charge of the finances of the City of Paris – 14 months suspended prison sentence and deprived of the right to hold political office for one year for allowing R.P.R. personnel to work full time for the party while being paid by the City of Paris.*

FRANÇOIS LÉOTARD. *Former Defence Minister – 10 months suspended prison sentence for money-laundering and illegal party funding.*

RENAUD DONNEDIEU DE VABRES, *French Member of Parliament – fined €15,000 euros ($18,500) for money-laundering.*

However, another ruling by another French court has not been so helpful to Chirac. On 10 October 2001, the *Cour de cassation* (Court of Appeal) decided that while the president cannot be prosecuted by normal judicial means during his mandate, that immunity ceases the moment he is out of office. Chirac's term of presidential office runs out in 2007. And then he's up for grabs.

This might explain why some in the presidential entourage are already floating the idea of Chirac running for a third term in 2007. But by then he will be 74 and there is no guarantee he would win an election nor even his party's nomination (the young, dynamic Nicolas Sarkozy, and Chirac's bitter rival, seems a much better bet for the R.P.R. grandees eager to maintain their hold on power).

FRIENDS OF JACQUES (2)

There are eighty-five members of the Conseil Constitutionnel, *France's highest judicial body. Some pure jurists, others are political or honorary appointees. In 1999 Chirac personally appointed the 12-man committee from the court to decided whether he, as President, was immune from prosecution. The so-called Avril commission, which recognised this immunity, was led by former French Foreign Minister, Roland Dumas. In 2001 Dumas was obliged to resign from the court when his former mistress Christine Deviers-Joncour accused him of receiving millions of euros worth of gifts from a slush fund operated by the oil giant, Elf-Aquitaine.*

So, in January 2005, his parliamentary supporters began lobbying for Chirac to be given a unique position in French politics after his retirement from the presidency, senator-for-life. A French senator, after all, is immune to any kind of prosecution.

It is a sly ploy and has been brought into play with equal slyness. Because, you see, this proposal, say its supporters, is *not* about President Chirac at all, it is about former President Giscard d'Estaing.

"NOTHING TO DO WITH ME"

In May 2005, 47 people, including some of Chirac's closest former allies, went on trial over a vast kickback scheme allegedly run from city hall while he was Mayor. The businessmen and politicians accused in the case have told investigating magistrates that companies paid a total of €86 million ($107 million) in bribes between 1989 and 1996 – most of it going to Chirac's political party. Allegedly overseeing the scam was Michel Roussin, Chirac's chief of staff for more than a decade, Roussin, accused of "complicity in and receipt of the proceeds of corruption", is a former minister and commander of the French secret service. The R.P.R.'s unofficial treasurer, Louise-Yvonne Cassetta, has testified that it was Roussin's responsibility to inform Chirac of all corporate "gifts" to the party. The trial continues. Chirac's only comment has been: "This is nothing to do with me. It is a matter for the courts". And the courts, as he well knows, can't touch him. For now.

Under Article 56 of the 1958 French Constitution, all former presidential incumbents (there have only been five under the Fifth Republic) are automatically given a seat on the *Conseil Constitutionnel* after they leave office. It is largely an honorary position and comes with no political powers, let alone immunities.

The new proposal, which would require a change to the country's constitution ratified by national referendum, is being promoted by Senator Patrice Gélard, a leading Chirac supporter. It has already been formally tabled in the Senate. Gélard says that his measure is primarily aimed at Giscard d'Estaing, who is frustrated by the rules of strict neutrality that he is obliged to observe as a member of the constitutional council and wants greater freedom to speak out.

"It's not a question of any particular individual. But it seems to me incongruous that a former president such as Giscard should be forced to submit to a rule of non-interference in public debate," he said. "It seems perfectly normal that he should be able to share his ideas on any number of subjects. The question of the European constitution is the prime example," he said.

The issue is still under discussion in the French senate. Chirac's name has assiduously been kept out of the matter by the motion's sponsors, but so far the opposition has not been fooled. "Why senator-for-life and not simply president-for-life?" Jean-Marc Ayrault, the head of the Socialists in parliament, asked sarcastically.

...AND AT A STROKE, OUR HERO WAS FREE?

It seems the political moves to make Chirac a Senator-for-Life just aren't going to fly. However, Chirac has no intention of spending his retirement making number plates in some minimum security prison. In 2005, as the proposal to grant him permanent immunity was being laughed down, it was reported that Chirac had suffered what the doctors at Paris's Val de Grace military hospital described as "minor vascular accident" in one eye. No official explanation was given to what this means. A ruptured blood vessel? A mini stroke? What? The President's office isn't saying. The illness apparently was not so serious that he cannot continue his functions as Head of State.

In May 2006, his doctors gave him a thorough going-over and issued a clean bill of health – but warned that the "condition might worsen in the future". The media caught the scent. They speculate that the president's condition, whatever it is, will remain stable until the end of his term of office and then, just after that, it will deteriorate so badly that he will be totally unfit to face any kind of trial.

One magazine, Le Canard Enchaîné, suggests that this would leave him free to enjoy the proceeds of an account in the Tokyo Sowa Bank, Japan whose details have come into its hands. The balance of £30 million, paid in over a number of years, is allegedly controlled my President Chirac through a "cultural foundation" (Chirac is a Japanophile, speaking some Japanese and an avid Haiku poet). Investigating magistrates are, as ever, on the case...